THE THEOLOGY OF THE CROSS

Reflections on His Cross and Ours

Daniel M. Deutschlander

NORTHWESTERN PUBLISHING HOUSE
Milwaukee, Wisconsin

Second printing,   2009

Cover photograph: DesignPics

Scripture is taken from the HOLY BIBLE, NEW INTERNATIONAL
VERSION®. NIV®. Copyright © 1973, 1978, 1984 by International
Bible Society. Used by permission of Zondervan. All rights reserved.

The "NIV" and "New International Version" trademarks are registered
in the United States Patent and Trademark Office by International
Bible Society. Use of either trademark requires the permission of
International Bible Society.

Quotes from the Lutheran Confessions, where noted as Kolb, are
taken from *The Book of Concord,* edited by Robert Kolb and Timothy
Wengert, © 2000 Augsburg Fortress. Used by permission.

Library of Congress Control Number: 2008935156
Northwestern Publishing House
1250 N. 113th St., Milwaukee, WI 53226-3284
www.nph.net
© 2008 by Northwestern Publishing House
Published 2008
Printed in the United States of America
ISBN 978-0-8100-2187-7

CONTENTS

PREFACE

In every age the church has had to deal with litmus tests of orthodoxy. The litmus test helps the Christian to distinguish between genuine, biblical Christianity on the one hand and corrupted or counterfeit versions of the faith on the other. One famous theologian said that the tests over the centuries could be illustrated by the figure of a church building. During the first three or four centuries, attacks on genuine Christianity were directed chiefly at the cross on the top, as heretics attacked the Bible's teaching concerning the person of Christ. The Nicene Creed was the answer of the faithful church to those attacks. During the next thousand years, the litmus test of genuine Christianity dealt with the body of the church building, that is, the definition of what the church itself is, its fundamental message, the nature of its authority, and its work. The Reformation, in no small part, dealt with those questions. From the 18th century on, the litmus test has dealt with the foundation on which the church rests, on the origin and authority of the sacred Scriptures. In other words, are they the infallible and verbally inspired Word of God and the only ultimate authority for the doctrine and life of the church, or are they merely fallible human records of what people believed in the days when the various books of the Bible were written?

What is the litmus test of genuine Christianity today? The old tests can never be completely put away; attacks on the person and work of Christ, attacks on the purpose and nature of the church, attacks on the source and authority of the Bible are renewed in every age. And yet each age has its own special litmus test in addition to these universal and ever resurfacing ones. What might a special litmus test for our day be? Could it be the theology of the cross that separates genuine Christianity from corrupted and counterfeit versions of the same?

We see on every hand a desire to make Christianity fun and happy-go-lucky. Some churches and their leaders go so far as to claim that God really wants Christians always to be healthy, wealthy, and wise. Others turn worship services into hours of self-discovery; the goal is to give the Christian personal fulfillment and better character. If the individual can learn to get along better with himself, then he will get along better with everyone else too, and God should be happy about that. Still others are obsessed with the notion that the true church should be successful, big, and influential in world and national politics. Within the church, no matter what denominational label the particular church may wear, many members want to be their own bible; they want the freedom to pick and choose what doctrines to believe and what behavior to praise or blame. Their choices change with their circumstances of the moment, and woe betide any preacher who tells them on the basis of the Scriptures that they are wrong and their choices damnable in the eyes of God. All of that is a theology of glory, a theology which lets man be his own god and turns the God of the Bible into a creature subject to personal whims of the moment.

The God of the Bible—the one, true, and only God, however, is the God of the cross. Jesus calls us to submission under his cross and then to bear the cross that he sends us and by which he marks us as his own. He did not come to entertain but to redeem us by his blood. He does not call us to be our own gods but to bend low before his cross in total submission to his Word and then to the cross that he is pleased to send. The cross of his own sending always and of necessity and by definition means struggle for us. The cross is not merely a piece of jewelry worn around the neck but pain carried on the heart and in the soul. Jesus calls us to the cross and sends one after another for us to bear. He bids us imitate him in stumbling under its sometimes crushing weight and to cry out in anguish as he did in the midst of its pain. All of that seems so, well, so un-American. We pursue pleasure, and for every pain there should be an instant remedy. We are addicted to entertainment and want church to be entertaining too. We shun any notion that we live in a veil of tears, in *einem rechten Jammerthal,* as our forefathers put it. We think that anyone who is in physical or spiritual pain must be sick and in need of therapy that will make him happy again—and soon!

At the same time, the Bible tells us that in the midst of suffering and under the cross, we should rejoice. Yes, it tells us to rejoice constantly and precisely because we are suffering under the weight of the cross that crushes and threatens to destroy us. It assures us again and again that those who rejoice without the cross and those who suffer without joy understand neither true joy nor the value of the cross that God has sent.

So we come again to the question: Could the theology of the cross be the litmus test of genuine Christianity in our day? The corrupt and the counterfeit push aside the whole concept of cross bearing in favor of a joy without it. Fake Christianity offers the Christian an imitation of Christ's glory in heaven, not of his humiliation on earth. The phony and the artificial church turns worship into a spiritual happy hour devoid of repentance, with cheap absolution, with no thought of taking God seriously in either the law or the gospel. And people love it. They still get to be their own god, their own bible, their own source of ultimate truth and salvation.

In the pages that follow, we will search the mind of God, as he has revealed it in his holy and inerrant Word, for his definition of Christian faith and life under the cross, under his cross and ours. We will wrestle with the seeming contradiction of the necessity of cross bearing and rejoicing at the same time. We will strive to bend our minds and hearts and souls beneath his cross and our own. Then we will rise under the healing balm of the gospel in his Word and sacraments to rejoice evermore in his cross and ours, until he takes us from the imitation of his cross to the enjoyment of his glory in heaven.

May God bless our consideration of his Word and the cross for the glory of his name and the strengthening of our life from him, to him, in him!

1

What Is the Theology of the Cross?

Our first hearing of the phrase *theology of the cross* might give us no pause at all as to its definition. After all, the cross is what Christianity is all about—the cross of Christ. Surely by a *theology of the cross* we mean a theology that is fixed on Christ and his cross, on the work of our redemption. Certainly any theology worthy of the name is always stamped by the mark of the cross of him who died for us and for our salvation and then rose to proclaim his triumph for us over death and hell. His cross and resurrection are the beginning, the middle, the end, the all-in-all of our theology, our faith in this life and our hope of heaven in the life to come. But when we speak of the *theology of the cross* in dogmatic theology, we are speaking not only about Christ's cross but also about our cross, the cross of the Christian in his life of faith. While never losing sight of Jesus' cross, it is the cross he sends *us* that will also occupy our attention in this book. The centrality of his cross will never be far from our minds, and in the center of the book it will be our chief concern. But in much of this work our focus will be on the results of his cross in our cross; we will examine how the two are never separated, how they are intertwined, and how the one defines the other as to content and purpose. It is, as we shall have occasion to repeat often, his cross alone that saves. It is the cross he sends us that sums up so much of our life of hope and expectation for the glory yet to be revealed in eternity.

Jesus himself gives us the reason to speak thus about the connection between his cross and ours, about the centrality of his cross for our salvation and our cross in a life that is faithful to him and to his Word. He promises that we will bear the cross as a necessary consequence of following him. He spells it out for us in sharpest clarity when he declares:

> If anyone would come after me, he must deny himself and take up his cross and follow me. For whoever wants to save his life will lose it, but whoever loses his life for me and for the gospel will save it. What good is it for a man to gain the whole world, yet forfeit his soul? Or what can a man give in exchange for his soul? If anyone is ashamed of me and my words in this adulterous and sinful generation, the Son of Man will be ashamed of him when he comes in his Father's glory with the holy angels. (Mk 8:34-38)

In our consideration of the theology of the cross, we want to examine this promise of Jesus with some care. Every word he speaks on the subject of the Christian's cross is so carefully chosen. And the subject itself is so weighty and broad that it embraces all of the Christian's life without ever being exactly the same from year to year or from person to person. We will therefore consider first of all those aspects of the theology of the cross that define it and that apply universally. In subsequent chapters we will examine particular and changing aspects of the cross in the life of the Christian and in the life of the church.

Characteristics of the Christian's cross

Notice first that Jesus makes the cross for his followers a *consequence,* not a cause, of discipleship. He is addressing those in

2

whom the gospel has already created faith and who now wish to follow him. Immediately before the promise of the cross for his disciples, Jesus spoke plainly of his own cross, of his impending passion, and of his resurrection after his suffering. It is his cross that saves, not ours. Nor does our cross contribute to our salvation—no, not in the least part. Even our faith is a gift that comes from his cross, from the proclamation of the gospel that we have been redeemed by his cross alone and not our own. It was after he had announced the saving work that he was about to complete for us that he turned to the crowd and to his disciples and announced a *consequent cross* for all who in such faith would follow him.

How shocking those words of Jesus must have sounded in the ears of all who heard them! Indeed, Peter speaks for us all according to the flesh when he takes Jesus aside to instruct his Lord that such a thing as a cross for the Son of God was altogether out of the question. When Jesus then announced that not only he himself but all who follow him would bear a cross, Peter must have been stunned into silence. If he did not want Jesus to carry a cross, we should not expect that he would cherish the prospect of carrying one himself.

The cross for the Christian is a consequence of discipleship. It is a *necessary* consequence. No cross, no Christian! It is the cross that marks the Christian as a Christian. Those who are ashamed of the cross in this life, both his and their own, will see the Son of God ashamed of them at the last judgment. Could there be a more horrible prospect than that? Could there be a more pummeling hammer against our sinful flesh? The flesh wants to hear nothing of a cross and certainly does not want to carry one. But Jesus is insistent and makes the whole matter still more emphatic by putting it all into the singular. Not *all those* but *anyone*. Not *they* but *he*. Not a single soul who follows him should ever think that he will be able to hide cross-less in the crowd of cross-bearers and so escape its weight and its pain. Not one Christian should imagine that he could meet Jesus on the Last Day without the sign of the cross.

A third characteristic of the cross, a characteristic wrapped in the word itself, is that the cross is *heavy and painful*. The pain and even the awareness of the cross may change from year to

3

year in the Christian's life. But nevertheless a cross there is; a cross there must be. A sermon from the pulpit or a lesson in the classroom, therefore, that tries to make Christianity sound painless, effortless, easy, entertaining, or just a Sunday morning jaunt to the happy place of souls is counterfeit Christianity. Luther expressed it well in his Large Catechism. In his comments on the Third Petition of the Lord's Prayer he says this:

> For where God's Word is preached, accepted, or believed, and bears fruit, there the holy and precious cross will also not be far behind. And let no one think that we will have peace; rather, we must sacrifice all we have on earth—possessions, honor, house and farm, spouse and children, body and life. Now, this grieves our flesh and the old creature, for it means that we must remain steadfast, suffer patiently whatever befalls us, and let go whatever is taken from us. (Large Catechism, Third Petition, par. 65,66; Kolb, pp. 448,449.)

All of these calamities can come as a result of the gospel and have befallen many because of their faithfulness to the Word. That these calamities do not always come is only because God often has chosen to spare us. Luther's point is that we should have a mind-set that understands and is ready to let everything go because of the gospel. He makes the same point in his great hymn "A Mighty Fortress Is Our God," especially in the fourth stanza (*Christian Worship,* 200). Even if our cross does not have the dimensions and the weight of those described by Luther in the Large Catechism, nevertheless a cross there will be; a cross there must be!

The liturgy addresses the needs of cross-bearers

The Sunday morning liturgy assumes the constancy of the cross in the Christian's life. The liturgy is addressed to cross-bearers. We do not come to church to do our own thing, anymore than we go to the emergency room in the hospital to do our own thing. We go to both places wounded, in need of help that only comes from another. We go to both places for healing, where our opinion and preference is of no consequence; only that of the healer matters.

The confession of sins assumes that we come into the house of the Lord in pain, aching at heart for the balm and soothing ointment of pardon and peace from God because of our still sinful condition and the abundant proofs of that condition in our lives. The cry of the "Kyrie," "Lord, have mercy," is the cry even of the forgiven sinner, who recognizes his continuing weakness both in body and in soul. It comes from the heart of one whose life knows needs of both body and soul that cannot be supplied apart from the mercy of God. Even the exultant "Gloria in Excelsis" repeats again the refrain of cross-bearers through the ages: "O Christ, have mercy and hear my cry; O Christ, have mercy!"

From beginning to end, the whole of the worship service addresses the Christian's varied needs under the weight of the cross. And at the same time it gives abundant opportunity to worship and adore and give thanks to *the* Cross-Bearer for the help and rescue granted in Word and sacraments. Preaching and teaching that does not take the mark of the cross on the Christian into account is missing the mark. It is the presence of the cross that makes the Christian realize his need for comfort under the cross and the gift of strength to bear it. Without such comfort and strengthening, each believer will lose heart, be crushed under its weight, and finally fall into despair. And tragically, his heart may become so cold and his soul so blind that he doesn't even realize that he has been crushed; his despair may finally be a deadness to any spiritual life at all.

It is to the Christian, who is made aware of the cross by events in his life and by preaching and teaching, that Jesus promises rest and refreshment in the pronouncement of absolution, in the readings for the day, and in the sermon. And it is in response to these that the cross-bearer sings exultantly his thanks and praise to God in the rest of the liturgy and in so many of the hymns. So effective is the consolation to the cross-bearers that we join with one another in the confident expression of the faith worked by the Word to cheer and encourage one another: *I (we) believe!* we confidently declare on the basis of comfort and strength received in Word and sacrament.

Jesus sums up his response to our need as cross-bearers so beautifully when he tenderly invites us, "Come to me, all you who are weary and burdened, and I will give you rest. Take my yoke upon you and learn from me, for I am gentle and humble in heart, and you will find rest for your souls. For my yoke is easy and my burden is light" (Mt 11:28-30). If the Christian had no cross to bear, he would need nothing of what Jesus promises in these verses. Nor would he have the least yearning for it. But in point of fact the cross-bearer is often worn out in his heart and parched in his soul. He comes to the Savior in the Word and the sacrament, longing for relief. That longing is not, however, for a life of ease without the cross. No, that could never be! For Christ has promised the cross and promised that it will not go away until the Christian enters into the glory prepared for all who follow under the sacred sign of the cross. Jesus carefully words his promise in Matthew 11 with that in mind. The word translated as "rest" would be better translated as "refreshment." Rest, final rest, comes at the end, but that is not what Jesus is talking about in this promise. This is a promise for a refreshment that enables the cross-bearer to get back to the labor and the load. The labor and the load become light not because they have disappeared but because of Jesus' promise that the yoke is his yoke and the burden his burden. We therefore carry and endure it with him and in his company. That is the company of one who loved us all the way to his cross, to hell and back.

The pain of the cross is at the heart of the Christian's joy

The simple fact that the Christian's cross sends him running again and again to his Savior for help, for strength, for refreshment should be reason enough for us to rejoice in cross bearing. For without the cross there would be no such constant recourse to him in Word and sacrament. At best, the running would degenerate into a casual or occasional Sunday morning stroll; the confession under the cross that the flesh is unwilling and the spirit still weak would become nothing more than a polite formality. The exaltation of the *Gloria in Excelsis* that follows the words of absolution would be no more than routine ritual. Luther makes the point eloquently in his comments on the Sixth and Seventh petitions of the Lord's Prayer in his Large Catechism. Every hour, he says, the Christian is subject to torment and temptation; today he stands, tomorrow he falls; today it is this trial, tomorrow that. Therefore we have reason to cry out in every hour, not for a life of ease without the cross, but for rescue and help in bearing it. For temptation *(Anfechtung)* of every sort is what Christ has told us we will have in this life, and it is help and rescue in the midst of it that he promises in the Word and sacraments.

The cross and the Christian's will

Notice too an astonishing thing about this theology of the cross, as Jesus defines and outlines it for us. *It involves the Christian's will!* Jesus speaks in Mark 8, previously cited, of what we *want* to do. Who would have thought it? Again we call to mind Peter's protest when Jesus spoke of his own cross. But Jesus had to take up the cross if the world was to be redeemed. And just as Jesus had to take it up willingly, so too must the Christian. Jesus does not say that he is going to impose the cross contrary to the will of his followers. He calls on the Christian, expects the Christian, to embrace the cross and to embrace it willingly. St. Paul understood that perhaps better than anyone when he declared:

> Therefore, since we have been justified through faith, we have peace with God through our Lord Jesus Christ, through whom we have gained access by faith into this grace in which we now stand. And we rejoice in the hope of the glory of God. Not only so, *but we also rejoice in our sufferings* . . . (Ro 5:1-3)

Jesus embraces and captures the soul in the proclamation of full redemption, full forgiveness as an accomplished fact and received by faith alone. So fully does he capture us by that message that the new will of the Christian, given by the Spirit through the gospel, rejoices to follow him under the cross of suffering. Only a Christian or a lunatic could understand that! The new will of the Christian may be weak in its embrace of the cross. Its weakness consists of a still-powerful sinful nature that surrounds it, that threatens to engulf and swallow it up. It may take a long time under the cross before the Christian will so triumph over the sinful will that he not only surrenders to the cross but rejoices in it. And that surrender may be a roller-coaster ride that lasts a lifetime. But ultimately the reality of the cross as a blessing (in German we always called it *das liebe Kreuz!*—the *dear* cross) sinks in, in part now, in full when we arrive at its consummation in glory.

Only the proclamation of the work of Jesus on his cross and its blessed result can move the Christian to imitate Christ in a willing and even joyful embrace of the cross. St. Paul inspires the will and kindles that joy in the great *sedes doctrinae** for Christ's states of humiliation and exaltation in Philippians 2:5-11. He begins that whole glorious section on the work of Christ for us with an appeal to the Christian's will. He says, "Your attitude should be the same as that of Christ Jesus." The apostle has just that short line about our will and then a long and graphic account of Christ's will accomplished in lowliness for us, in suffering for us, on the cross for us, and then in resurrected glory also for us. It is all that Christ did in his humiliation on the cross that moves us to an attitude and will that imitates his. Just so, Jesus speaks first of his cross and then of ours in Mark 8, as he works to conform our will to his. The writer of the epistle to the Hebrews speaks in the same way. First he exults in Christ's suffering for us, and then he speaks of our suffering at the hands of a loving Father who only disciplines us for our good (Heb 12:1-11); it is that love of the Father which moves our will to submit to the momentary pain of the Father's discipline.

But what if our attitude is not the same as the attitude of Christ? What if our will resists the cross? The simple fact of the matter is that our will is not yet completely renewed. The renewed will, as already noted, is still weak because we still have the old will, the will of fallen man, which always resists the cross. That is why St. Paul's appeal, like that of Christ himself in Mark 8, is to the *Christian* will, the will that has been born through the proclamation of the gospel. For the Christian always has two natures; he retains the fallen will inherited from Adam and Eve. At the same time, through the proclamation of the

---

*Sedes doctrinae is a technical term in theology. It means the "seat of the doctrine." The *sedes doctrinae* is usually one passage in the Bible that most completely sums up that particular doctrine. Other passages may speak of the same doctrine, may add depth and dimension to it, but it is the *sedes doctrinae* that best sums it up.

gospel in the Word and in the Sacrament of Baptism, he receives an altogether new will, a will that wants only what God wants, a will that loves its source—Christ in Word and sacraments. These two wills remain in conflict our whole life long, as St. Paul so graphically testifies in Romans 7:14-25. In the matter of cross bearing, it is only the new will that truly submits to the cross. The old will hates it, resists it, and tries with all its waning powers to throw it off. St. Peter uses the analogy of a newborn baby when speaking of the new will; still weak, still immature, it yearns for the pure milk of the Word that it may grow and become stronger (1 Pe 2:2). Again, the need for that milk to strengthen the new will is an ongoing one; it lasts a lifetime.

It is a fact that each Christian carries the cross as he follows Christ. It is a fact that such cross bearing is not optional but a necessary consequence of faith. It is a fact that the cross is often difficult and painful. It is a fact that the Christian embraces the cross willingly, even joyfully according to his new man. Though all of this is nonsense to the world, it is the ultimate rationality for Christ and those who follow him. Jesus makes that clear when he sets up the alternative in Mark 8. The alternative to cross bearing is the forfeit of the soul, that is, the forfeit of eternal life.

Why would anyone want to forfeit eternal life? What a horrible thing to contemplate, much less actually do! But that is exactly what those do who are ashamed of Christ and his Word, who therefore shun the cross that comes to those who follow him. It's an axiom: No cross, no Christian! Would someone trade in the cross in exchange for the whole world and all that it has to offer? A poor exchange indeed, even if it were possible! For the temporary and perishing world would come at the expense of eternal blessedness and would finally result in eternal torment. In reality no such exchange is possible. In point of fact, those who aim at such an exchange never get the whole world. They settle for far less. They get tinsel, not gold; they get baubles, not treasure; they get the fleeting and transitory, not the durable and the eternal. If the whole world weighed in the balance is a fool's bargain, how much more so isn't its tinsel and perishable pleasure? Thus, for example, the one who buys popularity with one compromise of principle after another ends up ashamed and disgraced often in this life and certainly in the one to come. The one who trades listening to the Word for work and wealth ends up with health ruined, wealth gone, and an eternity of the utmost poverty with the rest of the damned. The one who shuns the cross of struggle against the flesh and chases after pleasure as the goal of existence ends up frustrated and always dissatisfied in this life and covered with disgrace and eternal suffering in the next.

Joyful cross bearing

Jesus' brilliant discussion in Mark 8:34-38 of the alternative to cross bearing helps move the Christian's will to embrace what appears to many as a glaring contradiction in the Bible. It helps move the Christian will to embrace *joyful suffering.* Joyful suffering seems to be such a contradiction in terms that we need to focus our attention on the nature of joy in suffering. For both the suffering and the joy are real. The cross is indeed painful. The writer to the Hebrews recognizes that when he says, "No discipline seems pleasant at the time, but painful" (Heb 12:11). Yet so many passages in the Bible exhort us to a constant joy. To cite but one of the more striking examples, St. Paul makes joy a Christian imperative in Philippians 4:4 when he says, "Rejoice in the Lord always. I will say it again: Rejoice!" The astonishing thing about the insistence on joy in Philippians is that this epistle is one of Paul's prison epistles. He wrote it while he was shut off from much of the work he lived for. He wrote it while separated from beloved members of the churches he served and from many of his friends and coworkers. Still he insists on joy! How can the Bible insist that we should rejoice when it speaks with equal insistence about the necessity of suffering?

Each one of Paul's epistles is an answer to the question, and Peter's first epistle is a commentary that deals with the seeming paradox in every chapter: Suffering and joy are two sides of the same coin in the Christian's life. That elemental fact is what distinguishes the Christian's suffering under the cross from the suffering of the unbelieving world. Suffering without joy is the sorrow of the world in the ordinary course of things; it is sorrow and nothing but sorrow over the pain of sickness and death, over the anguish of loneliness or of human failure, over the bitter fruit stolen from a tree that promised pleasure but gave only guilt or shame. The sorrows and suffering of the world find no relief in the promise of rescue and redemption in Christ. For the suffering of the world apart from Christ is the consequence of being apart from Christ. Those who suffer thus receive no comfort in the assurance of the Scriptures that all things work together for good to those who love God (Ro 8:18-39). In sorrow those without Christ cannot rejoice in the truth that suffering in Christ bears a rich and abundant harvest for the soul even in this life (Ro 5:1-11). The sorrow of the unbelieving world is unrelieved by the companionship of Christ on the cross and at the empty tomb.

All that those who suffer without the gospel can wish for is that maybe the suffering will end, that maybe it will have some point or purpose. When even such vain hope dims and fades with the realization that death is man's ultimate reality, the worldling is left with only temporary relief in his favorite sins. He turns to drugs or alcohol, to fleshly pleasure or work in order to take his mind off of what seems to him a vain and futile existence. He does that even when he must know that much of his suffering is a direct result of such behavior in the first place! What he turned to initially for happiness, he now turns to for relief from the misery brought by his initial quest. Indeed, so deep does the despair of some become that they rush headlong into the ultimate crime, that of suicide. Much of modern philosophy ends up in just such a truly dead end: Life has no point and its suffering knows no purpose; therefore, if it becomes too much for you and you can no longer escape it, end it all! So deep is the pain apart from Christ, so profound the sense of futility, that in order to relieve it, worldlings try to make suicide sound like something noble! But as with so many of the world's solutions to problems, so the suicide solution creates more misery than it relieves. For apart from Christ, the sorrow and suffering of the present is but a foreshadowing of the far greater and the eternal suffering of the damned in hell.

And just as the suffering of those without Christ is very different from the suffering of the Christian cross-bearer, so too the joy of the worldling has nothing in common with the joy of the Christian, a joy that the Christian has even under the heaviest of crosses. For the joy of the worldling has no roots in the joy and

11

comfort of the gospel. A joy without the cross and apart from Christ is often nothing more than something superficial. When it is superficial, it is folly and silliness; consider, for example, the mania for sports, as though a game were the goal of life itself. When it is not superficial, it is idolatry and depravity; consider the addiction of so many to sex and violence, as though they were the only way to prove that one is really alive and important. Whether superficial or depraved, the joy of the world is in fact a joy that always has the smell of death about it. The birthday party ends with the realization that the end of life is one year closer. The ball on New Year's Eve gives way to the reality of uncertainty and still more struggle in the year to come. Even the happy recovery from illness holds in it only the assurance that illness will return, that finally virus or bacteria or organ failure will end in the triumph of death over life. In the face of these grim realities, the joy that the worldling knows is little more than "whistling past the graveyard." All joy apart from Christ must ultimately disappoint. It must end, either in a return of worldly sorrow and loss, in death, or in its aftermath of endless suffering under the just judgment of God.

By contrast, the suffering of the Christian, the bearing of the cross, has the blessed purpose of bringing him back to or closer to Christ, who at the end will give a crown to those who have carried their cross after him. That is Paul's point in Philippians 4. He wrote the epistle from prison, where there was little outward reason for joy. He wrote under the weight of nonstop suffering. He shows us that the two, the pain of the cross and the joy of its outcome, must always be presented together. Jesus does that so beautifully when he tells us that the Christian life is one of pain and joy inseparably linked, like the pain and joy that accompany childbirth for a woman. He was speaking of the time when he would remove his visible presence from the disciples. But the analogy applies as well to the whole of the Christian's life of faith. A woman has pain that is turned to joy once the child has been born (Jn 16:20-22). Were there no child, there would be no pain; were there no pain, there would be no joy in the birth of the child.

Thus the Christian does indeed have joy in the midst of suffering. In taking up the cross, he experiences it again and again: *joyful suffering*. For the Christian knows that what joy he has in this life is the gift of his gracious and loving Father in heaven. And he knows as well that not the least of God's gifts is the gift of the cross, which prompts him to draw ever closer to his Lord. In that fellowship of the cross, the fellowship of experiencing his own cross while following after the Crucified, the Christian rejoices. And as Paul reminds us in Romans 5, his hope in Christ will not be disappointed. It will only bear rich fruit in patience and still more joy as the Lord draws closer still to the cross-bearer in his Word and fulfills his promises there, promises of renewed strength, of help, of ultimate rescue.

The essence of the cross

What then is the essence of the cross that each Christian must of necessity carry and carry willingly, even joyfully? Jesus defines it for us with all its flesh-piercing splinters and slivers. He defines it in such a way that there could never be a time when an aware Christian would be unaware of his need for the compassionate Christ, who gives rest to the weary and refreshes the burdened. The essence of the cross in every stage of life and in every changing circumstance is this: *Self* denial. He tells us, "If anyone would come after me, he must deny himself and take up his cross and follow me" (Mk 8:34).

Again, with what mastery Jesus sums up the whole matter in Mark 8! *Self* denial will always be difficult, will always be a struggle. Hence, to undertake such is to take up a heavy, flesh-ripping, backbreaking cross. For what is it that everyone wants by nature? What is it that is at the very heart and core of each one of us? Each wants to save his life and not to lose it. And to fallen man the essence of saving life is not merely the continuance of bodily functions. It is rather that one's own will be done. To do the will of another or to have one's own will denied is to lose life.

The nature of *self*

That point is perhaps not immediately obvious. It requires some reflection. Disappointment in work, disappointment in family, disappointment with the circumstances of my life is the suffering that comes from the defeat of my will by that of others.

There would be no disappointment and no frustration if everybody else would just yield to *my* will, or at the very least, get out of *my* way. In the very least things in life, that is evident. If you doubt it, note your own annoyance in traffic or while waiting in a line. The goal of man by nature is to get his own way, to see the triumph of his own will. We may swallow hard when that is not possible. We may put on a pleasant smile to mask annoyance or anger or even hatred. But that does not change this fundamental fact of life: Life apart from Christ has meaning to the extent that I get my own way, that my will is victorious over the will of just about everyone else.

To be sure, we are loath to admit that the whole aim of our life is to get our own way, to accomplish our own will. But just examine the dynamics of family members who are masters of manipulation and other family members who refuse to be manipulated. Read the history of the world's great rulers. What will you see as the common theme, the constant in the crowd, the family, the history of the world? You will see individuals struggling to save their lives, that is, to give their lives point and purpose by getting their own way, accomplishing their own will. We only need to look in the mirror. When we examine our own lives, we will not run short of times when we either struggled just to get our own way or were annoyed and worse that we did not succeed. To the extent that such is the case, to that extent we did not carry the cross, to that extent we did not deny *self*.

Wars in the world and in the workplace, wars in the family and in the neighborhood always have that as the common denominator: Someone is trying to gain a victory for his own will over the will of someone else. Maybe that is the bottom line reason why we fear death and would prefer to imagine that death happens only to other people, that somehow we will escape it. For death is the final and complete defeat of one's own will. Death makes it impossible for my will to gain any further victories over the wills of others.

The desire to see our own will triumph over that of those around us manifests itself very early in life. We do not need to be taught how to do that. By nature every breath we take is in the hope of accomplishing our own will. In infancy we figure out how to speak because we want something, whether it is food, attention, or just a changed diaper. As soon as the most basic wants or needs have been satisfied, we lust for more. With the passing of time we become obsessed with the infantile formula: "If only I had . . . , then I would be happy." The getting of the *if only* satisfies the will for just a few minutes, to be replaced over and over again by a brand-new *if only*. That many of these *I wants* may only be satisfied at someone else's expense or loss bothers our obsession with our own will very little, if at all.

The getting of one's own way, the accomplishment of one's own will, getting things, getting ahead even at the expense of another, all of these are basically the same thing. They are the outward evidence of the assertion, indeed the worship, of *self*. Someone described as an "egomaniac" is, in fact, not a maniac at all. He is what we all are by nature. The only real difference between the one considered a pathological egomaniac and the rest of us is that he has not been able to hide his passionate love affair with *self* as successfully as those not so described. He has not grasped what the rest of us have come to understand: In order to get our own way we have to learn how to hide our real intention of achieving the triumph of our own will over the will of another.

We may have to settle at times for a partial triumph. We may have to limit or find a way to control our greed or our ambition or our lust, lest through a lack of self-control we lose other things that we value. We may have to smile pleasantly at the victory of another and wait for our own to come on another day. But no matter how much we smile or succeed in hiding our real aim, the desire to assert *self* lies festering at the bottom of the soul. That desire is never extinguished this side of the grave; it gnaws; it burns; it erupts in everything that we do apart from Christ. It is the opposite of *self* denial. And no matter how nicely we cover it up, its ugliness never goes away.

The role of *self* in the "good" done apart from Christ

That is a truism which applies even to the noble acts of those called humanitarians. At the very heart of even the most noble unbelieving humanitarian is the yearning to carry out his own will for his own reasons. He does what he does because he wants to. Whether he wills to do it because it just makes him feel better or because he thinks that somehow his works will please his God makes little difference. Whether he wants to do good because he secretly covets the praises of the world or convinces himself that such praise is a matter of indifference to him likewise matters not. At bottom he serves his own will. In the words of Mark 8, he seeks to save *self,* to save his life. His seeming self-denial may be of great benefit to humanity and indeed worthy of the world's highest accolades. But as Jesus says elsewhere and in a slightly different context, "They have received their reward in full" (Mt 6:16). That reward, whether the praise of the world or the praise of one's own feelings, is not the praise that Jesus gives at the last judgment to the works which flow from faith and thus are done to and for Jesus (Mt 25:40-46).

The role of *self* in the good done for Christ

The one doing the works praised by Jesus at the last judgment may not always even be conscious that what he is doing is done for Jesus, is done as a work of *self* denial. In Matthew 25 those praised for their works express surprise; they did not think the works were all that memorable or important, much less worthy of note by Jesus at the last judgment. Nevertheless, their works were the fruit of *self* denial; they were the result of a relationship with Jesus.

To others and even to the one doing the works, those works may have seemed insignificant and worthy of no notice at all. It could be the work of the child helping his mother with the dishes or the dusting. It could be the patient kindness of the mother to her own child or the child of another. It could be the work of the laborer done faithfully when "It's good enough" satisfied everybody else. The work was the lesson faithfully taught, the sick call, or the sermon completed in love for Christ and his people. It was the meal prepared for the family or for a stranger in a shelter. It was the kindly "Here, let me help you with that!" when there was neither hope nor expectation of payment or reward. The work done in *self* denial is, in sum, anything that the Christian does as a Christian; the Christian may not be fully aware that the work is a fruit of faith; the Christian may be on automatic pilot, so to speak. Nevertheless the work was done not for *self* but to one extent or another out love for God and for the benefit of his neighbor.

To be sure, many of these works can be done outwardly by the unbeliever too. But the unbeliever or the hypocrite does them only on the outside. The motive stems from, in the case of the works of parent or child for one another, the natural love of kinship. In the case of the worker, it might be a good outward pride in one's work, a good work ethic. And those motives are not absent from the Christian. But at bottom for the Christian, for the cross-bearer, the work is done to Christ, out of love for Christ, as a result of a relationship with Christ. To be sure, the work will be more joyfully done if the Christian is aware of the relationship of his work to Christ. We do well to think of that relationship and to remind one another of it more often than we do. It is by faith in Christ that both the worker and the work are cleansed by the blood of the Lamb of whatever still remaining selfish motives might stain the work. By virtue of that cleansing, God sees the work as perfect, so that both the worker and the work are prized and praised. We do not think of that connection often enough. If we did, we would rejoice more in the nobility that Christ has given to our lives as we follow him under the cross. We would cherish all the more the opportunities he gives us to serve him in things great and small.

It needs to be pointed out that the cross bearing of which Jesus speaks, the cross bearing that we are talking about under the heading of the theology of the cross, is not self-chosen or self-inflicted suffering. It is not the self-chosen poverty of the monk or the solitude of the hermit. It is not the celibacy inflicted by the papacy on those who wish to serve in the public ministry. Rather it is the self-denial that lives in submission to the law of God, in works of service to one's neighbor out of love for Christ. Sometimes such service may appear easy and convenient, sometimes difficult and unappreciated; sometimes such service matters to others or to all; sometimes it is unseen and unheralded by any. It is the *self* denial of putting the other first at work, in the family, in whatever station in life we may occupy. It is a willing, cheerful understanding that we live not for *self* but for him who loves us and gave himself for us. It is a life that is lived in harmony with the law of God because that pleases God. And that law is summed up in loving service.

How is suffering related to *self* denial and cross bearing?

Many think that cross bearing is any and all suffering that we have in this life. That is not what Jesus says in Mark 8 or anywhere else in his Word. Cross bearing is not the suffering that is the natural lot of mankind as a result of the fall into sin in the Garden of Eden. That which people suffer as the result of the wickedness of others or their own wickedness is not in itself a cross. Suffering from natural disasters of every sort, from earthquakes and famines, from war and bloodshed in which one's own will and behavior are not in the least involved is also not necessarily cross bearing. Losing loved ones in sickness and in death, getting sick and suffering pain, and finally dying is likewise not, by definition, in and of itself, cross bearing.

While this kind of suffering, which is the lot of all humanity since the fall into sin, is not necessarily *self* denial and cross bearing, it may *become* cross bearing. It may end up requiring *self* denial. For our sinful nature in the face of human misery, whether our own or that of others, may rebel. Our sinful nature may cry out with the unbelievers and scoffers of the world: "Where now is your God? Where is the promise of his mercy and love? Where is his rescue and deliverance? How can you believe in and trust a God who permits or sends such misery and such suffering?"

When we are pained by such questions, whether they come from others or arise from within our own hearts, then the suffering becomes a cross. It calls for *self* denial, the denial of our own will and reason in favor of God's Word. *Self* rejects God's Word and his promises in Romans 8 that nothing can separate us from his love and that all things work together for our good. But we cling to the promises of God and to his Word, even and especially when the outward evidence of the moment seems to contradict the Word. The suffering requires us to deny our own instincts and doubts and fears. It requires us to turn our backs on and reject the ridicule of the scoffer. It requires us, even if it seems to be foolishness and folly, to confess: "No matter how great the pain, how horrible the suffering, God remains my God and Savior because that is what his Word says. Let all the evidence say the opposite. Let the whole world shake its fist in his face in the presence of pain and misery. I will yet praise him, my help and my Savior. For his Word remains true when all men are liars. His grace remains sure when the ugliness of death itself says the opposite. My will I resign to his gracious providence. My will I deny in favor of his Word, his promise, his grace, his mercy."

Thus, in addition to the *self* denial that serves others out of love for Christ, cross bearing is that *self* denial which embraces the Word of Christ even when the sufferings of the moment seem to contradict his promise of grace and help in every need. Doing that at times can be very difficult, very painful. Every bit of that struggle is cross bearing. For it is a denial of the most basic instincts of the sinful *self*.

Yet another aspect of cross bearing is *self* denial that confesses trust in Jesus and in his Word in what Jesus calls an "adulterous and sinful generation" (Mk 8:38). An adulterous and sinful generation is by definition hostile to Christ and devoted to the satisfaction of its own will. We were created and redeemed so that we would be the bride of Christ. That marriage to Christ involves the surrender of our will to that of the Bridegroom. The worldling, who is not married to Christ, lives for another, for *self*. The worldling is therefore in his whole existence part and parcel of an adulterous and sinful generation no matter what he does. He follows his own will, whether that appears good on the outside or utterly wicked. Married to Christ, the Christian follows Christ under the cross in the surrender of his own will in favor of the will of Christ.

As Jesus tells us in Mark 8, the cross-bearer follows him with a loyal and faithful submission to him and to his Word, while surrounded by an adulterous and sinful world. The cross-bearer follows him especially when Christ and his Word are under attack. The attack will come sometimes from the world. The attack will come as well from our own sinful flesh, which is always in cahoots with the adulterous and sinful world. But *self* denial turns the back on *self*, rejects *self*, wars against *self* because of Jesus and his Word. Such *self* denial from beginning to end is unnatural for our fallen sinful nature. For the *self*, the old *self*, would much rather be married to the adulterous generation and devoted to its idolatrous pursuits.

To be sure, some works of *self* denial are easier than others. The parent tending a child has natural affection that will make

19

self denial and service easier than at other times when there is no such natural tie. But even in those works made easier by natural ties of kinship and affection, an adulterous and sinful generation may attack. It often ridicules the parent who insists on raising the child in accord with the Word of God. The parent who at home and even publicly opposes parts of the school's science or family life curriculum will not enjoy the praise of this adulterous and sinful generation. The parent who refuses to go along with the "Everybody does it" morality of the child's classmates may not experience much appreciation even at home.

That same parent who patiently bears ridicule for faithfulness to the Savior will find such *self* denial difficult, often very painful. But the essence of the easier acts as well as the more difficult ones is the same. Both, the one easier and the other more difficult, flow from a connection to Jesus and his Word. Thus in essence both acts have *self* denial as their common root, Jesus and his Word as their common source. For the care of the child stems not only from natural affection; it flows as well from a love for the Savior who gave the child and a desire to imitate Jesus' love by showing love. And that care includes care for the mind and soul as well as care for the body. Unquestionably, care for the mind and the soul is the more difficult of the two assignments. It requires a much greater degree of *self* denial and a still greater appreciation for the importance of carrying the cross behind Jesus in an adulterous and sinful generation.

The connection between the old man and the new man under the cross

It should be obvious, then, that the *self* denial of which Jesus speaks requires a new will if we are to embrace the cross willingly, even joyfully, no matter how light or heavy the cross may be. To the old will, the natural will, a cross is painful and presses heavily on the always unconverted old man in us. It is in the old man, that is, in the fallen nature we have inherited from Adam and Eve, that the old *self* rules. The cross is and remains painful for us precisely because we are never completely free of the old man and his corrupt, rebellious will in this life. But, and it's important to remember, the one that is crushed and pained and grieved by the cross is the old man—not the new man.

The new man is the Christian nature that is ours by faith in Christ, the nature born in Baptism, created and sustained by the gospel. The new man rejoices in the cross, sees it as a powerful tool for beating back the never-finished assaults of the old man who remains wedded to the adulterous and sinful generation. Make no mistake about it: the old man comes well armed to the conflict. His weapons are unbelief, the love affair with *self*, and his love of this adulterous and sinful generation. Our difficulty in understanding the theology of the cross and our difficulty in dealing with it can be traced directly to this fundamental reality of our life on the way to heaven. We remain, as Luther put it in Latin, *Simul justus et peccator,* that is, *at the same time,* and on our best day, *both saint and sinner.* The struggle between the two is very real and as difficult and painful as it is real.

This whole matter of *self* denial and of taking up the cross for the sake of Jesus and his Word is really just another one of the brilliant examples that Jesus used in teaching the First Commandment. At its core, *self* denial and cross bearing are exactly what the First Commandment requires. Luther surely understood that in his short summary explanation of the First Commandment: "We should fear, love, and trust in God above all things."

What could be more difficult, more contrary to the flesh, and more painful to the *self* than that? By nature we *fear* anything disagreeable to our own will, be it the effort involved in surrendering it or the ridicule of the world when we do surrender it. By nature we *love self* most of all and before anyone or anything else. By nature we *trust* our own will, our own cleverness, our own instincts, our own selfish and often very twisted definition of right and wrong: What suits me and is convenient is right; anything else is wrong. Of course, the First Commandment involves also all of the other commandments at the very least by implication. That is why Luther in the Small Catechism begins his explanation of each of the other commandments with "We should fear and love God that . . ." Those words are a constant reminder of the First Commandment. It is not too much to say that all of our conscious sins and many of the sins of which we are not even aware are connected to or caused by the refusal to carry the cross, that is, a refusal to deny *self*, a refusal therefore to fear, love, and trust in God above all things.

Crucial differences between Christ's cross and ours

There are a number of significant differences between Christ's cross and ours. Those differences begin in the difference between his will and our will. Our still sinful and fallen will continues to resist the cross; in fact, much of its weight is the result of the struggle between the old will and the new will. That resistance in our will prevents us from ever carrying our cross perfectly; our obedience is always imperfect, always stained by that struggle between the old will and the new will.

Although Christ prayed for his cup of suffering to be removed, he also prayed that the Father's will be done. So even then he yielded in submission to the will of his Father with the cross as his goal. He did everything for the benefit of mankind and at the greatest cost to himself. The bearing of his cross at the end of his life was the capstone and summation of his entire obedience during his earthly life. Christ died on the cross at the end with the same attitude that he had at the beginning. He lived to please his Father and to benefit us, and thus to conform his mind and life, and then his death, to the mission that he had from his Father. Thus his cross was suffering very unlike ours. Much of our suffering comes from the resistance to the will of God, which still remains in us. Christ's suffering, on the other hand, came to him entirely from outside of himself. His burden was the opposition of the world and the guilt of all humanity, which he bore on the cross. His was never a battle of some evil force within him that resisted the will of God and really wanted to sin rather than to obey the Father's will. Thus his cross bearing was unique, because it was perfect in every respect.

Finally, Christ's cross bearing was unique because it accomplished what no other cross bearing could accomplish, namely, the redemption of the world. We bear our cross trusting in the merit of his cross bearing, a merit sufficient to gain for us eternal life and salvation. As necessary as our cross is, it could never accomplish that or contribute in the least to what Christ alone has already accomplished for us with his cross.

That Jesus' work was unique in its perfection and its ultimate consequence should not be used, however, as an excuse for us to avoid or minimize either the necessity of Christian cross bearing or its importance. To put it another way, Christ's call to us to bear the cross and deny *self* is not merely another preaching of the first use of the law; that is, it is not intended only to help us see the greatness of our sin and our desperate need for his saving work. Of course, it is that. But it is not only that. While we in our fallen state always have reason to confess that we have not carried the cross as we should, that confession does not give us an excuse to cast the cross aside. Nor is absolution, the proclamation that our sins have been forgiven, a license to leave the cross behind at the church door. It is an abomination whenever confession is considered the easy way out of guilt and absolution the nullification of the will of God. Those who preach or teach that way fall under Paul's judgment in Romans 3:8: "Their condemnation is deserved." Or as the King James Version translates it more graphically if not quite as literally: "Whose damnation is just" (cf. also Ro 6:1ff.). Rather, the absolution serves as an incentive to go home refreshed and with a renewed embrace of this cross of *self* denial. For I want to express my joy in absolution in the way that Christ himself has chosen for me to express it, that is, in *self* denial.

Why *self* denial is so difficult

What then is so difficult about this *self* denial that it should be compared to and always is a cross? That is indicated already in the equation of the struggle to take up the cross with *self* denial. *Self* is so near and dear to us that its denial is, on the face of it, extremely difficult. In fact, there is nothing more difficult than to deny *self.*

Just to contrast our *self* with Christ's *self* helps to put the whole matter into sharper focus. Every thought, every word, every deed in Christ's life was a thought, a word, a deed that consciously and perfectly worshiped God, loved God, and benefited mankind. There was nothing haphazard about it, nothing merely coincidental. It was all—from beginning to end—conscious, deliberate, willing, joyful obedience and submission on the way to the ultimate obedience and submission in Holy Week. We see that even in the miracles of Christ during the years of his earthly ministry. Not a one of them was done for his own comfort and ease and convenience. They were all done for the benefit of others. Even in secret, during the temptations in the wilderness (Mt 4:1-11), he refused to use his almighty power just for his own benefit.

It is, on the other hand, impossible for us to imagine a day or even an hour or a moment in which we perfectly love God with all of our heart and soul and mind and strength. It is impossible for us to conceive of a day during which we consciously do everything out of perfect love for God and for the benefit of those around us. *Self* is just too close, too near and dear, for us to have any real nearness to that kind of perfection, except as we see in it in Jesus. The old *self* is so much a part of us that it is even hard for us to recognize the old will as sinful. In fact, we would never grasp that point, were it not for the testimony of the Scriptures (Jn 3:6; Ro 7:18; Eph 2:1-3).

So complete is the corruption of our old *self* that it may even use the perfection of Christ as an excuse to wallow in and justify its own sin and corruption. For unlike us, Christ could not fail in his obedience and submission. The personal union in Christ, that is, the union of his divine and human natures in one person, made sin an impossibility for him. His service therefore, strictly speaking and as already noted, cannot be his cross in exactly the same way that *self* denial is a cross for us; for there was never any resistance in him to his Father's will. And so, our *self* may argue, his suffering was not real, since his success was assured from the start. He cannot therefore expect us to be victorious over sin and temptation the way in which he was—or so our sinful flesh would have us think. For him it was easy; for us, it is just too hard to even attempt it.

But that his victory was assured is not the same as saying that the obedience and ultimately the cross were easy for him. No, not at all! In so many ways the cross of Christ is unique. But this much our cross has in common with his: The cross is painful. His was infinitely more painful than ours, because he suffered for the sins of the world on it. Even before his suffering in Holy Week, his struggle against Satan and sin was a real struggle, even though his victory was a foregone conclusion. Just consider that creatures, the holy angels, came to serve him at the close of his temptations in the wilderness (Mt 4:11). Had there been no real struggle for Jesus in his human nature, such service would have been pointless. Consider his anguish in the Garden of Gethsemane as well, where again an angel came to strengthen him (Lk 22:43). Hear his tormented cry from the cross, when for us and for our salvation, he was forsaken by the Father he so perfectly loved and obeyed (Mt 27:46). All those passages that speak of Christ's temptations and his suffering would become meaningless if his struggle and his suffering were not real. In point of fact, a temptation by definition entails struggle; if there were no struggle, no need to resist, there would be no temptation. But he did resist; he did struggle; he did suffer; and all of it he did perfectly.

We certainly would not say of something merely human, which to our eyes appears perfect, that it was therefore easy because it seemed perfect. Tell the swimmer whose perfect form in a dive won a gold medal at the Olympics or the ballet dancer after a flawless *Swan Lake* that the performance must have been easy since it was perfect. Then see what looks of contempt you receive! Indeed, the reverse should be the case: the closer something comes to perfection, the more difficult it is to achieve, much less to maintain. How foolish then to assert that Christ's submission and his cross were easy because they were carried out perfectly and without sin. The obedience of Christ, even with all the perfection of his human nature in its union with the divine, even with the impossibility therefore of sin, was nevertheless a struggle. All by itself the concept of perfection bespeaks the greatest difficulty: the words *never* and *always* are, after all, such big words. He *never* sinned. He *always* loved God with his whole heart and mind and strength. And still he was a true man. It boggles the mind! Such perfection is beyond our imagination and worlds away from anything we ever experience ourselves. So too is the enormity of Jesus' struggle. The gospel accounts certainly say so. The testimony of the apostolic writings agrees. When they speak of Christ's suffering and urge us to bear our suffering patiently as we follow him, they are not talking about pain that for him was a mere illusion or insignificant or a metaphor (e.g., Heb 5:7,8; 1 Pe 2:21-23). His struggle was real; so is ours. His cross was real; so is ours.

Thus the perfection of Christ's struggle and his triumph on his cross offer us forgiveness for our imperfection and our resistance to the carrying of our own cross; they do not offer a way to justify the idolatry to which our old *self* is addicted or to wallow in the muck and mire of our remaining imperfection. Again: Christ's struggle and cross were real. The cross and struggle to which he calls us is also real. Christ's struggle and his cross came to him from outside of himself. Our struggle is from inside, against our old *self*, aided and abetted by the devil and the world.

If we examine that struggle, how especially it works itself out in the better moments of our lives, we may understand a little better why Jesus calls our *self* denial a cross. What will we find in our every effort to do what is pleasing to God simply out of love and gratitude for his grace? *Self* resisting! At the very least, *self* provokes hesitation in obedience to his Word, then reluctance, followed by some measure of opposition and even regret that *self* was vanquished.

The most common of examples may demonstrate the point. The Christian in his renewed or Christian will wants to pray. *Self* doesn't. At the beginning of prayer, *self* holds us back. In the middle, *self* distracts and interrupts with foolish and wandering thoughts. At the end, *self* says: "It's about time; now let's get on to things that matter!"

The same pattern with but slight variation is easy to trace when we meditate on God's Word. When, for example, we are trying to listen to a sermon, *self* is perhaps busiest of all. Can't you hear the devil conducting his own service right on your shoulder, with *self* as the preacher in your ear every time you try to listen? The devil's sermon may go something like this: "Oh, no, not that again! Didn't he say the same thing last Sunday? I know all this already! And look what that girl is wearing. See how that fellow is yawning. Why can't that woman take the screaming baby out? Look at that hypocrite over there!" And on and on it goes.

When the collection plate comes around, *self* may howl its protest: "That much (even if it were but a penny!)? Think what you could have done with that. Compare that with what the rest give. Let them carry the load for a while. Well, at least it wasn't more than it was!" And if the flesh does not thus howl, it is probably because it won the victory earlier; it got the offering to be so small that it wasn't worth a howl of protest when it was finally made. Our Lutheran Confessions are at pains to remind us of the point that even in our best works, we still need forgiveness (e.g., Formula of Concord, Solid Declaration IV:8; VI:21,22). And why? Because *self* opposes and, to some extent, stains all our works, even the best ones. With just these trivial examples, it should be easy to see why we can put no trust for our salvation in our works, no, not even in our carrying of the cross. For too near is *self* ever to be rid of it this side of the grave. The simple and basic fact that *self* often succeeds in convincing us that its sins really are not sins and worthy of no struggle already tells us how difficult the struggle against *self* will always be.

The cross and repentance

Repentance in particular, whether for transgressions that seem trivial or for iniquities that cry out to heaven for vengeance, is perhaps the hardest *self* denial of all. The flesh clings tenaciously to self-service and opposes nothing so vehemently as the confession that it is utterly damnable. Close to the bosom it clutches its favorite sins, often unwilling even to consider that they are sins. One cannot help but reflect on what a great victory the flesh has won when the call to repentance and the cry of the *Kyrie* are turned into mere routine. There is not much of *self* denial and cross bearing in routine. But the gut-wrenching realization that the refusal to submit to Christ and his Word is the same as being ashamed of Christ and rejecting him—that is quite another matter. To look at the horror of Christ's crucifixion and to grasp the reality of God's anger against *my* sin, to hear the sermon of Nathan to David in 2 Samuel 12 ("*you* are the man!") in the deepest part of our being, oh how the *self* hates it. Yes, and ultimately to say to God, "Forgive everything! For there is nothing in me, nothing in my whole life, nothing at all that does not deserve hell. Anything that is good is yours. Everything else is wicked beyond description. And so, O God, forgive it all! Then the worst in me will be washed away, and the best which you have given me and which I still manage to corrupt will be cleansed by the blood of your Son."

What a horrible burden the soul carries around, whether recognized or not, when it refuses to repent! David did recognize that burden; he described the anguish of his soul when he did not want to repent as the wasting away of his bones and the groaning of his soul all day long (Ps 32:3). His guilt festered like a sore on which he was pouring vinegar by his refusal to confess his guilt. That pain, however, is not the cross of God's sending but the self-inflicted wound of the sinner who still holds fast to his sin. But in David's case, God used well the pain of David's self-inflicted suffering. It became so great that when confronted by Nathan, David let out the simple cry: "I have sinned against the LORD." He did not deny his guilt or excuse it. He did not make comparisons with others who had done things just as bad or worse than he. He repented. He mourned and lamented his guilt for which he could not atone by any amount of sorrow or by any future good deeds. As we see in 2 Samuel 12 and in Psalm 32 and elsewhere, the law did its work of crushing David. But the gospel did its still greater work. For repentance is not only the heartfelt grief over sin and sinfulness; it is also the new man's trust and confidence that the sin is forgiven, blotted out, removed as far as the east from the west.

Repentance has two great obstacles, the one as bad as the other, that confront us every day. The one obstacle is the refusal to repent at all. It is to treat sin as though it were of no importance or consequence. It is to imagine that God is not serious about his Word and will never call us to account.

The refusal that minimizes guilt and harbors the illusion that God is not serious about his law also ends up minimizing the gospel. For where there is no understanding of the crime and the punishment deserved, there will be little appreciation for the rescue won by Christ and the release given in absolution. With contempt for the law comes disdain for the gospel. The impenitent has an attitude of self-righteousness that casts aside the cross. All that remains of faith in the self-righteous one is what is called *historical* faith. That kind of faith merely grants that the history of Jesus' life, death, and resurrection actually happened. It is a "faith" no different from the devil's "faith." He knows that the history is true better than we do; he was an eyewitness to all of it. But mere historical faith saves no one, as St. James reminds us (Jas 2:19). There must be added to it the trust that the Holy Spirit creates through the gospel; there must be the trust that these truths apply to me, that Christ did not just die for everyone else. He died for me. And why did he die for me? Because I could not save myself or even contribute in the least to my own salvation. Because I had, therefore, in my wretchedness, my sin, my guilt, a *desperate need* for a Savior. That conviction, that faith, is the opposite of self-righteousness.

The equal and opposite second great obstacle to repentance is despair. The one who refuses to repent is self-righteous; he imagines that he is so good and God's law and gospel so trivial that he needs no repentance. The one who despairs, likewise, has an exalted opinion of himself. He imagines that his sin is so great that not even God can forgive it, not even Christ on the cross could pay for it. His repentance ends with sorrow over sin, like the sorrow of Saul and the sorrow of Judas. He casts aside the gospel, so that repentance never reaches its final goal of trust in forgiveness.

Without such trust, a new life under the cross is virtually impossible under the heavy burden of the sins of the old life. In fact, without trust in forgiveness, the despairing sinner really has self-righteousness as his only goal; he hopes to get to the point where he is so perfect that he has no need for sorrow over sin. It may sound strange, but it is nevertheless true: self-righteousness and despair are two sides of the same coin. The one in despair was probably self-righteous before he committed the sin that he now thinks cannot be forgiven. And in reality, as already noted, his goal is to get back to that condition in which he thinks that he needs no repentance. Thus the self-righteous Pharisee and despairing Judas are "twins."

As self-righteousness is not the cross but a refusal of it, so despair is not the cross either. Despair is the refusal first of Christ's cross and its infinite merit, and then the refusal to walk forgiven under the burden and in the battle of memory. For memory in those prone to despair always seeks to drag the forgiven sinner back either to the old sin or to the old guilt. The cross is the fight, the struggle, to stumble one's way back again and again to the cross of Christ in an ongoing repentance. That repentance grieves each day over its shame and its guilt. But even more important, such repentance embraces each day the forgiveness already won by Christ; then it takes up the cross anew for battle against temptations new and old, for battle against despair as well.

The cross of Christ should serve as a magnet to the one who struggles with the temptation to self-righteousness and a magnet as well to the one who must struggle with the temptation to despair. One must be drawn by the cross to see how great his guilt is and to bow low before it for the forgiveness that comes only from Christ's cross. And the other must be drawn by the cross to see how complete the love and work of Christ is in making the sacrifice that pays for the sins of the world and, therefore, also for his sins.

Thus the confession of those who struggle with the temptation to self-righteousness is the prayer of Jacob: "I am unworthy of all the kindness and faithfulness you have shown your servant" (Ge 32:10). It is the prayer of Isaiah: "All our righteous acts are like filthy rags" (Isa 64:6). And the prayer of the despairing is the confession of John the Baptist: "Look, the Lamb of God, who takes away the sin of the world!" (Jn 1:29). It is the assurance of St. John the apostle: "The blood of Jesus, his Son, purifies us from all sin" (1 Jn 1:7). Both the one struggling against self-righteousness and the one struggling with despair have a heavy cross. For the old *self* does not give up his claim to merit, nor does he wish to surrender his guilt to another. It is only because of the grace of God and the power of his Spirit in the law and the gospel that such a struggle is even possible. It is only because of the grace of God and the power of his Spirit in the Word and sacraments that such a cross can be and is carried successfully by countless saints in common life.

To put it briefly, cross-bearing *self* denial is to take Christ and his Word seriously in both the law and the gospel. *Self* strenuously and with all its might always resists every attempt to do that. Therefore, the work of such *self* denial is well called a cross.

As already noted, the cross may change its outward appearance from age to age, from individual to individual, from one time in life to another. The slivers may move and the splinters be differently configured, but its essence remains the same. It is the struggle to deny *self* and instead to follow Jesus. It is the struggle to follow him willing, even joyfully, in defiance of the adulterous and sinful generation that still remains in one's own heart as well as in the world. It is a *self* denial that begins with a struggle in the will, continues with struggle in the mind, in reason, and is plagued with obstacles from beginning to end in the emotions.

Much becomes clear when bearing the cross is defined as Jesus defines it in Mark 8. Cross bearing is *self* denial for the sake of Jesus and his Word. Thus anything that tempts us to turn away from Jesus and his Word is in cahoots with this adulterous and sinful generation. The struggle against temptation is a cross because of the appeal of temptation to *self*. The stronger the appeal to *self*, the more difficult resistance will be. *Self*, for example, loves to be flattered and pampered; accordingly, the approval and praise of the world makes it harder to trust in Christ and his Word, since I like hearing from the world that I'm already good enough and better than most. The pleasures that the world has to offer in abundance easily turn my eyes from the cross of Christ and from his Word to comfort and ease as ends in themselves that are worthy of all my attention.

On the other hand, outward persecution that may come because of a confession of faith in Christ or ridicule that follows such a confession is a cross. Why? Because in and of itself it is painful? No doubt. But even more than that, it is a cross because the flesh, the *self*, loathes the real cause and source of the pain, namely, Christ and his gospel. And the *self* is quick to point out that persecution and ridicule would be very easily avoided just by keeping quiet, by keeping the connection with Christ and his Word a secret, that is, by divorcing faith from life. *Self* strives without ceasing to do just that; for if faith can be divorced from life, faith itself will soon die. It is only by the death of faith that the cross disappears in this life. Then the marriage with the adulterous and sinful generation is complete, and the exchange has been made: Christ gone, the world's tinsel gained; eternal life gone, the soul doomed and damned.

Here it is worth noting a contrast: There are times when the *self* does not mind the hostility of the world. The greedy person or the lazy one may care little about the hostility of the world. The drunkard and the open adulterer and the thief may have long since overcome any interest in what the world thinks. All pain, all hostility, and even the possibility of pain and hostility, scoundrels are willing to bear in the pursuit of their own will, in the satisfying of the *self*. But the hostility of the world for the sake of Christ and his Word? That's quite another matter. The flesh howls in protest. *Self* shrieks that if God were really God, he would guard and protect his own. *Self* turns our eyes from Christ and his promises to the visible and to the pain of the moment. *Self* cries out that it is all Christ's fault. *Self* is willing to endure all manner of hostility in the interest of self-satisfaction; but it shuns and flees and loathes the least inconvenience or bother for the sake of Christ and his Word. That the self-satisfaction ends in nothingness, in frustration, in death, while Christ and his Word have eternal blessing with them does not alter the hostility of *self* in the least. Is it not clear? We have indeed a struggle that is very painful and a cross that is hard to carry. The struggle is against *self;* the cross is to deny *self.*

Thus not all suffering is a cross and suffering in and of itself is not a cross. Suffering *becomes* a cross not just because it is painful in itself but because it tempts the soul to turn away from Christ and his Word. All suffer sickness. But sickness becomes a cross when *self* uses it to cast doubt on the promises of God's gracious presence. Death comes to all. It becomes a cross when *self* uses death to argue that we are alone in the world, that death ends all, and that we should therefore serve *self* while we still can. Personal struggle with a besetting sin is a cross when *self* uses the temptation as an excuse to despair of the mercy of God if we fall and an excuse for self-righteousness if we do not fall. It is the connection to Christ and his Word that makes suffering and temptation a cross. It is the allure of the adulterous and sinful generation to the always adulterous and sinful *self* that makes resistance a struggle and a cross. It is these connections that distinguish cross bearing from the suffering which is the lot of all humanity to one degree or another.

The theology of the cross, therefore, is that study of the Word of God that looks for the connection between his cross and ours. It examines our cross as that necessary gift of God under which we enter finally into the kingdom of glory when God determines that the time for cross bearing has ended and the time for crown wearing has come. In heaven we no longer bear the cross, because in heaven the sinful *self* has finally been completely set aside and Christ has become all in all.

2

The Paradox

The theology of the cross contains a number of riddles that are impossible for us to solve with our unaided reason. To understand and embrace the truth of the gospel always requires the miraculous working of the Holy Spirit through his Word. Without his work in our hearts through the Word, we stumble in the darkness. That is true of the whole of the gospel and certainly, therefore, true also of the theology of the cross. How can we make any sense out of it? The crosses that God sends to us are good gifts of a gracious God. How can that be? The terms *crosses* and *good gifts from a gracious God* do not seem to fit in the same sentence. The theology of the cross confronts us with some of the most difficult paradoxes of the many that the Word of God presents to our faith. On the one hand, the cross is a precious gift from our loving Savior. On the other hand, the cross is a cruel instrument of torture, always painful, never easy. On the one hand, it is the dear cross, even the holy cross (again: *das liebe Kreuz!*). On the other hand, the cross is always stained by sin and in many important ways the result of sin; for in the struggle to deny *self,* we still have the old will resisting, so that we remain far from perfect on this side of the grave. To some extent, it will always be a cross of shame precisely because the victory is not yet won; its pain consists, to some extent, in that sinful will remaining in me that wants to sin, that wants nothing else but to serve *self.*

The twofold pain of the cross

Thus the pain of the cross is really twofold. On the one hand, it is the pain and frustration experienced deep down inside of the sinful *self* that it cannot get its way. The rest of the world with its dog-eat-dog mind-set prevents *self* from getting its own way; but more important, the Christian nature never stops its harassment of the old *self.* The Christian conscience condemns the old *self* both for what it wants to do and for what it actually succeeds in doing. Yes, to some extent the Christian in me robs the old *self* of the pleasure he was hoping to get from his sins! Imagine that! He sins and doesn't enjoy it as much as before because his conscience condemns him and drives him to his knees; hopefully as the law crushes and condemns the old nature, the old *self,* the gospel will bring the Christian in me back to the cross of Christ for forgiveness. That makes the old *self* all the more frustrated and angry.

The Christian in me even puts the brakes on the old *self,* so that sometimes *self* doesn't finish carrying out the evil that it had its heart set on. So, for example, the angry gossip chatters on to the hurt of another. But the gossiper's conscience judges and condemns, so that the mouth stops its evil before it is finished and the heart feels ashamed of the tawdry behavior that was not stopped soon enough. Or the old *self* pursues its lust with impure thoughts and a will that wants to run wild into acts that defile both body and soul. But the Christian conscience condemns and judges both the acts and the person as unclean and guilty. The Christian side robs the old *self* of the pleasure it sought in sin and, again, puts the brakes on so that depravity does not reach its ultimate depth. So the pain of the cross is in part the frustration of the old *self* when the old *self* does not get its way.

But the pain of the cross is also the frustration of the Christian nature, the new *self.* The Christian nature is frustrated because it does not completely conquer the old nature, the sinful flesh/*self*. The Christian new man wants to obey and serve God perfectly, really wants to. He wants to think and speak the best about his neighbor. He wants to put off once and for all impure thoughts as well as actions. He wants to say *good-bye!* for good to all greed and envy, to jealousy and spite, to bitterness and complaining, and especially to any lingering indifference to God and his Word. But the old *self* keeps banging on the door and barging in. It keeps staining even the best efforts with sin. How full of anguish is St. Paul's expression of that pain in Romans 7, which ends with his exclamation: "What a wretched man I am!"

The cross hurts. The struggle inside the Christian between the new man and the old man leaves the old man angry and frustrated; it leaves the new man frustrated and sometimes exhausted. How can that be good? How can that be called the *dear* cross, the holy cross, given to us by a loving and gracious God? Would it not be far better if God just zapped the old man, the old *self,* out of us as soon as we became Christians? Then there would be no struggle. There would be no pain. There would be no defeats for the Christian in battle and no guilty and accusing conscience in the face of such defeats. Yes, then we would be very close to heaven itself, where our will would be perfectly conformed to the will of Christ and our behavior would follow our now perfected will. Would that not be far better than this constant battle with *self* and its perpetual nagging and tugging at the robe of holiness that we really want to wear? Would that not be far better than the never-ceasing anguish of the guilty soul that always has to plead for mercy in the face of its shabby record of halfhearted battles and only partial victories?

To make the dilemma more pointed still, it is not too much to say that for many a saint the closer one comes to a life of cheerful submission to the will and Word of God, the heavier and more painfully the cross presses and oppresses as the old *self* struggles to reassert itself and regain its control. It always has a new tactic, another strategy designed for our ruin. We might have expected the opposite to be the case, that the closer we would come to victory, the lighter the cross. But that is often not the way things work out. For the closer the Christian gets to God in the Word and sacraments, the fuller will be the conviction of utter unworthiness and weakness. Indeed, his very success may bring with it a whole host of new opponents. And it is not difficult to list them:

✠ Temptations to pride, self-righteousness.

✠ Fleshly security that is content with the progress already made.

✠ Happy comparison of one's own spirituality and sanctification with the evident lack of the same in others, a pietism that often is the last refuge of a guilty conscience—"I did it; I won! Why haven't you?"

So no matter how far we have come in our Christian life, no matter how experienced, we nevertheless remain under the cross, the dear cross, the cross of struggle that comes from our loving God and Savior.

The cross that *God wants* us to bear and that *we want* to carry

St. Paul helps us see and accept the divine rationality behind this riddle: A *loving God* wants us to carry a heavy and painful cross, and *we* want to carry that heavy and painful cross as well. Consider his words, especially in Romans 7:24–8:39 and then again in 2 Corinthians 12:7-10.

In Roman 7 and 8 the apostle gives voice to his frustration in the struggle that goes on inside him, the struggle between the old man and the new man. He cries out, "What a wretched man I am! Who will rescue me from this body of death?" Then he quickly and beautifully gives answer to his own question. He shows us why the cross is the *dear* cross, the gift of a loving and gracious God, dear to him and therefore dear to us as well. He says, "Thanks be to God—through Jesus Christ our Lord! . . . Therefore, there is now no condemnation for those who are in Christ Jesus."

What a powerful point! Read the rest of chapter 8 and see how fully Paul delights in that point. The cross is dear and a gracious gift precisely because it keeps pointing me to and driving me back to the cross of Christ! Were there no cross and no struggle for me, I would not be singing endless praise and thanks to him for his cross and his struggle. As necessary as my cross and struggle are—again: no cross, no Christian—it is Christ and his cross, Christ and his struggle that have won my salvation. That is the essence of faith, its heart and core, its source and content and goal. Because of what he did, there is no condemnation, none at all for me as I limp and stumble along behind him under the weight of the cross he sends me. Assured is the final triumph, because he won it. Granted already is the joy of the coming resurrection, because he has fully paid for it. Therefore, *thanks be to God—through Jesus Christ our Lord!* I could never appreciate that truth or grow in appreciation of it year by year, were it not for the pain of the cross I bear.

How that must gall the devil! His great hope is that the cross will separate us from Christ. God's great intention accomplished by his gospel and carried out under the cross is exactly the opposite. And the great irony is that without the pain of the cross, there is no joy in the redemption accomplished by his cross alone. Therefore, the cross is the gift of a truly loving God. Therefore, we want it, no matter how painful it may at times become.

In 2 Corinthians 12:7-10, Paul answers the question about the cross and its pain on the basis of his own experience. Except for the virgin Mary, probably no one was ever blessed more richly than Paul. He saw Christ and was instructed by him after Christ had risen and ascended (Gal 1:12). He had the strength of a Samson to persevere in persecution and hardship (2 Co 11). He had received revelations directly from God, revelations that he knew would benefit the church as long as time would last, as the verbally inspired letters that he wrote and that God has preserved for us in the New Testament. And beyond such abundant blessing, he was even able to see heaven while he was still alive, to see it in a splendor so great that he could not describe it in mere human language.

With such great blessing came two temptations. One was that the people who saw and heard him would conclude that the church was successful because Paul was so great. The other was that Paul himself might be tempted to think so too. But Paul had a cross to bear, a suffering greater than the persecutions described in chapter 11. It was a cross because it required *self* denial on the part of Paul, a *self* denial that submits to what is painful, accepts it, even ends up boasting in it. He calls it "a thorn in my flesh, a messenger of Satan, to torment me" (12:7). He had some affliction that so tormented him that he begged God to take it away, begged three times. Was the affliction physical, perhaps as some have suggested, very poor eyesight? Was it some other physical ailment, some kind of constant stinging pain that could be compared to pain caused by a thorn? Was it an ailment that attacked his faith and tempted him to doubt the mercy and love of God? Was it an altogether spiritual thorn, perhaps even the temptation to despair that poked and prodded his conscience, as he recalled his earlier life of self-righteousness and of persecuting the church? After all, he says of himself that he *is* the chief of sinners—not just that he *was* at some earlier time the chief of sinners (1 Ti 1:15).

We do not know the exact nature of the thorn. And it is just as well that we do not know. We can imagine that his is perhaps the same thorn that we may suffer in our flesh, that pain of body or soul that never completely goes away, that always threatens our destruction. It is enough for us to hear him call it a thorn. It hurt. Its pain was relentless. And for all its pain, yes, because of all its pain, Paul considered it among God's greatest blessings. For God himself explained to the apostle the necessity of such a cross, such a thorn in his flesh.

The explanation that God gave is at once so simple and so profound: "My grace is sufficient for you, for my power is made perfect in weakness" (2 Co 12:9). Would that each Christian had the time to write his own autobiography with this verse as the title! Comfort and ease, success as the world judges success, outward praise and glory—these are not sufficient for life. Health and wealth, an abundance of friends and family, freedom from pain and frustration and failure—these are not sufficient for life. Deep insight into all mysteries and into the secrets of the human heart, including the secrets of one's own heart, total victory over every weakness and in every temptation—no, not even these are the stuff of life.

One thing alone is sufficient: *grace!* And only the bearing of the cross makes it clear that the meaning and essence of real life and everlasting life is *grace!* That is, God freely chooses to love me. And he chooses to love me for reasons of his own, reasons that have nothing to do with any good that I have done or ever will do. Even before the world began, when he knew already all of the reasons he would have *not* to love me, he nevertheless loved me. In such love and in Christ, he did everything, absolutely everything, that was necessary for my eternal salvation. He even ruled over all history, so that my hearing of the gospel and my trust in it would not be mere coincidence, much less the result of my will and choice; it would be altogether and alone his gracious doing in accordance with his gracious good will!

Without the cross that comes as a consequence of faith and, at the same time, as the result of my own sinful nature, I would never know that grace was sufficient, that grace is what life is really all about. I would assume perhaps that grace was a good start. I might think that grace was a nice help. I might conclude that grace was even necessary. But I would never either realize or experience the truth: Grace is sufficient! Grace is everything! Instead, I would confront and doubtless fall before the temptation to pray like the Pharisee in the temple (Lk 18:9-14). I would congratulate God for the wisdom of his choice in calling me; for see how I have proven myself worthy of that call since my conversion; see how I have risen above the common herd and its temptations; see how noble I have become and how fit for the company of the saints.

Ah, but the cross and its struggle, the cross and its frustration, the cross and its pain keeps knocking me down. It keeps crushing me under its load. It keeps bringing me back to the cross of him who loved me and gave himself for me and to his grace. For it is on his grace alone and on his cross alone that I rely. It is on him alone that my whole hope of victory depends. If the pain of the cross brings me to a deeper appreciation of that truth, then thanks be to God for *das liebe Kreuz,* the dear cross!

The corollary to the sufficiency of grace is this, that God's *power is made perfect in weakness.* That is, God's power shows itself and reaches its goal in the weakness of the one who bears the cross. In Galatians 4:13,14, for example, Paul expresses his appreciation both to God and to his fellow Christians for the fact that they received him when his weakness was evident to them. In Philippians he rejoices in his imprisonment. For under the cross of weakness and persecution no one will confuse Paul's power with God's power. Paul had no power to convince anyone of anything while in chains. But when in chains he proclaimed the gospel and people believed it, it was quite clear where the power was: it was in God and in the gospel message through which God worked faith in the hearers. Thus *God's power* was made perfect in weakness. *God's power* in the gospel reached its divine goal. That was a great joy and comfort for Paul, to see the power of the gospel at work. It was as well a great joy and comfort to Paul's hearers and to the recipients of his letters. Yes, and the power of the gospel sustained Paul in his own weakness, in the weakness that was his in chains, in the weakness that was evident when he could not overcome obstacles to his work on every side. Just as the faith of others clearly did not come from Paul but from the gospel, so too Paul's own faith. Paul could rejoice together with his hearers: Our faith is based, not on Paul—see how weak he is. Our faith comes from God in the gospel—see how powerful he is in his Word! If the pain of the cross brings me to a deeper appreciation of that truth, than thanks be to God for *das liebe Kreuz,* the dear cross!

The pattern of joy and suffering together is set in Jesus' own cross

So the cross is a symbol of suffering and yet dear. It is painful and yet precious. It is a sign of weakness and yet a forerunner of victory. The mystery and the paradox are evident and resolved even in the passion of Christ. To be sure, in dogmatic theology we make the very useful and scriptural distinction between Christ's state of humiliation and his state of exaltation (Php 2:5-11). In the state of humiliation, which began at the moment of his conception, Christ veiled the divine majesty and almighty power that always is his and which he never for a moment gave up. In the state of exaltation, he no longer hides behind the veil of weakness and lowliness; he uses his divine power always and not just occasionally as in the state of humiliation. The state of exaltation began at that moment when Christ became alive in the grave on Easter Sunday. That's when he entered into his glory. But look at how Jesus links suffering and glory at the beginning of Holy Week, when his humiliation will reach its lowest point. He links suffering and glory so closely together that in his mind there is hardly a distinction between them. In John 12 Jesus rejoices and speaks of his coming suffering, and ours after his, in the most exalted of terms. Philip and Andrew had reported to him that some Greeks wanted to see him. Jesus' response takes our breath away (as his words so often do, especially when he speaks of his cross and ours):

> The hour has come for the Son of Man to be glorified. I tell you the truth, unless a kernel of wheat falls to the ground and dies, it remains only a single seed. But if it dies, it produces many seeds. The man who loves his life will lose it, while the man who hates his life in this world will keep it for eternal life. Whoever serves me must follow me; and where I am, my servant also will be. My Father will honor the one who serves me. Now my heart is troubled, and what shall I say? "Father, save me from this hour"? No, it was for this very reason I came to this hour. Father, glorify your name! (vv. 23-28)

Jesus can hardly wait for his suffering to begin. But his heart is so deeply and profoundly troubled that it would be understandable if he had asked his Father to take the cross away. And still, he can hardly wait to reach the cross and its glory! There is a roller coaster of emotions in the heart of the Son of God and Mary's son, our Savior, as he confronts the real horror of the cross and the matchless glory of its fruit.

Thus Jesus links the joy and the suffering. The cross and the crown are inseparable. Where there is no cross, there is no crown. How can a loving Father inflict such pain on his only begotten Son and his Son then call that suffering the beginning of glory? How can he, knowing full well the agony that is approaching, speak in the same terms about the suffering that he expects his followers to endure, suffering which he himself will send? The seed must die to bear fruit. The Son of God must endure the cross to redeem the world. The Christian must die with him to rise with him.

The paradox of wickedness and the dear cross

Everything is made to fit under this necessity of the cross before the crown, even the wickedness of the devil and the world. The devil and the wicked world are forced to serve against their will the glorious goal of Christ's ultimate triumph. For it is the very wickedness of a Judas, together with the wickedness of a corrupt government and a fallen church, that Jesus uses to bring about his suffering and thus to enter into his glory. To spite the devil, to make him spit and rage, Christ is victorious in defeat. Out of death comes life. Out of the utter wickedness of the crucifixion comes the restoration of true holiness. What divine irony!

In our life and experience too, God lets evil serve his own loving and saving purpose for us. An analogy here may be useful. The devil is like a vicious pit bull. He growls and threatens, wants nothing more than to bite and kill. But he is on a leash in a pit. We are in the garden of God's grace and mercy, hedged about by the law and nourished richly by the gospel. Outside the garden, in his pit, the devil snarls; threats of painful consequences for sin are in his jowls. Sometimes the threats of consequences for sin are enough to keep our sinful nature in check, to keep us from going out of the garden. Nevertheless, at other times, our sinful nature gets the upper hand through neglect of the Word and sacraments. Foolishly and perversely we leave the beauty of the garden for the pit with the pit bull. In spite of both our knowledge from the Word and our repeated experience in life, we decide that we can get away with sin and somehow evade its consequences. And so we leave the garden. It may take a while, but out of love God lets the dog bite us, and sometimes he bites us very hard and painfully indeed. We suffer the consequences of our sins and of our greatest sin, the neglect of the Word. The pain should send us struggling back out of the muck and away from the pit bull, back to the garden. The jaws of the dog and the muck of the pit make our task an impossible one. But our Father is waiting for us. He sends his Son rushing to our rescue. Through the promises of the gospel, the Holy Spirit pulls and tugs us back into the Father's arms, arms rich in mercy with a voice filled with grace. The devil, the old evil foe, has served his purpose. God has used him to help in our restoration, quite contrary to the devil's intent. Again, what divine irony! (For God's own examples, cf. Ps 107!)

In the case of Jesus' cross, the answer to the question of how suffering can be the source of joy and glory is found in the redemptive result of his suffering. Jesus knew perfectly how it would all end on Easter Sunday and in his glorious ascension to the right hand of the Father (Heb 12:2; Php 2:8-11). Jesus knew perfectly that the result of it all would be the redemption of the world. He said so many times, and many times it was said of him, that he would save by his sacrifice. We think of Genesis 3:15, of Psalm 22, of Isaiah 53, to mention just a handful of promises about the results of his redemptive work in the Old Testament. Indeed, the whole system of blood sacrifices in the Old Testament, especially those at Passover and on the great Day of Atonement, bespeak a redemption and a forgiveness that comes only with blood, with suffering, with death (cf. Ex 12:21-23; Lev 4–7; 16:1–17:22, et al.; note especially the sum of it all in Heb 9:22). From the beginning of his earthly life to its end, we hear one promise after another concerning the redemptive significance of his suffering and of the inseparable connection between suffering and redemption. Even his name, Jesus, that is, Savior, carries with it the promise of suffering. Simeon spoke of it in the temple (Lk 2:33-35). John the Baptist pointed the disciples both to the pain and to its saving results when he identified Jesus as the Lamb of God, who would take away the sins of the world (Jn 1:29,36); a lamb is an animal of sacrifice for sin. And Jesus himself made frequent and unmistakable references to both his suffering and its result during his earthly ministry (e.g., Jn 3:16; 8:27; 10:11-18, to mention just a few of the most commonly known references).

And all of this suffering happens through the instrumentality of wicked and evil men who remain nevertheless accountable for their wickedness. They had no intention of playing a role in the redemption of the world or in their own redemption. Like the devil himself, their father (Jn 8:44), they wanted to prevent any good, much less salvation, from coming into the world through the work of Jesus. Nevertheless, these evil, vile, cruel henchmen of the devil became instruments in the hands of God for the redemption of the world! They must bear the shame and guilt of their evil. But

God and God alone brings about the good, the redemption that comes from it. How the devil must choke on that fact!

Differences that distinguish our cross and crown from Christ's cross and crown

In the case of Jesus' glory and his crown, suffering comes from beginning to end by way of the sin of others, since he has no sin of his own. His crown, therefore, is altogether his by right and merit, because he suffered in innocence. In our case, things are reversed. The suffering that is called our cross is rooted in our own sinfulness, while the crown comes from another, from Christ. But suffering there must be if there is to be a crown of glory. The suffering may be the cross itself, that is, the never finished struggle to deny *self*. Or it may be a suffering that begins with some event outside of our *self* but worms its way into our innermost being. It could, for example, be the loss of earlier gifts of God, of health, family members, wealth, position, or friends. Such losses, as we noted earlier, the *self* uses to incite us to doubt the mercy, the love, the grace of God.

All such losses may be very painful to us. We miss what we once had and assumed or hoped that we could keep. But the pain points us back to the fundamental nature of the cross, the denial of *self* and the acceptance of whatever God sends. For what he sends is the gift of a loving Father, even when what he sends is pain and loss. In the time of loss, it may not occur to us to give thanks for the gift so graciously given earlier. It may not occur to us to praise God that we had the gift to enjoy for such a long time. Instead, our *self* behaves as though it were entitled to what it had and that it is the height of injustice now to be deprived of it.

To put it another way: We would not complain about any loss if we considered Christ to be all in all. To the extent that he is not all in all, we suffer in the presence of outward loss. Our complaints, therefore, in the face of pain and loss are evidence of failure in the struggle against *self*. What a difficult lesson that is to learn! What a difficult cross to bear! What a difficult problem within our own soul to solve! Luther sings in the fourth stanza of his great battle hymn: "And take they our life, goods, fame, child and wife, let these all be gone, they yet have nothing won; the Kingdom ours remaineth" (*The Lutheran Hymnal* 262:4). But who really believes that? If one of these gifts goes, we grieve and understandably so. Indeed, not to grieve at all would suggest a lack of appreciation for the gift in the first place. Nevertheless, there is usually more at work than just a sorrow that stems from appreciation for the now-lost gift. The loss and the grief usually press harder than that. If more or all of the gifts go, the loss would press very hard indeed! How difficult it is for us to give God our hearty thanks for his gifts and at the same time be perfectly ready to lose them all, if it should please God to take them from us! It is certainly true that we rarely realize how unwilling we are to part with his gifts until one is gone. Only in loss do we begin to grasp how overly dependent we had become on the gift for our joy rather than on the giver of the gift.

That is exactly the lesson God is teaching when he inflicts or allows pain. He is drawing and tugging us back to Psalm 73:21-28, to Lamentations 3:17-26, and to Paul's beautiful confessions of this truth in Philippians 4:11-13 and in 1 Timothy 6:6-8. He is bringing us back to the realization that in having him we have everything. He is taking us back into Mark 8, to the recognition that having even the whole world is a loss without him. In our weakness we may object: "Ah, but if only we had known the outcome of our suffering from the beginning, the way Jesus did. If only we could know with his divine certainty the purpose of it all." To which objection we must answer: "But we do know! For he who does not lie has told us in his Word what the purpose is and how it is all supposed to come out!" St. Paul sings of the outcome and the end of it all in one of the most beautiful and exultant hymns in the Bible in Romans 8.

The bridge connecting the pain of the cross to the victor's crown in the resurrection

It is clear from the life and work of Christ that the cross and the crown are inseparably connected. It is clear from the lives of the saints—we will note David and Paul as examples—that the cross and the crown are inseparably connected for us too. But how do we get to the point where we can really embrace both that truth and the cross itself? How do we get to that point where we with mind and heart accept the cross as an instrument of pain for us and still a gracious gift from a loving God? God sees perfectly and with crystal clarity the end from the beginning. But we have a hard time appreciating the truth that it is enough for us that God knows exactly how it will all turn out for our good. When the cross begins to press hard, we tend to see only the pain. But *we* want to know and *we* need to know its end. The Word is the bridge. With the cross and its pain at one end, the love and grace of God in the gospel pave the way and lead us on to the glory of the resurrection and the promise of the victor's crown at the other end. That bridge is covered and paved with the love and grace of God.

It is the Word that shows us that the cross is a loving gift of our gracious God. The Word does that, whether we experience the cross as the struggle to deny *self,* or the reminder in earthly losses that we have not yet conquered *self.* It is in the Word that the suffering is explained. It is in the Word that we see our desperate need for the cross if we are to reach that blessed shore on the other side. There on the other side is the final triumph over our *self* and the ultimate crown of glory in heaven given as a gift of grace. It is in the Word that the grace of God shines forth and brings us to trust God even in deepest pain and loss, even in the hour of death. On that bridge, in that Word, the Spirit of God descends to us full of grace and mercy; he gives triumph, in part now and fully in heaven. Paul makes that so beautifully clear in his great hymn and confession of faith in Romans 8: Nothing, no pain or loss, no sorrow or cross can separate us from the love of God that is in Christ Jesus!

But we are still left with the nagging question: Couldn't God accomplish all of that in another way, without so much outward suffering and loss? And how is it an evidence of God's love and grace?

God shows us in the Word how *self* easily triumphs when all is going well, when there is no suffering under the cross. *Self,* like a child at Christmastime, fastens onto the gifts and quickly forgets the giver. Think for a moment about the gifts of God and what *self* does with them. *Self* assumes that the gift of time is ours to squander as it pleases us in the moment. *Self* simply assumes that other people exist only for our enjoyment. *Self* squanders health and wealth as though they were guaranteed to last forever. *Self* takes family and friends for granted. *Self* considers comfort a right and ease an entitlement. *Self* always worships *self* and therefore considers everything created its due. In the Christian on his best day, *self* is busy reasserting this creed of the religion of *self* worship that is at the heart and core of man's fallen nature. The greatest of the saints learned that from their own experience. Consider just two of them. David had it all. He knew more about the favor of God than most of us will ever know. But he too was that child at Christmastime. It was when all had gone so well for him that he got careless and lazy. Worse still, he became too comfortable in his relationship with God; he took God's favor for granted and no longer feared his wrath against sin. And so he fell. He neglected the duty of his office, toyed with lust, then plunged headlong into adultery. He lost all pity. He used another in order to murder a man more righteous than he.

In sum, David despised the law, showed contempt for God, lost his taste for the gospel, and gave free rein to the passions of *self*. That summary describes David in his adultery with Bathsheba (2 Sa 11) and later in his numbering of Israel (2 Sa 24). At the close of both instances, God sent suffering as a consequence of the worship of *self*. But suffering served for David's rescue from *self*. David repented at the preaching of Nathan, and his sin was forgiven. But the suffering in the form of violence did not depart from David's house. It served as a constant reminder of both the need for grace and of how precious grace is. Suffering came quickly on the occasion of the numbering of Israel. Death came to the people as a result of the sin of their king. Grace stayed the plague, but the memory of that plague and the reminder of its cause surely never died in David. In grace God removed the guilt of David's sins forever. But David's penitential psalms (Ps 6, 32, 38, 51, 102, 130, 143) show that he never forgot his sins or the greatness of grace made manifest in God's forgiveness.

In both instances, that of David's adultery and his numbering of Israel, the struggle against *self* resumed but not without suffering, pain, and even death. In both instances suffering was evidence of God's love and grace. Suffering reminded David, most of all, that his salvation was because of God's forgiveness (Ps 6). It reminded him of the greatness of grace, which removed the eternal punishment and restored David again to faith and favor.

Without suffering, David could easily have taken his own sin lightly and gone on to live in impenitence, resulting in ultimate eternal misery for his soul. Only the Word of God could make those connections for David between his sinful *self*, his need for grace and forgiveness, and the necessity of suffering that comes from the hand of a loving and gracious God.

In the case of David, there is the added factor that the sin was public. If there were no consequences for his open sin, others would be emboldened by his bad example to think that they too could sin with impunity. Others would think that God was indifferent to his own law and that his people had a license therefore to ignore it. Public sin needs to have a public consequence. Sometimes that consequence is imposed by those in authority in church, as in the case of an excommunication for open impenitence. Sometimes the consequence comes from the state when civil or criminal law has been broken. And sometimes it comes from the home, as when parents discipline their children. Sometimes God himself visits the sinner with the reminders that God's Word always needs to be taken seriously, as when the drunkard destroys his health and reputation or the gambler ruins his name and estate.

Where the sin is not public and not known, the consequence of suffering may long remain seared into the conscience of the guilty one, even long after the guilt has been removed in confession and absolution. Sometimes that pain is the worst pain of all. We cannot know when we preach or teach, when we visit in home and hospital how many secret crimes and how much deeply hidden pain there may be in the hearts of those we are serving. But we should always be aware of the probability that among our hearers there are those who desperately need the soothing balm of the gospel for pain that only God can see.

Whether the consequence of sin is public or hidden deep within the wounded but pardoned soul, it is the Word alone that makes it possible for us to understand the pain and even to receive it with thanksgiving. The gospel in Word and sacraments remains the one and only bridge between the pain of the cross and crown of glory at the end.

Consider the example of St. Paul. Already the promise of great success for his coming labor is accompanied with the promise of great suffering. For what does Jesus promise concerning Saul at the advent of his apostolate? "This man is my chosen instrument to carry my name before the Gentiles and their kings and before the people of Israel. I will show him how much he must suffer for my name" (Ac 9:15,16). Jesus himself told Paul the meaning and the grand purpose of it all some time later in that famous passage already considered, 2 Corinthians 12:7-10. There Paul bears witness to the necessity of his own outward suffering and pain, if God's grace and blessings are not to be trampled underfoot, taken for granted, and lost.

To put an even sharper point on the matter, Paul tells us that he never forgot his greatest crime, his sin of persecuting the church before the day of his conversion (1 Co 15:9,10). Indeed, he used the memory of his sin to magnify the glory and power of grace for himself and for those he served. Gratitude for the grace that covered his sin moved him to be most zealous in sharing the gospel which saved him. For if God's grace was so great that it could cover Paul's sin, then all others should draw comfort from that example of grace and conclude: God wants to forgive me too, just as his Word declares; for though I am no better than Paul, I am no worse either!

In both of these examples, suffering is so closely linked to the struggle against *self* that both the struggle and the suffering together are considered the cross of God's own sending, the dear cross, the cross necessary for salvation, even though it is not a cause of salvation. In David's case the suffering came as a constant reminder of the need for that struggle. In Paul's case the suffering came to remind the apostle that the struggle against *self* would not end. But in both, the suffering is inseparably linked to the end result of salvation and the glory yet to be revealed. In both, the suffering is tied up with the inability of the individual to triumph over *self* without it. In both cases, *self* is the root of the problem. In both, the Word is the key to understanding the nature of suffering as a gift. In both, the Word is the bridge on which the Lord carried believers from the cross to the crown.

The cross imposed by others

Just as in the suffering of the Savior, so also in us, God may even use the sins of others to spark the struggle against *self*. In

David's earlier years it was Saul whose persecution of David and of the church taught David to rely on God's promise alone in the midst of his afflictions. All the outward evidence suggested to David that God's promise of the kingship for David would not be fulfilled unless David himself acted contrary to God's Word. Even David's friends urged him to take matters into his own hands and kill Saul when he had the chance (1 Sa 24, 26). Later it would be members of David's own family, more than his obvious enemies, who would cause him to suffer. In that suffering too, David had only the promise of God to rely on. And on it he did rely, in spite of the outward evidence that suggested that his trust was in vain. How sweet and rich to David were those promises, when, contrary to all merely human expectations, the promises of God were kept! How little would be his gratitude and awe in the presence of the God who keeps his Word, had not so many others made his life miserable with their sins against him. Again, as with the Savior himself, God used the evil and the ignorance of others for his own good and gracious purposes. He does so without becoming the cause of sin but remaining the ultimate cause of the triumph of the Christian against the fallen *self*. If the Word did not make these connections clear, we would never see them. We would flounder and drown in a sea of confusion and despair.

Psalm 73 is perhaps one of the most beautiful of the psalms precisely because of its usefulness in showing the bridge between the love of God and the cross of the Christian. The psalmist's particular suffering is this: He sees what seems to be the ease of the comfortable sinner compared to the suffering of the saint. That unhappy contrast makes no sense until the Word of God, as seen and as heard in the temple, makes everything clear. For consider the end of the sinner; he loses everything. Consider the end of the saint; should he lose everything, he still has everything because he has his Savior. In fact, if there were no suffering, the saint would never even realize the emptiness of everything apart from the Savior; he would never grasp and appreciate that in the Savior he already has everything.

The whole of the book of Job is devoted to much the same point. Job has great difficulty understanding what has happened to him and reconciling it with his earlier relationship with God.

At the beginning he accepts suffering without seeing a need for it to be explained or for God to justify himself in sending it. But as the pain grinds on day after day, Job is worn down by it. His suffering is increased by the judgmental attitude of his friends, who seem to know nothing except the law and who torment the suffering Job with unfounded accusations. But notice that Job comes to his senses once God speaks. He again worships and adores his Maker, and he does that *before* God restores or even suggests that he will restore to Job his family, his health, his wealth, and his earlier enjoyment of peace with God.

Were it not for the connection that the Word makes, we could just as easily have Homer's *Iliad* for our bible. There the gods are capricious and their purpose is never clear; men fight and struggle, but in the end their only prize is the hoped for loyalty of their comrades, the fleeting favor of the gods, and the enjoyment of the moment. Or we could choose a more modern bible with Jean-Paul Sartre. His novel *Nausea (La Nausée)* leaves us with a world that makes no sense at all, a human existence that is meaningless with death as the ultimate proof of that meaninglessness. But the Word makes the connection and the purpose of suffering clear. For it demonstrates the faithfulness of God in his zeal for our salvation. So great is that zeal that he allows us to suffer, even sends us suffering, so that we will not fall in love with the fleeting world and the service of *self* in it. He does not turn us into robots and destroy our humanity in order to make us saints by forcing perfection on us. Rather, he continues as God the almighty and the all-merciful by leaving us our humanity and using our very humanity to triumph over our fallen nature. What a riddle! What a paradox! What a solution! Only the Word of God can make any sense of it and solve the mystery.

The doctrine of the means of grace and the theology of the cross

But that's only the beginning of the connection with the Word. The Word does more than merely explain the necessity of suffering if our *self* is to be contained, controlled, and defeated. Even more important, it is through the Word as an *effective means of grace* that God gives the Christian the power both to bear the cross and even to rejoice in it. It is not enough for the Word to make the connection, to give us the information, and then to leave us to our own devices in carrying on the struggle. We are much too weak and too perverse in our fallen nature for that to happen. If the cross is in its essence the struggle against *self,* and if that struggle requires suffering as an indispensable motivator for carrying on the struggle, then God will have to give us the wherewithal, the desire, the energy, yes, the joy and the confidence to persevere in that struggle.

That is exactly what God does in the Word. That is exactly the purpose of much of our preaching, our teaching, our meditating, with the Word of God as the source of it all. That the Word is an *effective* means of grace that makes it possible for us to bear the cross willingly, even cheerfully, is something that we need to remember especially in counseling situations. We are too addicted in our age to the false notion that every problem has a solution, with any luck at all a quick and easy one. In point of fact, not every problem has a solution. To be sure, some do. But often our counseling must be directed toward the goal of patient endurance, of bearing suffering that may last a long time. The husband whose wife is terminally ill or bedridden may be tempted to adultery. There is no simple or easy end to his struggle; his *self* denial may be very difficult indeed. The Word as an effective means of grace is what he needs to sustain and strengthen him so that he can endure. The wife in such an instance may be angry with God that she now considers herself a burden instead of a help to her family. There is no easy fix for her anger and her anguish. The Word as an effective means of grace must not only explain the need of the cross; even more it must give grace in time of need to accept and to carry it.

The theology of the cross, therefore, cannot be separated from the doctrine of the means of grace. That is, the gospel in the Word shows us God's grace and then miraculously brings us to trust in him and his grace. The Word is not only information. The Word is power.

To be sure, the Word exerts that power even before it acts as a means of grace. In the law the Holy Spirit effectively moves to convict and condemn us because of our idolatry. In the law the Holy Spirit rips away every shred of pride in *self* when we enter into the presence of God. In the law the Holy Spirit brings us to that desperate and despairing cry of *self* loathing, the cry that *self* loathes beyond everything else: "God, be merciful to me, a sinner; sinner is what I am; sinner is all I can claim to be; sinner is my name, my occupation, my destiny, my doom, my damnation." Only the law of God can create that conviction and conclusion in us. It may be as obvious and as plain as the nose on my face that it is so; but so great is my corruption, that I would never fully recognize it, far less admit it, were it not for the effective working of the Holy Spirit through the law. The Bible says so and convinces us that it is so in John 3:6; in Romans 1,2; and in so many other places. The Lutheran Confessions bear witness to that truth, especially in the Formula of Concord, Article I.

But the law, powerful and effective as it is in the hands of the Holy Spirit, is not a means of grace. The law can indeed show us how difficult the struggle will always be, the struggle to deny *self*. But the law cannot help us carry on the struggle, want to carry it on, or rejoice in it. That office is reserved for the gospel. In fact, the law, by driving us to despair of ourselves, makes all the more glorious the office of the gospel; it magnifies the power of the gospel, which causes and creates and sustains in us a joyful embrace of the promises of God, of forgiveness and eternal life.

It is the gospel that creates faith in Christ's cross as the be-all and end-all of our salvation. And it is the gospel that gives us the desire to bear the cross to its end and even to rejoice in it. Notice how Paul connects the gospel to the bearing of the cross in his many chapters on sanctification. Those chapters are filled with what we customarily call the third use of the law. That use identifies for us those works that please God when done by the forgiven and believing children of God. But in those chapters Paul never leaves the gospel behind. Quite to the contrary, the gospel is the fuel for the engine, the reason for the struggle, the source of both joy and triumph in the midst of struggle and under the cross. Consider, for example, Romans 12. After the apostle has described in exquisite detail the work of God in accomplishing our salvation and in creating faith in that saving message, he begins his discourse on the Christian's life, that is, life under the cross, with this gospel motivation: "I urge you, brothers, *in view of God's mercy,* to offer your bodies as living sacrifices, holy and pleasing to God" (v. 1). It is by calling to mind all of the mercy of God in the face of all our perversity that the Christian is willing to take up the cross. For to sacrifice our members in the service of God and our neighbor is the opposite of what our fallen nature wants to do.

The very word *sacrifice* implies suffering. Even the seemingly painless sacrifice of thanksgiving runs counter to our fallen nature. But it is because of the gospel, because of the mercy of God, that the new *self* wants to make an entire sacrifice, to take up the cross. Yes, and the fact that the gospel has already made the sacrifice a holy one (Ro 8:1) wards off the sense of futility that there would be in such sacrifice, always stained by imperfection and sin as it is. For the assurance of forgiveness covers the future as well as the past. God's mercy covers the stains on good works just as it blots out the sin that had not the least good attached to it. Therefore, the sacrifice of all and everything can be a joyful one—pure and perfect because it is covered with the blood of the Lamb.

In Romans 8, Paul links as tightly as he can the sufferings of the Christian with the promises of the gospel; for it is the gospel as an effective means of grace that makes suffering not only bearable but a joy. He is not simply encouraging Christians to keep a stiff upper lip in the face of difficulties that come into the lives of all. He is transmitting the confidence only God can give, a confidence that God does give through the gospel. He speaks of the groaning of creation. He speaks of the painful sighing of Christians for the ultimate fruit of their redemption in paradise. And then he exults in the confident expectation of the glory to be revealed, a glory already enjoyed in hope, and declares: "The Spirit helps us in our weakness" (v. 26), so that we are more than conquerors (v. 37), and that in the midst of our weakness. It is the delightful paradox revealed only in the gospel, that the Christian, because of that weakness to some extent, loses every battle but, nevertheless, is assured of victory. For the victory is Christ's victory. And it is the power inherent in the gospel which causes us to trust that the victory is indeed ours. It is the victory given when sin is forgiven. It is the victory accomplished fully when yet another paradox is brought to completion, when through temporal death, we pass into the full enjoyment of eternal life. Confidence in that ultimate victory does not come merely from the gospel as information. It comes from the gospel as power; it comes from the gospel as an effective means of grace that creates faith and sustains it in struggle, beneath the cross, even in the hour of death.

Thus the Word is not only the connecting bridge between the pain of the cross and the crown of glory in heaven; it also enables us to carry the cross from the one side to the other and to rejoice in it. For that very reason the Bible throughout urges us to cling to the Word. As the effective means of grace, it is the life-giving seed of faith (Lk 8:11; 1 Pe 1:23), food for the soul (Isa 55:1; 1 Pe 2:2), the all important weapon in the struggle (Eph 6:17). It is the fact that the gospel is an effective means of grace that makes the simple salutation at the beginning of his epistles more than just a pious wish. That salutation, repeated at the beginning of so many sermons, is power. It contains within it the Spirit's power implanted always in his Word. The apostle says, and we repeat after him, "Grace and peace to you from God our Father and from the Lord Jesus Christ." That salutation conveys God's blessings in the gospel, a blessing that will be doubled and tripled in the proclamation of the gospel in the sermon and then made so personal in the celebration of the Sacrament. At the close of the service, all of the gospel blessings will be summarized and reconveyed in the benediction.

Not the least of the blessings in the gospel is the will and the ability to take up the cross and follow after Jesus in his triumphal but tortured procession on the way to Easter. That, after the kindling of faith in the proclamation of forgiveness, is or ought to be one of the primary purposes of the sermon, as it was of the apostolic letters. With the application of the gospel, we want to strengthen the cross-bearers in that procession, lest they lose heart and fall by the wayside. The awareness of the need for such a mighty aid as that afforded by the means of grace should keep us from turning worship into entertainment. Worship is serious business. It is serious business because sin is serious business, the cross is serious business, and the gospel is serious business. The Word is a mighty weapon, which our pastors take into their mouths when they speak for God in the pulpit. It is a two-edged sword for life and for death (Heb 4:12). It is the sword that kills when they preach the condemning Word of the law. It is the sword that brings back to life when they proclaim the forgiving grace of God in the gospel. God's struggling cross-bearers always need both. If the holy writers, and the Holy Spirit through them, do not waste our time on the cute and the clever, we should learn from them and not waste our hearers' time either. Our task is sacred and too important for that.

An extra special case: *When God seems to be the enemy . . . !*

What an absolutely and utterly horrible thought, that God could appear or seem to be the enemy! Luther, however, says on more than one occasion that this is exactly how God presents himself many times in his Word. It is how God appears to the greatest of the saints. It is at just such times that the point we have been making about the means of grace shines most brightly; the means of grace are *effective*. The gospel in Word and sacraments is not only the bridge between the Christian's cross on one side and the crown of glory on the other; it is as well the wagon that must carry us over from the one to the other. Indeed, it is the only means that God has promised through which we will survive when God himself is the enemy.

Consider just a few examples. In Genesis 22:2, we read that God came to Abraham and said, "Take your son, your only son, Isaac, whom you love, and go to the region of Moriah. Sacrifice him there as a burnt offering on one of the mountains I will tell you about." Could God have been more cruel? See how he demands of Abraham the one gift that Abraham valued above all other, not least because it was through Isaac that the Savior should come. See how God twists and turns the knife in Abraham's heart: "your son, your only son, Isaac, whom you love." See how God appears to contradict not only the wonderful gospel promises that he had made concerning Isaac but even the elemental law given in the heart of even natural man and given by God after the flood (Ge 9:5,6). God tells Abraham that he must murder an innocent man. But that is still not enough; the place is a three-day journey away. Abraham must walk with his son with nothing else to think about than the horror that lies before him. Who can bear to think of it? The horror of the deed demanded is bad enough, but the demand has come from the God of love whom Abraham and Isaac love, from the God of grace who is worshiped and adored, and the God of mercy in whom we trust.

Then there is the example of Jacob in Genesis 32. The pre-incarnate Christ appears to him in a night filled with horror. Jacob already has troubles enough. He is in dread of the impending meeting with his brother, Esau, whom he had cheated out of the blessing of Isaac. Coupled with his fear of Esau's possible bloody revenge, he must cope with his own guilt for what he had done. And now to make matters infinitely worse, Christ attacks him. All night long the wrestling match goes on. Even when morning comes and Jacob is allowed to win the match, Christ shows that he is really the victor. He does it by inflicting a wound on Jacob that Jacob will never be allowed to forget; for the rest of his life he walks with a limp whose source is Christ the enemy!

Nor can we forget the whole book of Job. There God uses Satan to strike at a man whom God himself calls blameless and upright (1:8). One misery after another he heaps on innocent Job, the loss of his family, of his wealth, of his health, and then of any comfort that he might have received from his friends. In Job's discourses with his friends there are things that Job does not understand. But this he does understand: the source of his pain and loss, of his utter misery and desolation, is God himself, the God whom he loved and served, to whom his whole life was devoted. God had become the enemy.

The psalms too sometimes cry out to God who has appeared as the enemy. Just to mention one of them, Psalm 60 begins with a cry to the God who has armed himself against his people and brought them to the brink of despair.

Nor are examples lacking in the New Testament. The one that springs most quickly to mind is the case of the poor Canaanite woman (Mt 15:21-28). Could Jesus have appeared more heartless, more cruel? He ignores her cries. He calls her unworthy of his even speaking to her since she is not from the nation of Israel. And when she still persists, he compares her to a dog! Where is gentle Jesus, meek and mild? He is first the enemy.

Even in the Lord's Prayer, is there not a hint at the possibility of God as the enemy? We cry to him: "Lead us not into temptation." St. James tells us (1:13-15), and Luther echoes the thought in his explanation to the petition, that God is not the source of temptations to evil. But still, given the examples mentioned, does not God at times *appear* or allow himself to be perceived as the source of temptation? And is not that the reason for the constant plea of the Christian in this petition, as though he would say to God: "O God, do not deal with me thus, that you seem to want me to fail and fall and perish in my sins and finally despair of all help or mercy from you! Do not appear as the one who would lead me into temptation!"

We could go on all day with examples from the Bible and from the lives of the saints. Luther thought of God as the enemy during his days in the monastery. How could God demand love from him when he could see God only as an angry judge who seemed to want nothing more than man's damnation. How could he love a God who seemed to hate him?*

It may well be that the reader at some time in life has experienced the excruciating torment of the soul, the agony of mind and conscience that comes when God appears as the enemy. At such times no one needs to convince the one thus suffering of the reality of hell; the tormented soul already smells its sulfur and sweats from the heat of its flames. The abyss of despair is all too near, and he totters at its edge. The child died, in spite of the anguished prayers and the river of tears to the God who could save if he wanted to. A temptation gnaws like a cancer in spite of God's promise that he would not let us be tempted beyond our capacity, and then the guilt crushes; there seems no escape from either the sin or the crushing load of guilt. The one problem that makes all of life bitter and miserable begins its haunt at the first dawn of day and lingers through the night; like Hezekiah the anguished soul turns its face to the wall and weeps through the night, but there is no relief either in sleep or in the morning. The

---

*The reader will find Luther's comments on the subject of God as the enemy very worth while. Cf., for example, his comments on Genesis 22 and 32 in vols. 4 and 6 respectively of the American Edition of *Luther's Works*. Those with access to either the St. Louis or Erlangen German editions will find Luther's consideration of *Anfechtung*, as rendered in the *Tischreden*, likewise very worthwhile (St. Louis: XXII:784-481; Erlangen: 60:80-186).

patient can look forward to no cure, and death refuses to come; both the pain and the medication to alleviate it make meditation and even prayer all but impossible. In such circumstances the cross is crushing indeed; the temptation to utter despair is ever present. For the earth is rock that will not soften, and heaven is flint beyond which it seems that no prayer can reach: God appears as the enemy! How did the saints of old survive their experience of God as the enemy? How does anyone endure and not despair at such a time as that? The answer, the only answer: The gospel remains an effective means of grace, even and especially when God appears as the enemy! Reason may dress itself in the robes of Job's wife and counsel: "Curse God and die!" (Job 2:9). But the devastated soul still gives the answer of the men before the fiery furnace: "If we are thrown into the blazing furnace, the God we serve is able to save us from it, and he will rescue us from your hand, O king. But even if he does not, we want you to know, O king, that we will not serve your gods or worship the image of gold you have set up" (Da 3:17,18). The answer may be a feeble and tormented one, coming from a soul that wriggles like a worm on a hook. But that is still the answer. It is the answer that will not let go of the promises of God, even when God appears as the enemy. It is the answer born of Abraham's certainty that God would yet prove true to his Word of the gospel, that God would raise his son from the dead (Heb 11:17-19). That's how powerful, how effective, the gospel is! The cry of the *Kyrie,* the persistence of Jacob who will not let go of Christ until he blesses him, it is all the result of the gospel's divine power to preserve faith in the God of all grace and mercy, even and especially when God himself seems to be the enemy. It is with such miraculous faith (and again, faith is always miraculous!) that Paul *expects* us to join with him in rejoicing in suffering (Ro 5:1-5). Could there be a more eloquent demonstration of the power of the gospel as the effective means of grace than this, that it preserves faith and trust in God even when he appears as the enemy?

Johann Gerhard, in a sermon on Romans 8:31-34, points to the doctrine of election as a special comfort in such times. He reminds us that *God spared not his own Son:* God did not just give him for us; he did not spare the Son who was his crown and joy any suffering or pain. And all of the Son's suffering, his groans and sighs, the Father's sparing him not, are mighty proofs of the Son's measureless love for us against our despair under the cross, when God appears as our enemy!** A point worth remembering—no, a point worth clinging to for dear life!

The role of the doctrine of justification in the theology of the cross

Just as there can be no real discussion of the theology of the cross apart from the doctrine of the means of grace, so too there can be no true discussion of either the theology of the cross or the doctrine of the means of grace without a consideration of the doctrine of justification. We cannot help but call to mind the fact that many of the orthodox Lutheran theologians declined to use the word *doctrine (die Lehre)* in the plural. For them there really was no such thing as "doctrines"; there is but one doctrine. That doctrine is all that the Bible teaches. It is a whole cloth, so to speak. Nowhere is that point of emphasis more obvious than in these three teachings (*Lehrpünkte* instead of *Lehren*), or if you would insist on it, in these three doctrines. Not one of the three is really complete without the other two. These three show the teachings of the Bible as a magnificent tapestry through which are woven strands and threads of purest gold and silver; take out any one of them and the tapestry will be ruined beyond recognition.

How then is the theology of the cross connected to the doctrine of justification by way of the doctrine of the means of grace? The adulterous and sinful generation goads on the weak and the sinful *self.* The world entices the *self* along the broad and easy road that leads to destruction. The world knows, so to speak, all the right buttons to push in the *self.* For the young, it is the excitement of hormones and the urge to rebel. For the more mature, the ambition to make a name for *self,* to get ahead or get even. For the elderly, buttons of bitterness or disappointment

---

** Joh. Gerhard, *Postille,* vierter Theil, J. C. Hinrichs'sche Buchhandlung, Leipzig, 1878, pp. 249-262.

in work or family or friends are large and easy to find. The fear of loneliness, sickness, and death is never far away. Luther often lamented that with the passing of so many centuries, human nature had become steadily weaker in the face of the onslaughts of the flesh and the world. What would he say in our day? With the temptations of the Internet, the greed of the marketplace, the host of predators on the young and on the weak and on the elderly, it is a wonder that any survive. Has the day come when the last trumpet must soon sound because scarcely the elect can persevere?

Faced with the strength of the temptations and the wretchedness of our still sinful nature—indeed, its love of weakness and temptation—we have ample reason to go back again and again to the ultimate reality of our faith and the cornerstone truth of the Scriptures. And that is the doctrine of justification. It is this, that God has declared the whole world *not guilty!* because of the work of Christ, who bore the sins of the whole world on his cross (Jn 1:29; 3:16; 2 Co 5:14-21). While we stumble along in our weakness and in the perversity of our still remaining fallen nature, this rock-solid truth sustains us at the foot of his cross and under our own: Since the sin of the world has been paid for, so too has my sin been paid for; it is true because God says so; I believe it because the gospel means of grace has moved me to believe it. Were it otherwise, we would be back with Homer and the *Iliad* or with Sartre and *Nausea* for a bible. We would be left with nothing but confusion, then despair, then death, then hell.

It is, however, not only my sinful flesh that the gospel of justification must overcome. To make the matter of my salvation still more difficult, the flesh is attached to the world and these two are joined in an unholy threesome by their master, Satan. He sows error and heresy of every sort in the church and doubt in the heart of the Christian struggling under the weight of the cross. Error, heresy, and doubt are not merely hindrances to cross bearing; where they triumph, they are themselves a refusal to bear the cross. And we can be sure of this: Just as sin is never content to be alone but always wants the company of more sin and other sinners (Eve proved that already in the Garden of Eden!), so too are error and heresy and doubt. There is no such thing as just one; each breeds another and then another, until the means of grace and justification are lost to superstition, sentiment, and mere opinion.

Ultimately all error aims at using a rejection of *my* cross to get to the rejection of *his* cross, that is, to a rejection of the heart and core of the gospel, the doctrine of justification. False doctrine always puts *self* in front of the Word, *self* in front of Christ and his cross. False doctrine always seeks to replace the revealed will of Christ with the fallen will of man. Heresy is Satan's wedge into Christ's dominion in the heart. If the devil just gets in there with a little, he can always expand his own territory until what seemed like a little error turns into a full frontal assault on the cross of Christ and the doctrine of justification.

A few examples may suffice to illustrate the point. Does the creation account in Genesis 1 and 2 seem too difficult for people to accept these days? Out it goes! What ends up in its place? A fuzzy theistic evolution with a God who sort of started a process that works itself out somehow with or without him. The error is bad enough by itself. But still worse is the notion that man can sit in judgment on the Word of God and deal with it as he sees fit. It will not be long before many who cannot accept the creation account reject also the doctrine of original sin embedded in the account in Genesis 3 of the fall into sin. Out it goes too. And what takes its place? Usually the notion that man is basically good, or at the very worst neutral, when he comes into the world. Shortly after that, the miracles of the Old Testament find their way to the dust heap as legends suited for an unsophisticated age but certainly not historically true. And again man sits in judgment on the Word of God and decides what is and what is not true in the Bible.

Some may try to defend themselves by saying that only the parts of the Bible that deal with faith and morals are God's Word; those parts dealing with history or science are merely human additions that came as men tried to explain or account for how things happened. That the Bible is a whole cloth, all of it verbally inspired (2 Ti 3:15-17), they dismiss out of hand. It is just a matter of time before the greatest miracles of the New Testament go the way of the miracles in the Old Testament. The virgin birth of Christ and his resurrection become for such people the pious wishes of early Christians, not the facts whose gospel power made them Christians in the first place. Then the devil has reached his goal: no virgin-born and risen Savior equals no faith. For faith without the Christ of the Bible as its source, its content, its goal is impossible. Faith in the biblical sense of the term cannot exist apart from the gospel.

The doctrine of justification dies without the Son of God and Mary's son as the sinless sin bearer. Without the Christ of the Bible and the doctrine of justification, the church becomes a lodge with a cross on top of it, the preserver of "faith traditions." It is no longer the household of faith but the museum of an all but dead culture. In it only an arrogant deism will be found with man at the center, man deemed basically good and wiser than his Maker. Do too many doctrines appear out of harmony with one another? Let them go in favor of "Let's all just love one another." Does the preaching of hell upset people? Get rid of the doctrine of hell, and while we are at it, of the doctrine that there really is such a thing as sin and unbelief and that these anger God. In sum, don't take God's Word seriously and don't take him seriously either.

Such are the threats of the devil, the world, and our own sinful flesh. And still we want to speak of the *dear cross* in the face of such perils? The risk in carrying it is enormous for those who imagine that it is easy, that they could do it either by themselves or with only a little help now and then. The number of those who have stumbled under the cross and been crushed by its weight is beyond counting. How then can it be a precious gift of God, an indispensable mark of a Christian, a necessary piece of equipment for anyone who expects to enter into heaven? Only by constant recourse to the means of grace. Only by a constant recourse to the cross of Christ and its proclamation of justification. For justification remains that doctrine by which the church stands or falls. And the means of grace alone will convince us of it and keep us under its saving mantel. The cross of the Christian is designed and given by a gracious God to bring us again and again to those saving and central truths. Without the cross, we wander from the means of grace. Without the means of grace, we cannot carry our cross and will forget about his cross and the justification won for us by it. Without justification, we will stumble and be crushed under the weight of the cross and Christ's cross will become for us a scandal and an offense. Therefore, we give thanks for our cross as we flee to his and cling to it in the gospel for our rescue in time and for eternity. So may it ever be!

3

Slivers on the Cross

**The assumptions of our culture that are hostile
to the theology of the cross**

In earlier times it was common for people to consider life difficult. The further back we go in history, the more often we encounter in the writings of seers and sages the assumption that life's difficulties are rooted somehow in the interaction between God and man. Most people assumed that storms or plagues, famines and floods, all alike came from God or the gods in response to man's wickedness and as a punishment for man's sins. In the days, for example, of the Thirty Years' War (1618–1648), Lutheran pastors and theologians wrote prayers for rescue and deliverance from the scourge of a war that had come over Germany. They took it as a given that the war was a result of the indifference of so many to the Word of God. When the war was over, many were the hymns written and sung in Lutheran churches in thanksgiving to God for at last delivering his people from the scourge of sword and the plagues that always accompanied the sword. Even during the midst of the war, the city of Ulm, surrounded by Catholic armies outside and devastated by plague and famine inside, held a special celebration; it was the hundred-year anniversary of the presentation of the Augsburg Confession and the birthday of the Lutheran church. The celebration was to thank God for the restoration of the gospel through the work of the Reformation, for which God's people were most grateful, even if they would soon perish in the war! Can anyone imagine such a thing happening today?

It was not long after that war that the so-called and misnamed Age of Enlightenment began. Beginning in France in the 18th century, a new breed of philosophers arose who wanted to push God from center stage and put man there instead. Voltaire (d. 1778) and writers like him considered Christianity a hindrance to progress; they viewed faith in the Word as nothing more than superstition. Sadly the corruption in much of the church at the time gave speed to the course of this new and militant unbelief. Contributing to the loss of confidence in the church was the cynical marriage of the altar and the throne after the Congress of Vienna in 1815. Rulers used the church as a means for keeping the masses quiet. The promise of heaven after death in exchange for submission to powerful rulers and injustice in this life was supposed to keep people from revolution. The declaration of Marxists and Leninists at the end of the century and in the early 20th century that religion was the opiate of the masses shocked no one. Quite to the contrary, that sentiment summed up fairly well the way that many viewed the church by the end of the 19th century.

The advent of evolutionary theory as an alternative to the biblical record of creation increased both the number and the influence of ideologies opposed to the gospel. By the end of the 19th century, direct assaults on the Bible had become so common that the only arguments left in the scholarly world were between different schools of unbelief. Only a relative handful of scholars still defended the proposition that the Bible is the ultimate source of truth, verbally inspired by the Holy Spirit, and therefore without error in all that it teaches. They were dismissed as ignorant miscreants from a bygone age.

Sadly, that rejection of the inspiration and the authority of the Bible has found a home within most church bodies that call themselves Christian. Books published even by some Lutheran publishing houses now compete with one another in advancing theories about the *real* source of the books of the Bible. They debate with one another over how many, if any, of the words attributed to Jesus in the gospels actually were spoken by him. Some even wonder if he ever existed at all. If they concede his historical existence, they nevertheless have little use for his virgin birth, his death for the sins of the world, his resurrection, and his promise to return on the Last Day. They dismiss heaven and hell as notions held by prescientific people who were trying to make some sense out of life with notions that have no relevance for modern man. This supposedly scholarly rejection of the Bible and its God as the ultimate source of truth is assumed by now in every field of human endeavor.

Therefore, it comes as no surprise that the role of God in nature and in the course of history rarely comes into the modern mind. The notion occurs to few that sickness or famine, war or storm have God as the source and director who judges and blesses according to his own counsel. Sickness is caused by germs and viruses. Storms come from weather fronts. Earthquakes are the result of moving tectonic plates deep beneath the surface of land and sea and nothing more.

While all of these findings about nature and natural laws are very useful, they tell us nothing about the ultimate causes in nature. But very few people think about that. Few wonder at God's goodness and generosity in weather, storm, and tempest. Fewer still consider that God controls and rules over all these natural phenomena also in judgment, to punish the wicked and to call people to repentance. Instead, modern man has the same arrogance that ancient man had; ignoring the God who blesses and judges with his rule over nature, people still twist nature as best they can to their own ends and to the satisfaction of their own passions (Ro 1).

In the social sciences, the recognized and leading authorities assume that human behavior likewise has only natural causes, causes that have nothing to do with sin—original or otherwise. Crime comes from a deprived environment, poor parenting skills, or substandard education; get rid of poverty, improve child care, and spend enough on education, and we will get rid of most if not all criminal behavior. No one will deny that physical environment, family life, and education play an important role in social development. But even the best in all of these will not eliminate evil, crime, deviation, corruption, vice of every sort. It is a wonder that anyone would think otherwise, given all the evidence of evil and perversity of every kind also among the most privileged in society.

So pervasive is the influence of unbelieving philosophy in both the natural and the social sciences that for many even defining what it means to be human has become all but impossible. Many suppose that we are but a random conglomeration of genes, hormones, and electrical charges in the brain. These are said to be conditioned and programmed mechanically in such a way that the concepts of free will, morality, good, and evil are impossible to define. What then is the difference between a human being and any (other) animal? What is the difference between human and machine? The notions of morality and moral choice are an illusion if man is nothing more than a complex of electrical charges fixed in his nervous system. We are destined by our "wiring" to act as we do, whether that be as a heterosexual or homosexual, a hard worker or a sloth, a humanitarian or an axe murderer. Whether even the best social scientists, the best psychologists and psychiatrists, can substantially alter that wiring is very much open to question and the subject of debate.

Death too becomes the victim of spin and propaganda in the culture that has lost even a hint of Christian mooring. Is death the end of all things, the ultimate proof of the meaninglessness of life? Or is it the beginning of some snowflake or sunbeamlike existence, as one popular funeral poem would have it? With either theory, people try to wish away death's horror. By one silly wish or another, they try to comfort the bereaved with a spin designed to remove death's sting. In the popular culture, people like to imagine that if we just eat right and exercise, we can postpone death indefinitely. Why anyone would want to postpone death if life is meaningless or if its aftermath is in a sunbeam is a question best left uninvestigated and unanswered. When death finally does threaten to overwhelm all of our efforts to hold it at bay or to deny its reality, we will avoid the dying in hospitals and nursing homes so that we do not have to think about it. When death at length claims its prey, we will get a makeup artist to hide its horror in the casket. Quickly the funeral takes place with a burial at a cemetery, out of sight and thus, as much as possible, out of mind.

While many of the advances in our understanding of the world in which we live are useful, they do not advance in the least man's understanding of his fundamental problems. Nor do they answer with a single syllable the questions that should rise up from the depths of human existence. Instead, advances in the natural sciences are offered as proof that we should look for truth alone where the natural sciences look for it, in experiments that are the essence of the scientific method. Irrelevant and unanswerable are questions and problems that go beyond scientific inquiry. That man's fundamental problem is his relationship with God occurs to few. Most doubt that the basic questions *Who am I? Why am I here?* and *Where am I going?* have any reliable answers at all; and most of the rest consider such questions the business of unenlightened religious fanatics. Listen to them and you will end up killing your neighbor in a religious war if your neighbor disagrees. It is better therefore to leave these matters uninvestigated.

Thus Pontius Pilate's question *What is truth?* has received one of two replies: Either there is no such thing as truth outside of the world of the natural sciences and mathematics, or if there is truth outside the scientific method, it is whatever I happen to think at the moment. About this latter kind of truth, I may change my mind tomorrow, and with that change, the truth changes. Nor is my truth necessarily your truth. Everyone's truth is uniquely his own, and no one has the right to say to another's truth: *I'm right and, therefore, you must be wrong, and I'll show you why!*

What happens to faith in a world like ours? *Faith* in such a world is not formed by facts; people do not *believe* something because it is true, that is, because it corresponds to reality, to facts. Rather, something is true only because we believe it. Is there a God? Only if I believe there is. Is there a hell? Not unless

I think so. Is there a heaven and a way to get there? There is a heaven if I believe there is, and the way to the heaven of my own inventing is the way that I plan to get there.

In short, there is truth in the physical world that is subject to scientific investigation. In the metaphysical world, the world of the soul, of God, of the ultimate meaning and purpose of life, of life after death, the only truth is the one I pick for myself.

But what happens to modern man with this jelly in his soul when he suffers? If he is sick or in want, lonely or afraid, when he endures pain and loss and ultimately death? In part, these are all intended by God to point man away from himself, to motivate at least a search for ultimate realities. For most, however, that is not the response to suffering and the threat of death. The responses cover a wide range, from a stoic acceptance of fate to attempts at mindless escape in the fog of drugs, alcohol, pleasure, or even work. None of these satisfies, but that keeps no one from seeking satisfaction in them. The fact that all of them only serve to increase modern man's suspicion that life is pointless causes few to look elsewhere for answers to the basic problems of life and death. In fact, the more he fails in his search for peace and in his quest for purpose, the more modern man flees for refuge to the same vanities that left him feeling empty in the first place. The famous prayer of St. Augustine in the *Confessions* would make it to the lips of almost no one, even if they had ever heard of it: "Thou, O Lord, hast made us for thyself, and our heart is restless until it finds its rest in thee." Stranger still would be those most comforting words from Psalm 73:23-26: "Yet I am always with you; you hold me by my right hand. You guide me with your counsel, and afterward you will take me into glory. Whom have I in heaven but you? And earth has nothing I desire besides you. My flesh and my heart may fail, but God is the strength of my heart and my portion forever."

We may be more the children of our culture than we realize

But what does all this have to do with us? What does it have to do with those who proclaim and hear God's Word, who believe it, and who strive to order their lives according to it? What does it have to do with the theology of the cross?

We need to remember that we are also children of the age in which we live. We absorb more of its culture than we realize. Its threats may seem harmless to us because we have become so used to them, because we live with them every day. We live in an age that denies any kind of absolute truth and any kind of ultimate accountability. There is no accountability to God, or even to one's own conscience, once God has been dismissed as an irrelevant superstition of a bygone era. Without any accountability in the culture, society descends into a new barbarism. Little in our culture has even the outward trappings of decency that Christianity once lent it. The thin Christian veneer that used to overlay the culture kept the most crude and coarse expressions of our vile nature under wraps. But no more. To be sure, much that passed for Christian culture was little more than Puritan or Victorian respectability. To be sure, such respectability was often just a front for hypocrisy. Nevertheless, one may argue that some hypocrisy in the culture is better than an honesty that boasts of its sins and wallows in the basest perversions of fallen nature. By comparison, old-fashioned hypocrisy would be a considerable step up. At the very least, in such a culture a consideration of God's role in history and in the lives of individuals was not dismissed out of hand or considered the crutch of the intellectual cripple.

So we pose the question yet again: How much of this culture have we made our own? With God removed almost entirely from the culture, it is all too easy also for us to reduce his role even in our lives to a role on the periphery. The commonly accepted culture puts slivers on the cross that we bear. The slivers are so sharp that we scarcely notice when they pierce our souls. The devil sticks them into us with the skill of a good nurse inserting a needle. It is easier than ever to thoughtlessly adopt the relativism of our age. It is so easy that we may not even be aware of the removal of God to the edge of our existence and to a fringe corner of heart and soul. As products of our age, our souls can become calloused to immorality. Mass media entertains us with material that teaches our youth that there is no such thing as innocence. We are merely animals. We have instincts that need to be satisfied and urges that are unhealthy to deny.

The educational system says an essential *amen*. We evolved from some lower life-forms. And as we have evolved biologically, so too we have evolved in our society, in our understanding of alternative lifestyles and alternative family structures. There is, in any case, no such thing as absolute truth outside of science and mathematics. There are only *values,* and these are all relative. Something has value only because I or someone else considers it valuable. Politicians like to boast of their support, for example, of *family values.* But they are very careful not to define the term. Each family is left to assume that it is its own family values that are being praised and supported. Few give the least thought to the simple fact that the term *family values* has no common definition; its meaning ends at one's own front door. In religion there are only *faith traditions;* each of these has something to offer and none of them possesses the final answer or absolute truth. Our goal should be the appreciation of every possible point of view; embrace what you want and leave the rest. The only absolute is that there are no absolutes. Therefore, respect every point of view and take none of them too seriously. Every man is his own bible. Each individual is his own ultimate source of truth.

When such notions of our age first assaulted our souls, we were shocked and cringed and turned away. But gradually we get used to these things. And little by little, habituation leads to embrace. Religion, morality, absolute truth, God, salvation, faith—all these are relegated to a small corner on Sunday morning or on some Sunday mornings. We even appreciate it when the service is shortened because the football game's kickoff is early this Sunday!

How can a culture like that lead to anything but hedonism, the worship of pleasure? How can it end in anything but the mind- and soul-numbing assumption that the only thing that is real is me and the moment? And that hedonism is by no means the province only of the pagan. The Christian is tempted, tempted so constantly to this same hedonism that he may not even notice the temptation anymore, much less realize that he has embraced it. In such a culture it is very easy to escape the ultimate and only important realities, the realities of sin and grace, heaven and hell, the cross and the crown. We can hide from other people and our duty to serve them by marrying the Internet. We can escape a sense of frustration in our lives by burying the self in music so loud that thinking is impossible. Or we can work so hard that there is no time to ponder the reason for all the work. We can get lost in mindless and endless recreational activities when work is no longer pleasant or possible. Should conscience nag, the philosophy of the day suggests that we may need counseling. The goal of such counseling will have nothing to do with sin and grace; it will be designed to help us conquer or dismiss conscience, to see it as the unhealthy voice of negative influences from our past. If the nagging of conscience continues, there is medication for it. Or if we do not want or cannot get counseling, there is just more of the same rat race of work and entertainment to drown out the voice of conscience and suffocate the soul.

Yet again, we have to remember this: We are children of the age in which we live. All of these things have an impact on us. No one is immune to the loud and insistent assaults of the culture against the soul. Whether we are always aware of it or not, we absorb never-ending blows of our culture against the realities of truth and error, heaven and hell, God and the devil. How in such a culture can the voice of Christ penetrate the darkness and the filth? Who will hear his call to deny *self,* to bear the cross, to surrender one's own will, and to embrace the pain that accompanies the cross as good for the soul and a gift of God?

The very nearness of these currents in the culture to our own bones and in our own soul threatens our hold on the gospel as well as the way in which we proclaim it. The world so entirely addicted to the pleasures of the moment is so alluring that we are tempted to let go of basic truths of the Bible in the interest of getting people to listen to any of it. We are tempted to make Christianity easy, painless, merely entertaining. For we fear that the call to the cross will put people off, offend them, send them running in the opposite direction.

Jesus' encounter with the rich young ruler (Mt 19) reminds us that the problem is not an entirely new one. The young man went away when Jesus made it clear that the cross, that *self* denial, was the cost of discipleship. But in Jesus' day Peter could still say, even if with a lot of misunderstanding on his part, that he and the other disciples had left all to follow their Lord. Given the competition that the Lord has today, how many would rather go away with the rich young ruler than leave all to follow Jesus? How many would be left if Jesus said to us what he had said to the rich young man? Too easily we dismiss Jesus' words to the rich young ruler with the observation that Jesus spoke those words to one who worshiped his wealth—as though none among us would ever do such a thing! We correctly emphasize the main point in the story, that salvation is a gift of grace; as such it is impossible for us to accomplish and can only be accomplished for us by the God-man. The point, however, that the young ruler went away and thus by his love of his wealth forfeited the salvation Christ came to win for him, and that such a forfeiture can also happen to us, that point often gets lost or ignored. To put it another way, we can end up covering over the cross of *self* denial with a gospel that has become a pillow and a couch for the rich young ruler in each of us.

The temptations of the culture to live for sensual satisfaction and to avoid the ultimate reason of our existence make it difficult to teach the theology of the cross, more difficult still to embrace it. The pressures of moral and metaphysical relativism offer an easy out for those who want to cling to at least some sins. The result is a smorgasbord Christianity; a little of this and a little of that, laws I think I can keep, and plenty of gospel as a cover for sins that I cannot or do not want to let go of. Pastors and teachers want to be understanding. They do not want to drive people away. Besides that, the church needs to grow. People won't come if we expect too much of them. If they want to remain outwardly Christian, relatively Christian, they can always go someplace else, where not so much is expected. Therefore, the application of the Scriptures should not expect, much less demand, very much. Encourage people to do what we already know they are doing or what they can easily aim for. Never probe too deeply into the First Commandment. Be content with superficial applications of Commandments Four through Seven. The Second Commandment doesn't seem all that important; and the Third Commandment can be too controversial, too disruptive of our unity, especially if we take Luther's explanation in the catechism seriously. The Eighth Commandment is too abstract, and the Ninth and Tenth Commandments come too close to the First.

How will we recognize these slivers on the cross, and how will we counteract them?

It may be that no one culture or age is any more resistant to the theology of the cross than any other. It may be that in each age, thinking Christians conclude that the end must be near, that things simply cannot get any worse. Many a church father thought that. Luther said it often. That the end is always nearer than it was is of course true. But the corollary, that each age is accordingly more resistant to the gospel, perhaps does not occur to us so quickly. What was the answer of the fathers to the inherent and natural resistance to the cross? What is the answer to that resistance fortified by assumptions in the culture that refuses even a consideration of the Bible's most important doctrines? What especially is the answer of a church in danger of becoming afraid of its own people because so many of its people have married enough of their culture to want nothing to do with the cross?

It is the bold and unflinching answer of the Bible itself. That must be the answer. That is the only possible answer. In the face of our fears we simply have to remind ourselves over and over again: Faith is always a miracle, a miracle which only God can accomplish; so too is the Christian life a miracle when it takes up the cross and follows him who carried it first and for us. It is the Word Incarnate who speaks through his written Word, speaks first to the heart and soul of pastors and teachers. Each pastor, each teacher must, simply must, go back to that Bible again and again, take it seriously, and let God do his work through it! As Jesus so often took the disciples aside and away from the crowd so that he could be the sole object of their attention, so he wants to take us aside. He wants by means of Word and sacrament to rip us away from the world and our culture to speak to us privately. What does Jesus say in Mark 8 about the cross? It is, as already noted, not optional. It is necessary. It is not something to be dreaded. It is something to be embraced. It is not imposed on the unwilling. It is a gift to those whose wills have been renewed by the gospel. Then the renewed, in love with the one who saved them by his cross and his Word of the cross, become cross-bearers in the footsteps of the crucified and risen Savior. From cross-bearers they become ambassadors who take his Word to those entrusted to their care and to the world. They take it to those who want to hear and to those who will refuse. They take it, trusting not in their own skills and cleverness but in the Spirit's presence and power operating through that Word. For those whom God has chosen he will save through that Word. The ambassador's care is not outward success but faithfulness to the One who sent him and to his message. Its success in ripping still others out of the doomed culture ripe for judgment is the business of the Spirit in his powerful Word. For, again, true faith is always a miracle.

And what does Jesus have to say to those too timid to preach and teach *his* theology of the cross? God warned against spiritual laziness and indifference no more dramatically than in his words to Ezekiel. Could he have been clearer than he was in Ezekiel 3 and 33? God reminded Ezekiel that the prophetic office was a serious one. If the prophet did not warn the sinner, the sinner would die; but God would require his blood from the hand of the prophet who did not warn him! Indifferent prophets become the false prophets that God calls "jackals among ruins" in chapter 13. They are those who

> lead my people astray, saying, "Peace," when there is no peace, and because, when a flimsy wall is built, they cover it with whitewash, therefore tell those who cover it with whitewash that it is going to fall. Rain will come in torrents, and I will send hailstones hurtling down, and violent winds will burst forth. When the wall collapses, will people not ask you, "Where is the whitewash you covered it with?" . . . I will tear down the wall you have covered with whitewash and will level it to the ground so that its foundation will be laid bare. When it falls, you will be destroyed in it; and you will know that I am the LORD. (vv. 10-14)

The point is inescapable. A different kind of suffering comes to those who reject the cross of *self* denial in favor of a gospel that is no gospel, a gospel aimed at pleasing people instead of pleasing God. Such people, such pastors and teachers, no matter how sincere their intentions, fear men more than they fear God. And it is

God who promises them suffering. They will suffer God's wrath and his just judgment because of their cowardice; called to proclaim his law and his gospel, they proclaimed instead their own preferences or what they thought would please their hearers. When judgment comes, the shame of the coward is laid bare and the foundation of his self-love instead of *self* denial will be all too evident. To put it another way, such teachers and preachers became true children of their age, devotees of this adulterous and wicked generation. They make the cross so smooth and light that it would not hurt them at all but rather be the key to an easy life and a popular "ministry."

St. Paul echoes God's words through Ezekiel when he calls the false teachers "belly servers," or as the NIV renders the passage, those who serve their own appetites (Ro 16:18). They cater not only to their own inclinations but also to those of their hearers. They adapt the message to peoples' preferences and so win them away from the cross, both the cross of Christ and the cross that Christ wants them to embrace. The subtle, perhaps even unrecognized, goal is to win people for the preacher instead of for the cross of Christ; the goal becomes to win people for the ambassador rather than for the one who sent him.

In Paul's day the popular thing to preach was the legalism of the Judaizers. They appealed to those who wanted a salvation that they could achieve by their own effort. But no matter how zealously and how rigorously they interpreted and pursued the law, at bottom they were *self* promoters. For whether recognized or not, that is always the alternative: either Christ and his cross and patient bearing of our own cross after him or *self* promotion. St. Paul argues that there is no halfway point between the two. And the proof of it is this: Those who reject the cross will inevitably end up persecuting those who embrace it. Paul makes that point very emphatically in 2 Corinthians 10–11 and in Galatians 4–5.

The Judaizers of Paul's day may be gone. But the quest for a following by a denial of the cross is still very much with us. In our day the popular preacher may be the pulpit entertainer with the pop psychologist at his side. He may be the pseudo philosopher or social scientist with the latest survey of what people really want to hear at the ready. Together these may have all the appeal that the Judaizers had in Paul's day. For like the Judaizers they make man the center of attention and the measure of all things. Their message may sound religious, but it is the broad and easy road. It has no more to do with Christ and his cross than a passing reference. It is as deep as the relativism on television and as empty as the "things may be better tomorrow" counseling offered the grieving soul or the one considering suicide. What it is not is the cross of Christ. What it is not is the call to the cross of discipleship. For such as those who preach that cross and for those who faithfully carry it, they have only the persecution of contempt and ridicule and often even anger. As in Paul's day so in ours, it is hard to oppose that spirit and easy to be sucked into its orbit.

There is no halfway house between the cross and the world

Some may look for a nonexistent halfway house between the cross and what ends up as mere *self* promotion. They may persuade themselves that they will eventually get around to the cross; just now however is not the time. They may think that they can still hold on to Christ while letting go of doctrines in the Bible that many find offensive. The end result is the same: Christ's cross remains as a scandal and an offense, and the cross of *self* denial is reduced to the triviality of "giving up something for Lent" or dismissed altogether as psychotic masochism.

But whether it is the Judaizer of Paul's day, the relativist and social Darwinian of our own day, or the equivocator who wants to find a place in our pulpit, the verdict of the crucified is the same: "I don't know you" (Mt 25:12). It is the verdict of "let him be eternally condemned!" (Gal 1:8,9). Paul's words should echo and reecho through the soul of the pastor who prepares to preach and teach that Word as a faithful servant of Christ: "Am I now trying to win the approval of men, or of God? Or am I trying to please men? If I were still trying to please men, I would not be a servant of Christ" (Gal 1:10). And behind the words of Paul are those of the Lord to Isaiah: "This is the one I esteem: he who is humble and contrite in spirit, and trembles at my word" (Isa 66:2).

So the obstacles to preaching and teaching the theology of the cross are in the world and the culture that surrounds us and so easily find a home within us. They infect like a virus and eat away like a cancer at our supposedly sophisticated civilization. And they find a home in our hearts to such an extent that we often do not even recognize the danger, the attack, the disease, the impending death. In pastors and teachers the slivers on the cross may be fear and timidity before the world and even before the members of the congregation. They may be the slivers of laziness and indifference. So cleverly have these vices been inserted into the soul that the called worker has not even noticed them. He has become a robed worldling. He is comfortable with the world and does not want the bother of opposing the devil and the world in himself, much less in anyone else. The sliver on the cross may even be the noble-sounding goal of winning souls for Christ but only with part of God's Word, a Word stripped of anything that might offend the flesh and therefore keep the church from growing fast enough.

Precisely because we are children of our own times, it is often difficult to see these poisoned slivers in ourselves. And precisely because we are children of our own times, it is often difficult to resist them, even when we do recognize them. As we quench our thirsty souls with the Water of Life and feed on the living bread from heaven who came down for us and won heaven by his cross, we need to hear the sad question of Christ: "You do not want to leave too, do you?" Inspired by his gospel the only answer possible for us should daily be that of Peter on one of his better days: "Lord, to whom shall we go? You have the words of eternal life. We believe and know that you are the Holy One of God." Then we still must hear Jesus' answer, both so comforting and so filled with loving warning: "Have I not chosen you, the Twelve? Yet one of you is a devil!" (Jn 6:67-70).

More than ever, therefore, our pastors and teachers and the people who support them need to immerse themselves in the Word of God. That seems or should be so obvious. But, again, because we are children of our age, so many things can crowd out that Word, even when we are working with it. All the more reason to examine and reexamine ourselves daily, as Luther encourages us in the catechism, so that the old man may be drowned and die, and the new man come forth to take up the cross and follow Jesus gladly. For what will it profit the pastor, the teacher, the person in the pew, if we gain the whole world and lose Christ? And what will we give our people in exchange for the warm embrace of Christ and the heaven he won for those who follow him under the cross?

That such a message is so countercultural, so jarring to modern man and to the modern man within each of us, makes it all the more important that we immerse ourselves in the message, that we marry it and depart not a hair's breadth from it. For after all, is it not the pervasiveness, the all-around-us-all-the-time nature of relativism that makes it such a threat to us and to our people? If the gospel could push out the poisonous sliver by being ever on our minds and in our hearts, then we would not be such easy prey for the isms of the day. Is that not exactly what St. Paul had in mind when he wrote, "Whatever is true, whatever is noble, whatever is right, whatever is pure, whatever is lovely, whatever is admirable—if anything is excellent or praiseworthy— think about such things. Whatever you have learned or received or heard from me, or seen in me—put it into practice. And the God of peace will be with you" (Php 4:8,9)?

Does that not appeal to the Christian in us? Does it not make the whole prospect of denying *self* and bearing the cross appealing to the soul of the new man? Does it not help us to understand even what Jesus means when he says that his yoke is easy and his burden is light (Mt 11:30)? Hear the joy in the voice of one who had a Ph.D. in *self* denial, in cross bearing: John the Baptist. With what great joy he confesses, "I am not the Christ" (Jn 1:20). Can you perhaps see his joyful embracing of the cross when he declares, "He must become greater; I must become less" (Jn 3:30). God be praised: *You* are not the Christ either! That's what those try to be who seek a following for themselves by compromising the truth of God's Word—*they* want to be saviors of the world. There is only one Christ, and he has already accomplished our salvation. In love to him who thus loved us, we join in the procession of the faithful who have gone before us under the cross. For that is our goal too, that we do nothing but decrease as he increases through the faithful proclamation of all of his Word!

The dread sliver of *acidia*

Once those of us who are pastors, teachers, and leaders in our congregations have begun the battle against the slivers on the cross that pierce us especially, then we need to consider an additional sliver on the cross of Christians in everyday life. It is a highly poisonous sliver indeed. It pierces the souls of young and old, of those in the pulpit no less than those in the pew. It is a sliver that is arguably more prevalent now than ever before. The very relativism of our day makes it so. It is an obstacle to Christian faith and life so common that we may scarcely recognize it. In ancient times there was a word for it. The word was *acidia* (or *acedia*). It is a Greek word. It means sloth or laziness of such a kind that the one afflicted knows what is right and true and good but does not pursue it as it deserves to be pursued. He pursues it only halfheartedly, casually, in a bored and uninterested manner. Dante treats it brilliantly in the *Purgatorio* of *The Divine Comedy* (Canto XVII–XIX). In his day, this *acidia*, this special kind of laziness, was considered such a danger to the soul that it was called one of the seven deadly sins. Luther often railed against this vice, and no more brilliantly than in his longer preface to the Large Catechism (Kolb, pp. 379-383). In his comments on the Third Commandment in the Large Catechism, he also properly identified the sin and railed against it. He writes:

> In the same way those conceited spirits should also be punished who, after they have heard a sermon or two, become sick and tired of it and feel that they know it all and need no more instructors. This is precisely the sin that used to be numbered among the mortal sins and was called *acidia*—that is, laziness or weariness—a malignant, pernicious plague with which the devil bewitches and deceives many hearts so that he may take us by surprise and stealthily take the Word of God away again. (Kolb, p. 400)

While the Bible does not spend time on the term, it certainly deals with the malady. This special kind of spiritual laziness, together with pride, is at the root of the fall into sin. Adam and Eve knew what was right and true and good. God had told them.

But when they fell, they did not treasure it or consider that its pursuit was what life is all about. Instead, they threw away holiness and righteousness and innocence and embraced sin and death, mortality, alienation from God—in a word, *unbelief.* In the gospel we see it in the parable of the talents in the person of the lazy steward who buried his talent (Lk 19:20-24).

We encounter a particularly virulent form of this dread spiritual disease in our day. It is as common as it is deadly precisely because of the relativism of our day. It is so easy for our people to think that the truth they hear in church is just one truth among many and one therefore that they need not actively embrace.

The materialism of our day makes the matter all the more difficult. People have so many material distractions that keep the Word from being the organizing principle of life. The gospel occupies only one of the many cubbyholes in the mind and soul; work, pleasure, family, friends, even the sports page may have bigger cubbyholes. The gifts of God intended to remind us of his goodness and generosity end up being ends in themselves; they cease being means to the end of grateful adoration and wholehearted commitment to him and to his Word. Those modern conveniences that make our lives easier and save time could free up energy and time that could be devoted to the Word and to a life of service. Instead, however, we so easily use them merely for transitory pleasure. The time saved goes to nothing more than accumulating still more "stuff" to enjoy. Would that we received all things with thanksgiving, enjoyed them with a pure heart, and then used them to deepen our life with Christ and in service to one another!

Sins with no apparent consequences embolden *acidia*

The ease with which we can sin and get away with it helps fill out the picture of slivers on the cross, slivers so sharp that we scarcely notice when they pierce and poison us. There are few if any social or civil sanctions against greed or immorality. And much that is vile these days can be hidden away on the Internet or in "creative" bookkeeping. Couples live in sin before they are married, and their parents defend their behavior instead of (as was the case years ago) running to the pastor and insisting that he "do something." So-called alternate lifestyles are considered just a reflection of different "values;" to object, much less to warn of God's wrath, is thought by many of our members to be unloving and unchristian. Try to exercise Christian discipline in many a Lutheran school and learn of the relativism of angry parents who attack with "Lutheran" vigor: "What's the matter? Don't you people know about forgiveness?" They want to hear nothing about repentance and less still about the consequences for sin. That Adam and Eve were forgiven but never got back into the garden and ultimately died, that David suffered greatly after he was forgiven receives no consideration from such people. Since they will not hear of such things, it is all but impossible to speak to them about these chastisements as loving gifts from a heavenly Father. It is all but impossible to share with them the virtues of the cross.

And that exactly is the problem. Spiritual laziness that pursues the truth and godliness with insufficient vigor accepts sin and tries to defend it with the gospel! Forgiveness is used as a license to sin and a wonderful and so sanctified-sounding way of escaping the cross! Should the conscience occasionally be troubled during the sermon, Rev. Sloth mounts the devil's pulpit and soothes away the trouble: "Don't be concerned about the sins the sermon rebukes; before he is done, he will tell you again that all is forgiven! Good thing too! After all, the cross hurts, it's hard to carry it, and the sins are dear." Ask people what they expect to find in heaven and the answers of some may be very enlightening. They may rattle off a list of afflictions that will no longer be there—no more sickness, no more hunger or thirst, no more death. And, of course, they will be right. But how many would be shocked to discover that the reason these will be gone in heaven is that their cause will be gone: There will be no more sin, not one, not my favorite ones either! No more lust, either open or secret; no more getting even; no more getting ahead of someone else; no more Me First! Instead, there will be—are you ready for it—JESUS. How many might be disappointed to hear it?

It must take a stick of dynamite to blast this spiritual laziness out of ourselves and our people or even to get us to take it seriously. And just such dynamite we will find in God's Word, if we have the courage to light that fuse. Jesus declares without apologizing and without flinching in Revelation 3:15-19:

I know your deeds, that you are neither cold nor hot. I
wish you were either one or the other! So, because you
are lukewarm—neither hot nor cold—I am about to spit
you out of my mouth. You say, "I am rich; I have acquired
wealth and do not need a thing." But you do not realize
that you are wretched, pitiful, poor, blind and naked. I
counsel you to buy from me gold refined in the fire, so you
can become rich; and white clothes to wear, so you can
cover your shameful nakedness; and salve to put on your
eyes, so you can see. Those whom I love I rebuke and discipline. So be earnest, and repent.*

And so we note it yet again: The cross is not optional. Felix
thought so to his eternal peril. So too did King Agrippa
(Ac 24,26). They were outside the church; they did not want to
come in just yet. Paying insufficient attention to the gospel, they
heard only of the cross, a cross whose heaviness seemed to them
greater than its blessedness. But Felix and Agrippa have a host
of companions who consider themselves to be inside the church.
Apart from repentance the tragic end of these saints, according
to the order of Cain, is no different from the end for Felix and
Agrippa. C. F. W. Walther in three brilliant sermons for the
Second Sunday in Lent on the Epistle Lesson, 1 Thessalonians
4:1-7 observed:

Many thousand times more fall again out of grace
through laziness and lukewarmness than through open
sins and vice. It is indeed true that sanctification preserves no one in grace; but it is just as true that whoever
does not want to pursue sanctification but wants to continue in his sins, pushes a good conscience away from
himself, suffers shipwreck in his faith and together with
his faith loses grace, righteousness and blessedness.**

---

*Note the Greek word that Jesus uses here for *love*. It is not, as we might expect,
from *agapao* but from *phileo*, i.e., the love of friendship, which shares common
goals and interests with the one thus loved.

**Carl Ferd. Wilh. Walther, *Amerikanisch = Lutherische Epistel Postille Predigten*
(St. Louis: *Lutherischer Concordia Verlag*, 1882), p. 131.

Take God and his Word seriously

Is it not abundantly clear that the proclamation of the gospel of free salvation and full forgiveness is not intended by God to be an easy escape from the cross? Is it not equally clear that the gospel has not turned God into an overindulgent parent, indifferent to the sins and faults of his children? We cannot say it too often, emphasize it too vigorously: God expects us to take him and his Word seriously, all of it, both the law and the gospel. Who then dares to imagine that God has become indifferent to the timidity or cowardice or laziness of those he has called into his service, be they in the pulpit or in the pew? To a godless life, the yawning soul with a deadened conscience says, "Well, we all make mistakes; nobody is perfect. Who should judge anyway?" So he relieves himself of any warning call from the law of God and brings down a fearful future under the wrath of God. For doctrinal errors, the same lazy soul offers the bromide, "Well, when all is said and done, we still worship the same God, don't we?" The amazing thing is that such an answer pleases both the one who said it and most of those who hear it. For now no one needs to think about what *God* has said in his Word; no one needs to think at all! How easy! How convenient! Everybody gets to be God and his own bible!

Too numerous to mention are the exhortations in God's Word that warn us against this spiritual torpor that uses the gospel as an excuse for vice or a license to sin or remedy for doctrinal disputes. Read the epistles of Paul. Almost all of them, especially in their closing chapters, have warnings against just this vice that plagues the lazy who think that they have been saved not from sin but for sin. Note especially Paul's warnings in 1 Corinthians 10:1-13. The Israelites compromised with wickedness and God did not wink: "God was not pleased with most of them; their bodies were scattered over the desert. . . . So, if you think you are standing firm, be careful that you don't fall!" (vv. 5,12). Or this from Galatians 5:19-26 and 6:7-9: "I warn you, as I did before, that those who live like this will not inherit the kingdom of God. . . . Do not be deceived: God cannot be mocked. A man reaps what he sows." Or this from 1 Thessalonians 4:6-8: "The Lord will punish men for all such sins, as we have already told you and warned you. For God did not call us to be impure, but to live a holy life. Therefore, he who rejects this instruction does not reject man but God, who gives you his Holy Spirit."

To bring the matter as clearly as possible back to the theology of the cross, call to mind Paul's sharpest exhortation of all in Galatians 5:24: "Those who belong to Christ Jesus have crucified the sinful nature with its passions and desires." There is no such thing as a lukewarm or casual crucifixion. There can be no doubt about it; the flesh squeals in horror at the prospect of separation from sin, let alone any accomplished separation. But the very essence of cross bearing is *self* denial. It is taking on this assignment so horrific to that flesh, the assignment of nailing passions and desires to a cross and doing that over and over again, every day, every hour. For the past act of *having crucified* is never really an entirely done business until we get to heaven. The passions and the desires keep trying to wriggle and slime their way off the cross to live again in our hearts and lives.

Our great difficulty is getting people to see that. Getting people, yes, getting ourselves too, to grasp that Christianity is the one and only real business of our lives. It is, again, the difficulty of getting people to take God and his Word seriously. Our prayer at the beginning of the day is not just for health and wealth. It is first and foremost for mercy that keeps on forgiving the past *and* granting new strength to struggle against the old *self* in the new day. The Word of God is filled with exhortations to see our life exactly in those terms, terms of cross bearing that is a conscious struggle which occupies our whole attention. It surely should be obvious that cross-bearing *self* denial cannot long be an unconscious undertaking. *Self* objects and protests and resists every step of the way.

The cross presses hard on the *self* in every attitude and act. That is why Paul uses such striking metaphors in his exhortations to sanctified living. In Romans 12, for example, the apostle compares the whole of the Christian's life to a sacrifice. The Christian acts as a priest. For such a priest, sacrificing is the Christian's entire occupation. In 1 Corinthians 9, Paul employs sports metaphors to show us that Christianity is not just a part-time avocation. Rather, the Christian is in training like the runner or the wrestler whose whole goal is to conquer first himself and then to win against his opponents. Such a one is single-minded in his devotion to the goal of victory and allows nothing to interfere with his training. It all takes effort. It involves commitment that is total. It is not for the lazy, the careless, the indifferent. They have no part in the struggle and none in the victory either! In Ephesians 6:10-18, Paul paints in the most striking terms the battle scene of the Christian against the hosts of hell inside of *self,* in the world, and from hell. Such a battle requires all of the warrior's attention and the best weapons that God himself and God alone can afford and provide in his Word. There is no place on this battlefield for the occasional warrior or the soldier addicted to *acidia* (lazy indifference). Jesus brings the whole matter to a conclusion for us with his parable of the wise and foolish virgins in Matthew 25:1-13 when he ends it by exhorting us all, "Therefore keep watch, because you do not know the day or the hour."

These are hard sayings, are they not? Who can hear them? Who can live by them? Who can live proclaiming them? The hearer fears the wrath and resistance of his flesh. The proclaimer fears the wrath and resistance of the hearer. For both it remains ever imperative that the connection between the theology of the cross and the doctrine of the means of grace with the doctrine of justification not be lost. Were it not for the promise that our salvation has already been won for us by Christ, we would give up before we even began the battle. Were it not for the power inherent in the gospel, the preaching of the cross of Christ and the justification that flows from it would be in vain, no matter how cleverly we made our presentation. Were it not for the power inherent in the gospel of Word and sacraments, the call to carry the cross would likewise be in vain; for only the gospel itself can give us a joyful and eager response to the message of the cross—both his cross and ours.

Neither the preaching of Christ's cross nor our own is in vain. The apostle was, as already noted, shown by Christ at the very beginning of his apostolate that he would have to suffer for the gospel (Ac 9:16). So powerful was the gospel that Saul became Paul. And when it was all over or almost all over, he could declare with confidence to his dear son in the Lord, "I have fought the good fight, I have finished the race, I have kept the faith. Now there is in store for me the crown of righteousness, which the

Lord, the righteous Judge, will award to me on that day—and not only to me, but also to all who have longed for his appearing" (2 Ti 4:7,8). He sees the final glory as a gift from God, in no way earned by his fight, his race, or even his faith. But he also sees that fight, that race, that faith as essential in his life, not optional, as defining his life, not just occasionally describing it.

So the slivers on the cross are indeed dangerous, no matter how easily they slip into the soul to pierce and poison it. Timidity in some and in others an ungodly marriage to success as the world judges it keep many a preacher and teacher from proclaiming the cross. And the same obstacles keep many a hearer from embracing it. The high hurdles of moral relativism, materialism, and spiritual laziness prevent many from even competing against *self* to which the theology of the cross calls each one of us. But there is no avoiding it if we are to be faithful to the Lord, who calls us to love him because he has loved us first. And this love for Christ, once we have come to faith in Christ, shows itself first and foremost by the ongoing, the full-time battle against *self*.

4

Slivers Under the Cross

To carry the cross in the grand procession of the saints on the way to heaven is to deny *self*. The parade is a messy one. The path is strewn with the dead souls of those who gave up along the way because they were spiritually lazy. Some were lazy because they never really listened to Christ's call in the first place. Jesus speaks of them in his great and paradigmatic story of the seed falling on the pathway, on stony ground, and amid the thorns and thistles (Lk 8:4-15). Some were aided in their laziness by preachers and teachers who themselves were lazy or timid or more busy winning followers for themselves than disciples for the crucified One. But the procession goes on, peopled by those who have taken Christ at his Word, those who have taken that Word seriously. For that is the essence of faith, that we take Christ and his Word seriously. We really have been redeemed from sin, death, and hell. We really are called to deny *self* in response to that good news. We really are called to follow Christ, carrying willingly, even joyfully, the cross he sends out of love for us.

The obstacles to triumph inside of us are those clusters of sins that infect the *self* and by which the *self* really wants to live. The obstacles inside of us come from our own sinful nature as well as from the devil and the world. They are obstacles of careless indifference to Christ and his Word on one side and ardent devotion to one's own will on the other. Even after we recognize these obstacles inside ourselves, we are not yet finished identifying and dealing with hindrances to *self* denial and cross bearing.

Luther on the freedom of the Christian under the cross

There are still other slivers on the cross that present an ever-present danger for the cross-bearer. If the chief obstacle inside us is our own sinful nature spurred on by the devil and the world, then a chief obstacle that remains outside us is the sinful nature of those around us. We do not carry the cross in a vacuum, and we do not exercise *self* denial on a desert island. We live, as St. John reminds us, *in* the world but are not to live as those *of* the world (1 Jn 2:15-17). And what of this life *in* but not *of* the world? It is not a life of splendid isolation. It is a life in a community, in a household, in a civil society, in the church, in a nation. It is a life with other people. And how does *self* denial, cross bearing, connect with a life with other people? Luther answers brilliantly in his famous 1520 treatise *The Freedom of a Christian* (*Luther's Works,* American Edition, vol. 31, pp. 327-377). Permit a brief summary of Luther's thoughts in this famous treatise.

Luther makes two chief points: First, the Christian is free and subject to no one; then second, the Christian is a servant and subject to all. He is free, since Christ has won our salvation entirely and alone; he is free, since in the gospel of forgiveness, Christ gives us all the perfection that the law requires. Therefore, no one can demand anything from us for our salvation, since Christ has given everything to faith; he has freely granted pardon and peace, heaven and eternal blessedness. In that sense, the Christian is entirely free from all laws and commands. For they have all been fulfilled for us by Christ. The soul that believes God, that trusts his promises, is united to Christ as a bride to the bridegroom. And in this sacred marriage an exchange takes place. The virtue and holiness and blessedness of Christ, the bridegroom, have become the possessions of the bride.

The sin and guilt of the bride have become the property of Christ, who has taken it all away on his cross. So the Christian with Christ as his bridegroom and head is a king and lord over everything; he is even a priest to whom God listens and whose prayers God gladly answers. And all of this is his through faith alone, altogether without works.

But while the new man is perfect because of the forgiveness earned by Christ and given in the gospel, he lives in the flesh, in the world, with people. And the new man living still in the flesh needs to discipline the flesh by means of those good works that are pleasing to God and useful to his neighbor. Thus it is that the Christian is the servant of all and subject to all, for the sake of discipline. Without such discipline he would again fall completely in love with the world; ultimately he would abandon Christ and faith altogether. But when he disciplines and crucifies the flesh, when he obeys the law, when he serves his neighbor, he pleases the God who has already made him a free child and heir. And so the Christian becomes subject to all because it pleases God that he discipline the flesh by serving his neighbor; and all the Christian really wants to do is to please God. Just as Adam and Eve in the garden before the fall needed no works to become God's children, so the Christian needs no works to become righteous; he is that already. But just as Adam and Eve had work to do in the garden, which before the fall they did gladly and freely, so too the Christian has work to do. He does the work gladly and freely. Yes, he delights in serving because that is what pleases God.

Thus good and pious works do not make a good and pious man, but a good and righteous man produces and does good and pious works. That is exactly what Jesus tells us in Matthew 7—a good tree bears good fruit; a bad tree bears bad fruit. To be sure, it is by the outward and visible fruit that we see if the tree is good or bad, but the tree nevertheless must first be good before it can bear good fruit. So too the Christian: when he does good works, the works are visible and outward and necessary evidence that he is a Christian; but they do not make him a Christian.

The Christian does not live isolated and alone but lives with others. Because he is a Christian, he wants nothing else for them than what is useful to them. To put it another way, he has no cause for greediness or selfishness in which he would seek gain at his neighbor's expense; for as a Christian he has everything already in Christ and the gospel. That makes him cheerful and generous in his life lived for the benefit of others. The love that he enjoys in and from Christ he cannot help but display and share with those around him. He does that by making himself the servant of all, so that all of his works are directed to the benefit of his neighbor. In so doing, he does nothing else than what Christ, his head, has already done for him. Christ freely and out of love did everything for me; now I freely and out of love do everything for my neighbor. And in doing it for my neighbor, I do it for Christ, who has given me my neighbor just for this reason, so that I can serve him. And who is my neighbor? Anyone and everyone whom I can serve is my neighbor, whether members of my family, my neighborhood, my church, my nation, or anyone else in the world that I have the opportunity to serve.

Obstacles in the path of a life of total freedom in total service

What a world it would be if these expressions of Luther became the reality of our lives with one another! Every life has an organizing principle. If the organizing principle in someone's life were total joy that he has everything in the gospel and is therefore free to live in total service to those around him, what a heaven on earth would surround such a one! Luther, of course, knew perfectly well, and better than most, how little this organizing principle finds its way into the hearts and lives of even the best among us. In the previous chapter, we considered some of the major obstacles inside us that war against such an organizing principle for life. In this chapter we look at the obstacles to *self* denial, to carrying the cross, that we encounter through those around us. They are splinters under the cross. Those splinters tear at our feet and make it difficult to walk on the pathway of service to all.

Luther was no rosy view, pie-in-the-sky idealist, out of touch with the realities of life as it is lived day by day in a family, a parish, a civil society. He expressed his realism so pointedly in his Large Catechism (e.g., his comments on the Fifth Commandment) that some have called him a hopeless cynic. But he was not a cynic or a depressing pessimist who had given up on service in a godless, thankless world. No, not at all. Quite to the contrary, Luther takes into account the reality of sin in self *and* sin in those around him when he echoes the call of Christ in the theology of the cross. It is so common in our day for people to say that there is some good in everyone, that people are by nature good and decent, kind and true. That is part of the Arminian heresy, which denied the doctrine of original sin. Arminianism is an essential component of Baptist and Methodist churches and their pentecostal and liberal cousin churches. Arminianism is virtually the state religion of the English-speaking world. Luther, on the other hand, together with all the apostles and prophets, had no such illusions about people. He had no such illusions about himself either. He took the doctrine of original sin seriously. The depravity and hostility toward God that still lives in the sinful flesh of even the greatest of saints finds ways to express itself; it does so in me *and* in those my Christian self wants to serve.

It is essential to the Christian's life of service that we recognize that basic fact—the fact of sin not just in ourselves but in everyone else as well. If we fall for the Arminian heresy that everyone is basically good, we will soon be disappointed, then disillusioned, then despairing and bitter. For people will prove that they are sinners. People will often not appreciate our best efforts in their behalf, may even resent us for them. Many will be ungrateful. Many will try to take advantage of our kindness and generosity. Many will abuse us for it, slander us or find other ways to persecute us, if for no other reason than that any sign of virtue in others gives them a guilty conscience and highlights their own vice.

Ah, but we know from the beginning—as the result of sin in the world, that is exactly what we should expect! And if we expect it, then we will not be so easily disappointed or deterred in our service. Indeed, on those occasions when things go well for us, when there is some understanding, even appreciation, then how grateful we will be for it! For we did not expect thanks and did not serve looking for reward. Some even will see our good works and come to praise God for them (Mt 5:16). Our example and our service may inspire them to listen to the gospel. Some of those, through the gospel's faith-creating power, will even believe

93

and join us in the procession that follows Jesus under the cross. When such things happen, it is a pleasant and delightful surprise, another kind gift from an always most generous God. On the other hand, if we expected people always to be good and welcoming, kind and appreciative, then we will become easy prey to bitterness when we see that so often they are not. We will soon retreat to curse the world, as we throw away the cross and return to a life lived only for self.

We need to get it straight. These are the only two alternatives. Either we live for others, expecting disappointment and then being pleasantly surprised when disappointment is replaced with appreciative acceptance; or we live expecting appreciation and end up retreating in bitterness when we discover that most people are just as sinful as we are and not afraid to prove it.

The theology of the cross and 1 Corinthians 13

It is with these realities in mind that we look at what Luther said in *The Freedom of the Christian*. It is with these realities in mind, together with Luther's comments in the Large Catechism, that we consider the theology of the cross and its connection to our lives in all the different associations we have with other people. A chapter of the Bible that is a must-read in such a consideration is 1 Corinthians 13. St. Paul had no illusions about man's nature as fallen, corrupt, and depraved. That is exactly what makes his inspired encouragement for our lives with one another so completely connected to the theology of the cross. Too often, as in many a wedding sermon, 1 Corinthians 13 is presented as a rather sappy and sentimental expression of the Christian life. It is anything but that!

Love and the theology of the cross

Crucial to any correct understanding of 1 Corinthians 13 is a correct understanding of the word *love* in that chapter. That is essential as well to any correct understanding of our lives with one another under the cross. The love of which the apostle speaks in Greek is *agape*. That is a love which in its essence, by definition, *seeks the good and the best interest of the object, of the one loved*. It is the most commonly used word in the New Testament for the love that God has for us, as well as the love that we should have for one another. A love that seeks the best interest of the one loved is not merely an emotion or a sentiment. In fact, such a love does not reside chiefly in the emotions; it resides in the *will*. It is a love of *choice*, not necessarily a love of *attraction*. It is a love expressed in *action*, not merely in sentimental niceties. *Agapao*, the verb form of the noun *agape*, is the verb used for God's love in John 3:16. This is how God loved the world: He *chose* to love the world and then put his love into action by giving his Son for its rescue. That goes way beyond sentiment! Likewise, it is this word for love that is used in Hebrews 12:6: "The Lord disciplines those he loves." Thus, while a sentimental love does not willingly inflict pain on the one loved, this kind of love may sometimes do just that. Again, it is a love that seeks the best interest of the one loved. As a father disciplines his child out of love that goes way beyond sentiment, so God disciplines us in ways that may be painful at the time. But he is seeking our best interest, and that is from a love which he chooses to have and to display in action.

Contrast this meaning for *love* with the way in which the word is so often used in English. In English we speak of loving a certain kind of food or weather. That kind of love is shallow and sensual, as fleeting as a meal or a sunny day. A television personality or a television preacher may often say something like this: "Now don't forget: We love you." But that love knows no action, gives nothing, accomplishes nothing, offers nothing, promises nothing. In a word, it is a love that is meaningless. Contrast it as well with the love of the romantic. He or she gushes and bubbles over with a love that may indeed be very real. But it is a love that wants something from the loved one to complete itself. It is not really free. It is not really unconditional. In fact, that's why it's gushing and bubbling, so that it can, at the very least, get as good as it gives. There may not be anything wrong with that in honorable relationships. But the point is, that it is not the meaning of *agape*.

To be sure, the love of John 3:16, the love of God, wants something too. But what it wants is to give, to rescue and redeem by the sacrifice of the cross. That is a love in which the cross of Christ is wrapped, a love that looks always to please the Father and to redeem the lost and fallen world. From the standpoint of the world, there is nothing that the fallen world can be or give or do to earn such loving action. In fact, the world does everything possible to spurn that love on the cross. Consider the passion of our Lord. His disciples abandoned him. His church plotted his destruction. His institution of government perverted justice to be rid of him. His best friend, his mother, and a few others could only stand at a distance and weep. Even Simon of Cyrene, who carried the cross for Jesus, did so unwillingly; by his action, he only hastened the process of execution. No one helped. All contributed to his sorrow and his pain. And this was his love: That is exactly the way he wanted it! The work of love that wins the world must be and was his alone. So perfect, so complete is this love of God in Christ for us! Again, consider the contrast with the way the word *love* is used in common expression; common usage of the word does not even begin to grasp what this kind of love is.

The imitating love of the Christian under the cross

This active, totally giving love of God in Christ inspires the love of the Christian. It makes imitation the goal of the Christian life in the world after he has received the saving benefit of God's love and Christ's cross. St. John sums up the matter beautifully when he declares, "This is love: not that we loved God, but that he loved us and sent his Son as an atoning sacrifice for our sins. Dear friends, since God so loved us, we also ought to love one another" (1 Jn 4:10,11).* St. Paul speaks the same way when he introduces his masterful summary of the Christian life in Ephesians 5:1,2: "Be imitators of God, therefore, as dearly loved children and live a life of love, just as Christ loved us and gave himself up for us as a fragrant offering and sacrifice to God." Jesus set the pattern for the disciples and for us when at the very threshold of the abyss into which he would so soon plunge, he said and then said it again, "Love each other as I have loved you" (Jn 15:12, see also v. 17).

---

*It is interesting to note that the word that is translated *friends* is not the usual word from the verb *phileo*. It is *agapetoi,* literally, *ones who are loved with* [God's] *agape.*

A correct understanding of this word *love* will go a long way to removing one of the major obstacles that people encounter when they read 1 Corinthians 13. The chapter does not call on us to *like* with a sentimental or emotional attachment. Even God in John 3:16 did not *like* the world as it was, with a mere sentimental attachment to it. For it was buried under the rubble of sin with the stench of death all over it. No, he loved the world and acted to bear the rubble of its sin on his own shoulders on the cross and wipe away the death and its stench in his own grave. To put it another way: Love that would have been a sentimental attachment to the world in its fallen state was impossible and out of the question. To be sure, the love that 1 Corinthians 13 calls for and calls forth may often have an emotional component to it. There are many people whom we love in an emotional way, people of whom we are fond and to whom we are attracted or attached. And there need be nothing wrong with that. But that is not the essence of the love spoken of here. If it were, then we would have to despair when Jesus tells us, "Love your enemies" (Mt 5:44). He is not telling us to be fond of them or feel some strong emotional or sentimental attachment to them. He is telling us to actively pursue their best interest at our own expense, whether that is accepted, understood, and appreciated or not.

It is crystal clear that such a love will require a high degree of *self* denial. Is it not then easy to see how the exercise of such a love is united to the cross? For apart from the cross of Christ, who would ever be able to undertake that kind of *self* denial? His cross is wrapped in the love of God. It is that love which makes it even conceivable that we would love in imitation of his love, that is, actively, selflessly, seeking only the good of those loved.

It is that love, the love of Christ for us, that makes bearable the slivers under the cross, slivers in our feet on the pathway of loving service to those around us. In 1 Corinthians 13 each line assumes obstacles to the love we are called to express. The entire epistle is an eloquent testimony to obstacles that the apostle overcame in his love for the Corinthians. Were it not for such love in the apostle, he would have given up on that congregation with all its evidences of lovelessness. They fought with one another over silly things, over which pastor or apostle was their hero. They missed the point that church discipline is a proof of love for the fallen; and so they did not practice church discipline, but lovelessly let the sinner go unreproved and thus unrepentant. They battled it out with one another in law courts to take advantage of one another. They apparently had members who thought that grace and forgiveness were a license for lust. They even turned the Lord's Table, that sublime expression of Christ's love, into an occasion for excess and for lording it over one another.

When Paul, therefore, writes his beautiful hymn of praise to Christian love, he is speaking of a love which for him too required *self* denial. It required a victory over obstacles that the congregation presented to his love. Read the chapter in the context of Paul's labors in Corinth and then the congregation's subsequent failure to put into practice what he had risked his life to teach them. Consider the specifics of the chapter with some care; then you will certainly see that the love of the Christian is not something laced with shallow sentimentality.

"Love is patient, love is kind" assumes that our neighbor often puts patience and kindness to the test. The neighbor who is a member of our family or one with whom we work every day often tests patience and kindness. It is sometimes easier to be patient with and kind to total strangers than to those we know, those we live and work with. However difficult a stranger may make patience and kindness for us, the obstacles he presents are short term. Patience with those whom we know is quite another matter. After all, some of those near and dear to us keep on making the same mistakes over and over again. It can be difficult to be patient with our own children when they are slow to learn, slow to behave as they ought. It can be difficult to be patient with a spouse or coworkers when either they or we are tired and irritable. *Be kind!* It's much easier to blurt out to a son or daughter, to a spouse or coworker: "How many times do I have to tell you . . . ?" Being patient and kind to a stranger may be easier by comparison. But even with a stranger, it can sometimes be difficult. By the time we have to deal with the telemarketer, the rude and pushy in traffic or in a line, the exhortation *Be kind!* may be a long way from the front of our mind and mouth.

"[Love] is not rude, it is not self-seeking, it is not easily angered, it keeps no record of wrongs." The apostle is not telling us that

love is indifferent to wrong. He had already rebuked the congregation for its indifference to the sin of the member who was living with his father's wife. He is speaking of the spirit of love that is forgetful of *self* and seeks only the good of the one loved, even when that requires discipline. Discipline without being rude! Discipline without self-seeking, that is, without the pleasure of getting even or of working off your own frustration in the disciplining of another; so often the child is spanked too violently simply because the parent was too indifferent to chastise at the right time; the parent waited until his own anger was the chief actor in the discipline, not love for the child. Then discipline becomes rude; then discipline is self-seeking. Pride in self gets in the way. Pride or stubbornness in the one needing correction likewise gets in the way and makes it easy to shout, to scowl, to dredge up the past.

Paul goes on: *"Love does not delight in evil but rejoices with the truth."* That there are people who take a devilish delight in doing evil is all too obvious in our society. But one can delight in evil even without doing it. Some people get a perverse thrill out of watching the wickedness of others. But there are more subtle ways of delighting in evil. We delight in evil when it gives us an excuse to boast of our own innocence, at least with respect to the evil we see in another: "Well, at least I didn't do *that!*" The truth that we might have wished to do evil and were only kept from it by fear is not expressed. The truth that we have done other evil that makes us just as guilty likewise is passed over in discrete silence. Truth gets corrupted by pride and self-righteousness. To rejoice with the truth is to grieve over the evil, to strive to correct it out of love for *the* truth—Christ died for all. In the case of a fallen Christian caught in a sin, it is to rejoice in the Christ who comes to live in that Christian too by the message of grace and pardon. Even in dealing with an unbeliever and the impenitent, we rejoice in the truth that Christ came to set that one free as well. No matter how great the evil, Christ carried it on his cross. No matter how shackled the sinner is to his sin, Christ died to set him free. We rejoice to share that truth with the fallen slave of sin, whether he will hear it or not, believe it not, come to rejoice with us or turn on us.

When is it *my* turn?

"[Love] always protects, always trusts, always hopes, always perseveres. Love never fails." We cannot help but notice in these words that there is not a syllable about when it will be *my* turn, about getting *my* rights, about *my* feelings. That is what makes these words so much an echo of Jesus' call to us to deny *self* and to follow him. Whether those who receive such benefits from me return them or not does not really matter when I am confident that the Lord will keep his Word and never leave or forsake me.

That is not an easy lesson to learn. Have you perhaps thought when reading Paul's exhortations to husbands and wives in Ephesians 5 that it would be a lot easier to be the kind of husband Paul says a husband should be if only the wife were the kind of wife she should be? Or it would be a lot easier to be the kind of wife Paul says a wife should be if only the husband were the kind of husband that Paul says he should be. But there is not a word in Ephesians 5 that suggests "You be this way if your spouse is that way." He does not even suggest that the spouse will be the way the spouse should be if you are first the way you should be. Each is to love unconditionally as Christ loves us—not necessarily as the other loves us, as desirable as it would be for the other to love us as he or she should. Again, showing love like Christ's love *may* at times be repaid with like love. But that is not the reason for showing it. Nor is it an excuse for withdrawing love when it is not repaid. If love is returned with love, then that is a beautiful thing indeed, a most delightful gift from God. But it is not the cause, the reason, or the condition for showing love.

But when is it *my* turn? The question keeps popping into our minds and getting in the way of love that acts solely for the benefit of the neighbor. Don't I have needs too that need to be addressed? The question cannot be ignored. The answer to it however is not to be found in the neighbor. It is to be found in Christ. He says, "Take up your cross and follow me." He remains the one who fills our eyes. If we were looking elsewhere or at another, we would stumble; we would lose sight of him and end up in the ditch. But we are looking at him. And he it is who fills our needs as well as our eyes. To put it another way: When is it *my* turn? That's his problem, not mine. When we need taking care of, he will find someone to take care of us. When there is a cry in the heart and an ache in the soul, he will provide a saint of his own choosing to dry the tears and sooth the ache. Turning away from following Christ to chase after and demand service from those we should serve is to lay down the cross before we get to heaven. He knows our needs better than we do. He supplies those needs in ways always better than the ones we would have found on our own and apart from him.

To put it most simply, he tells us through St. Peter, "Cast all your anxiety on him because he cares for you" (1 Pe 5:7). The solutions to the problems of *my* turn and *my* needs are Christ's problems, problems that he unfailingly deals with far better than we ever could ever imagine or prescribe for him.

St. Paul puts it in a slightly different and very interesting way in Galatians 6. He tells us, "Carry each other's burdens, and in this way you will fulfill the law of Christ" (v. 2). The emphasis is on what each should give the other. But the giving to each other presupposes or includes in it also a receiving; it presupposes that on some level others are doing the same thing. God will give others to help me carry my burden; but my *chief* concern is that I am the one who is busy helping others carry their burdens. Lest we miss the emphasis he adds, "for each one should carry his own load" (v. 5). The point could not be made more emphatically; our passion is service to the other; God's passion is service to us through others of his choosing and in his time. Perhaps the person of God's own choosing is right next to us—perhaps it is a wise parent or an understanding son or daughter; perhaps it is a kind teacher, a sympathetic pastor, a faithful friend. In his providence, God gives these gifts so that we can serve them; and in his providence, he gives these gifts so that he can show us his kindness when we need them to serve us. But even in their necessary service to us, our focus and goal normally will be to get back to normal, so that we can again serve them.

As we focus on the needs of others and trust God to provide for our own needs, we do well to bear in mind the analogy that Paul used immediately before his discussion of the Christian's life of love in 1 Corinthians 13. He tells us in 1 Corinthians 12 that we are the members of the body of Christ. Each member of a body has special abilities and functions. The parts of a body do not act with indifference to each other. Rather, they serve the whole by doing what each was designed to do—the eye to see, the foot to walk, the hand to do, the ear to hear. Each of us is a member of his body. Each member in love for the whole body, and especially for Christ the head, looks for its own function, its own abilities. Then it acts appropriate to its place in the body. Do the eyes say, "Since the foot is hurting, I will stop seeing?" Do the ears declare, "Since the hand is sore, I will not listen?" Certainly not! Each member does what is appropriate to it for the benefit of the whole, even if other members for some reason cannot or do not function as they ought. Indeed, we know that in a body, the hearing of the blind often becomes all the more acute in order to compensate for the lack of sight. So in the body of Christ: there may be many members who for whatever reason do not carry out all of their functions as they should. That only serves to heighten the need for other members to carry out their own function with particular faithfulness; that way they can to some extent compensate for the loss to the whole body that comes as a result of the failure or weakness of some of its other members.

Again, there may be many slivers under the cross, that is, people who make it more difficult for me to carry my cross. They increase the pain and may seem to add little to the peace and joy of the body of Christ. But their weakness, even as they cause pain to the body, provides us with an opportunity for loving, self-denying service. As our need moved Christ to compassion and action for our salvation, so their need and the need of the whole body should move us as well to compassion and action; for it is the love of Christ that has created our love. And beneath the cross is where that love is exercised.

The Table of Duties

Luther helps us think through our particular place and function in the body of Christ through the Table of Duties attached to the Small Catechism. The members in the congregation at Corinth got into trouble, in part, because so many thought that they could decide their own function and everyone else's as well. But if we think through the roles that God graciously grants us, we will go a long way toward figuring out ways of living the love of 1 Corinthians 13. Am I husband or wife, worker or employer, student or teacher, pastor or member, child or parent? God's Word addresses people in each of these roles.

The roles may change as time goes by, and we may fill more than one of them at a time. But this whole concept of roles, given to us by God, helps us to understand the special goodness of God to each of us. For in our station in life, God gives each one ways of serving him right here, right now. Our God-given roles also help keep us from being overwhelmed at the enormity of our assignment—that we should live to serve our neighbor. And who is our neighbor? Everyone is! But it is humanly impossible to carry everybody else's burden. The Table of Duties tells us where to begin. Serve where you are. Love according to your station in life. Husbands, love your wives in the self-denying way that Christ loved the church and gave himself for her. Wives, submit to your husbands out of love to them and to Christ, just as the church submits to Christ. Children, obey your parents as Christ's representatives. Parents, love and discipline your children as God our Father loves and disciplines each of us. Pastors and teachers, carry out your offices not for your own sake but for the sake of those whom Christ has entrusted to your loving care. Members and students, listen and obey with respect and reverence those whom God has given for your instruction. Employers and rulers, remember that you too have one who is over you and who rules in love for the benefit of those he governs. Employees and citizens, work and obey the law of the land as servants of Christ.

Again we need to call it to mind: There is not a word in the Table of Duties that suggests we should do these things only if our counterparts do their part. It is a fine thing indeed when such is the case; but we serve in our own roles out of love to Christ, not out of some naïve expectation that everyone else serves him too. That other people are doing their duty is not the reason for our doing our duty. Rather, that Christ did it all for us, that is the cause and the reason for our service to him through our service to one another.

Doing our duty in our own station in life is the most important way that we can show the love called for and called forth in 1 Corinthians 13. There can likewise be little doubt that showing love in our own station in life is often the most difficult place for us to show love. As already noted, sometimes it is easier to be

kind to strangers than it is to be kind to many of those we see
and deal with every day. Those we deal with every day may have
hurt us the day before. They may have irritated us for a thousand days in a row. They may have given us an almost infinite
number of reasons to be annoyed with them, impatient with
them, bitter toward them, and zealous only to avoid them. Who
among us cannot give names to a score of slivers under the cross,
to people whose very existence is like smoke in the eyes or ammo-
nia in the nose?

While the slivers considered in the last chapter are so sharp
that they slide under the skin often unnoticed, that is certainly
not the case with the slivers under the cross that we have considered here. These are all too obvious and apparent, like slivers
stuck in the sole of a runner. They poke and jab and leave behind
aches and sores on the soul that are healed only with difficulty.
Even after the sores are healed, their source may return without
notice to inflict new and greater pain. It is hard to love the parent, the child, the spouse, the neighbor who is a drunkard or a
drug abuser or a thief or a liar or just plain mean-spirited and
cruel. It is hard to love the pastor or teacher who just doesn't
seem to understand our needs or really care about them. It is
hard to love the member or the student who is impossible to
please or teach. It is hard to love the one whose whole aim in life
seems to be to make my life miserable. It is difficult to know how
to love or show love to such a one.

We need to keep reminding ourselves that the love which
Christ calls for from us in Matthew 5:43-48 and the love that he
wants us to show in 1 Corinthians 13 is that *agape* love, the love
that seeks the ultimate good of our neighbor. While it may be
impossible to *like* some people, it is not impossible to pray for
them. It is not impossible to hope and long for their salvation. In
fact we will find it difficult to despise those for whom we pray
and those for whose salvation we yearn. And then we may discover that it is not impossible even to seek opportunities to serve
and help them as St. Paul urges in Romans 12:9-21.

Our very difficulty is a reminder of the greatness of Christ's
love for us. It is as well a reminder of our continuing and desperate need for his forgiveness that pardons the smallness of our
love. And it is a reminder too of our need for his presence in

grace to help us carry the cross of his sending and to bear with the slivers under the cross.

The Table of Duties can keep us from overreaching

While we repent of our impatience with people who are slivers to us, it would be good to remember that we may also be slivers to some of those around us—and without any fault on their part. Humility in the face of that reality may be the mother of patience. Just as the Table of Duties is a good place to start in the practice of that *self* denial which consists of loving service, so also the Table can keep us from overreaching. It can help to keep us from trying to carry out assignments that God has given to someone else for our benefit. We easily *become* splinters under the cross for other people when we step outside of the Table of Duties and presume to know everyone else's duty better than they do. It may be that everyone would be better off if *I* were the boss, the pastor, the president, or the king of Prussia.** But I am not. It may very well be that many children could run the household better than their parents. But that's not the responsibility that God has given to children. It may be that some women would be better preachers and pastors than some men who are. But that is not a role God has assigned to women. God has given responsibilities to each, and each will give an account for his stewardship in due course.

Too many of the slivers under the cross are there because of the arrogance of people who thought they knew everyone else's business better than anyone else. Yes, in point of fact, by their behavior they seem to suggest that God himself has made a mistake in the roles that he has given them. All of the attention, of course, that such people give to other peoples' roles and business detracts from their carrying out their own roles with all the zeal

---

** We cannot help but note here the old German saying used by those who know everybody else's business best; the German before he proceeds to announce how everything would be better if he were running things may say, *Wenn ich nur König in Preussen wäre* . . . (If only I were king in Prussia, then . . .). German also has a special word of scorn for that kind of attitude by which one imagines that he knows everything better than the one who has some specific responsibility; the word is *Besserwisserei* (i.e., better-knowingness).

and faithfulness possible. To the extent that they are busy meddling in matters God gave to others, to that extent they weaken the body of Christ and become slivers under the cross.

Again, it is a matter of remembering that the church is the mystical body of Christ, as Paul says in 1 Corinthians 12. We exercise the love that he speaks of so beautifully in 1 Corinthians 13 when we remember the roles which he has given us in that body. Whether someone else carries out his role as well as we think he should or could is our business to judge only if God has placed us in positions of authority to make that judgment. Otherwise, even if we think we could carry out someone else's role better than he can, until we are actually in that role, we do well to learn humility. Maybe the member would be a better preacher than his pastor. If so, then either that member should go to school and become a pastor or learn to be patient and supportive of his pastor's efforts to grow and improve. Maybe the wife would be a better head in her household than her husband. But her role is to use her talents to help her husband to carry out his God-given role of headship in the family. When people rebel against the roles they have and without warrant interfere in the administration of others in their God-given roles, then slivers multiply under the cross. Resentment and misunderstanding irritate and annoy. The benefit someone intended turns into a loss and a problem.

Happiness and the cross

If we take this whole matter of bearing the cross seriously, if we understand 1 Corinthians 13 in the context of following Jesus under the cross, then we may make an astonishing discovery. The surprising and wonderful discovery is this: *We were not seeking happiness by bearing the cross, but we discover that there is no happiness without it.* Indeed, to the extent that we deny ourselves and follow Jesus under the cross, to the extent that we heed what St. Paul says in 1 Corinthians 13 and in so many other places, to that extent we will become and be happy human beings. That is another great paradox of our faith. Most human unhappiness is the result of self-service and the result of the very flawed assumption that other people exist primarily for the service of *oneself.*

Just think about the things that make people unhappy and reread 1 Corinthians 13. "I'm unhappy at work because I have a stupid/vindictive/demanding employer and I am surrounded by lazy/self-seeking/foulmouthed/ coworkers; no one appreciates my efforts; all they do is take advantage of me." But St. Paul says that love seeks only the good of others and in so doing takes it as a given that the world is evil. With that assumption in mind, love is not surprised by these hostile circumstances; love expects them and even sees them as opportunities to exercise patience, forbearance, and kindness. It is a great victory for love—and for my own peace and happiness—when the adversity is expected, then dismissed, then overcome.

"I'm unhappy because my spouse doesn't understand me or appreciate me and my children/parents/other relatives and friends just expect me to give and give and give." Love, St. Paul says, keeps no record of wrongs. Today is another day for me to deny *self* and to serve those whom God has mercifully placed around me; that's the goal for the day. The goal is not to receive but to give. And that is a goal, which under the cross, I can achieve in at least a limited way. If the goal is to get, then I can count on frustration and failure. As God gives me opportunity, therefore, I will aim for the goal he has set before me. And at the same time, I will remain confident that he will give the blessing of finding someone to serve me when that is what I really need. Indeed, the very thanklessness of some among those I serve should be a powerful reminder to be grateful to those who have served and helped me. For all too often I *expect* to be served and miss the point that the service of others is a gracious, undeserved gift.

So in all things, whether the blessing is to serve or to be served, my only wish is to follow Christ under the cross. The time may come when I am sick or weak, old and feeble; that will be time enough for the Lord to demonstrate his faithfulness to his promise never to forsake me. Then my only service may be to receive service with a cheerful acceptance and thanksgiving, even as I long for the days when I can again be useful and needed. But even then, even in receiving when I would rather be giving, love is kind and patient; love gives the other the opportunity to serve and receives such service with thanksgiving to

107

God and to those God may send to serve me when that is what
he decides is most needed.

Slivers that come from memory

Perhaps one of the most painful challenges to love is the cry
"But you don't know what they did to me." How difficult it is to
love and seek opportunities to serve those who have hurt us! The
most painful wounds come from those closest to us, a friend, a
relative. The resentment of past hurts, of cruel words, of injustice
and unkindness at the hands of those we trusted, of those once
near and dear, is hard to overcome. How many families have forever been torn apart by quarrels over an inheritance, by the
remembrance of some past harsh words, by some real or perceived wrong? The wounds burn deep inside and often last all the
way to the funeral and the cemetery.

But St. Paul says that *love never fails.* Again we need to
remember that the apostle is talking about love that seeks the
best interest of the one loved; he is not talking about a mere sentiment or an emotion. It may be impossible for us completely and
perfectly to forgive and forget a past hurt. That we cannot get
past it perfectly is just further evidence of our own desperate
need for the forgiveness of the One who alone perfectly and completely forgives. Our difficulty in following his example brings
into sharp focus the ongoing battle inside of ourselves against the
sinful nature still there, still not entirely conquered.

That we struggle and strive nevertheless to seek the best
interests of those who have hurt us most is a sign that we are
still in that grand procession of those following Jesus under the
cross. The abused child or spouse struggles to love the abuser.
That struggle may be difficult and painful because the slivers in
the memory are buried deep within the heart. That struggle may
often be tinged with hatred for the abuse that spills over into
hatred for the abuser. Yes, it is true; hatred in the flesh and love
in the spirit may fight it out with each other every day in some
families and relationships. But still: *Love never fails.* That is
most blessedly true of Christ's love. Our love is a work in
progress. It is often a pale imitation of his love. We trust his love
to forgive our still so imperfect love.

Paul was certainly aware of how difficult it is to live these words, *Love never fails*. In the Corinthian congregation, love clearly had failed. It had failed to such an extent that members even sought revenge in heathen law courts (1 Co 6:1-8). Someone's love failed. The aggrieved member sued to even the score or to put things right. Could there be a more public display of love's failures than that? Paul is talking about triumphant love when he exhorts, "Why not rather be wronged? Why not rather be cheated?" And Jesus says the same thing in Matthew 5:38-48 when speaking of the wrongs we suffer at the hands of persecutors.

The more we think about it, the more important it becomes to remember that the love we have been considering is located chiefly in the will, not in the emotions. Think of it this way: The will chooses to seek the best interest of the one loved, while at the same time repenting of the emotions that war against love, the emotions that remember and cling to past hurts and would rather seek revenge. That may be difficult to remember when the emotions burn hot with anger over things that happened in the distant past. But to let the emotions rule and not to focus on the choice of the will to act in love is a recipe for despair in the face of God's Word: *Love never fails*. Again we cannot help but call to mind that the cross presses hard against our sinful flesh; its slivers cut deep. The flesh wants nothing more than to escape it.

Yes, the flesh would like to dismiss this whole equation of crossing-bearing, *self* denying love = happiness. It would like to call it nothing more than dreamy pie in the sky, impossible to achieve and therefore not worth bothering with in practice. But just consider once more all the reasons people give for their unhappiness. You will quickly discover that the root of all or almost all of their unhappiness is a refusal to love. It is a refusal to serve in love. It is a refusal to see *self* denial and following Christ under the cross as the organizing principle of life. Where that refusal to love and serve dominates, where the cross is cast aside, there unhappiness and an always complaining, discontented life is guaranteed!

The love of the cross and the consequences for sin

Having said all these things about love that seeks the best for the one loved, St. Paul does not mean that there never should be consequences for sin. The consequences of sin also are slivers under the cross. They hurt; their pain can be very difficult and last for a long time. There are consequences that God himself imposes. Those consequences are further evidence of God's love. God loved Adam and Eve, but they never got back into the Garden of Eden. God loved David and forgave him. But the child of David and Bathsheba died, and as a further consequence of David's sin, strife and even violence never left his house (2 Sa 12:10-18). Zechariah repented, but he remained mute until the birth of his son (Lk 1:19,20). In all of these instances and in so many more, God demonstrated that he takes all of his Word seriously, whether we do or not. He demonstrated that man cannot sin without consequences. Were there no consequences for sin, even believers would become bold to sin yet more and more. Eventually they would abandon all of God's love and his gospel as well. They would perish in unbelief. It is therefore in love that God sends consequences for sin, a love that seeks the best interest, the eternal salvation of the one loved. Just so does a parent love and forgive a misbehaving child and proves it with appropriate discipline. Just so in a Christian school, discipline is practiced in love that goes beyond punishment for its own sake. That love may even require the removal of a stubborn and willful child, love not only for the one child but for all the others as well.

There are, however, two things that we need to keep in mind when we consider the consequences for sin and our own role in visiting those consequences on someone. The first thing we need to bear in mind is the role that God has assigned to us individually. It is not up to an individual to stand in the place of God apart from the role God has given that individual in life. The parent has a role to fulfill in disciplining the children in the family. The policeman and the courts have a role given them by God in punishing lawbreakers in the community. The administration of a school has the duty to exercise discipline in that school. It is not up to me, as an individual without a responsibility assigned by God, to sit in the place of God and visit God's vengeance on someone who has hurt me. Private vengeance is a sin against both God and the neighbor, no matter how much I may think the neighbor deserves it. In due course where vengeance is required, either God will mete it out or those whom he has charged with the responsibility will dispense it. David gives us a remarkable example of one who waited for the Lord to avenge the wrongs of Saul. David refused to get revenge, even when the opportunity was there for him to do so in fullest measure (1 Sa 24 and 26; note especially 24:12).

The second matter to bear in mind is the connection between consequences and love. Vengeance, getting even, when we do not have a God-given role to carry out (e.g., parent, teacher, judge, or police officer) rarely has anything to do with love. But when we act in the roles that God has given us, we strive to imitate the way that he is with us. The consequences that God visits on us for our sins are consequences born of love for us. He wants to call us to repentance. He wants us to see the seriousness of our sin as well as the seriousness of his love for us; that is a love which both forgives and then in love also disciplines. When we act as a parent or in some other God-given role, it is our aim to serve, even when disciplining, the best interests of the one we must discipline. That is quite different from vengeance or seeking revenge. To refuse to get even when the opportunity to do so presents itself must surely be a high mark of Christian love as Paul defines it for us in 1 Corinthians 13! To love when called on to discipline is likewise a very high and Christian art.

Still it must be added: Who is sufficient for these things? The further we pursue the mind and heart of God in his Word concerning a theology of the cross, the more readily must the cry arise from our hearts and lips: God, be merciful to me, a sinner! Even when it is clear to us that our own happiness is rooted and grounded in *self* denial and in bearing the cross after Jesus, even then we have the greatest difficulty in subduing the sinful flesh. Even then it rises up in rebellion and hinders what we have come to see is not only God's good will but in our best interest precisely because it is God's good will.

Accordingly, it should seem a strange thing indeed if one would become proud or self-righteous in following Jesus beneath the cross. There will always be more left undone than done, more to strive for than accomplished, more to repent of than to boast about. And even the boasting that is proper is the boast of Christ, that all is accomplished from him, to him, through him. All that is lacking is mine alone, to be covered up, not by my excuses but

111

by his blood. For the obstacles and slivers inside of me are beyond measure. The obstacles and slivers to my service in those I want to serve are just as daunting. Indeed, the most painful consequence of sin may be the vengeance that conscience takes with its constant reminders of failure. Even this consequence we should consider a gracious gift of God; for it drives us again and again to see our salvation in his cross alone, not in our cross so imperfectly born as we stumble along behind him.

So Jesus' words "Take up the cross. Deny yourself. Follow me!" still stand. It is our goal as Christians that Jesus' call may become in every way more and more the organizing principle of our life in him. We follow him in receiving grace heaped upon grace. We follow him in trusting that he provides all that we are and have and hope to be. We follow him in the embrace of his cross, which covers all that we are by ourselves as he washes us in his own blood. We follow him as he without our help wins heaven for us by his death and assures us that heaven is ours by his resurrection. We follow him by taking up the cross of *self* denial in the face of horrible obstacles in our still-remaining sinful flesh. We follow him in a life lived in love for our neighbor in the face of obstacles in our neighbor's sinful flesh. The goal remains that Christ should become and be all in all.

And as Christ becomes all in all, the Christian comes to appreciate more and more the truth and the beauty of his promise in Matthew 11:28-30: "Come to me, all you who are weary and burdened, and I will give you rest. Take my yoke upon you and learn from me." Given the pain that the cross inflicts on us because of the obstacles inside and outside of ourselves, it might be easy to conclude that the whole business is too difficult, even impossible, to bear. But Jesus says, "I am gentle and humble in heart, and you will find rest for your souls. For my yoke is easy and my burden is light." And, as Luther loved to say, God would not lie to us!

5

The Theology of the Cross and the Hidden God

By this time one might be pardoned for asking yet again: Why does it all have to be so difficult? The cross presses so hard against a flesh that never completely dies until we are carried off to the cemetery. The conscience grieves over the weakness of the Christian in me in this struggle with the flesh. The good is so difficult, the evil so easy; and that's true even after I have seen that the good and God-pleasing things bring peace and joy, while the evil never brings anything but pain and suffering—in spite of the devil's promises to the contrary! The pain of the struggle for the good against the evil only proves how far I still have to go before Christ has become all in all and the flesh has been pummeled fully into submission. Why does it all have to be so difficult and take so long?

The answer is the one repeated from the beginning to the end of the Scriptures. It is this: *God remains hidden in and under the cross, in weakness and in struggle, and he chooses to be found nowhere else.* As he is found in the weakness of his Son, weakness in the manger, weakness on the cross, so he finds us and lets himself be found by us in our weakness, in our struggle, in our failure, in our sin and guilt. In this chapter and the next one, we will consider that little-appreciated but central truth of the Bible and of the theology of the cross. God's love and grace hide in weakness, on the cross; they hide on the Savior's cross; they hide in ours as well. Where his cross is not, there his grace, his mercy, is not. Where the cross is not, there he refuses to be and refuses to be found as Savior. And so it is that he is found in suffering and in struggle, both his and ours, and not for very long apart from it.

That is not the way we would have arranged things, had God sought our advice. We would have told God, had he asked us, that he should always show himself in his glory, not in the suffering of the cross. That is what people have always wanted from him; people want glory not shame, victory not pain, strength not weakness, yes, sight not faith. Adam and Eve in the garden were not content with his righteousness and perfection hidden within them. They wanted to be his equal in glory, to fetch his divine essence in their experience and in their intellect and in their emotions. They chose not to believe his Word. They wanted to see for themselves. And so they fell terribly; they lost innocence, holiness, and righteousness. Yes, they lost God.

And how is God found again? How does he reveal and then give himself again? In suffering. He promises Adam sweat in this life and the dust of the grave at the end. He promises Eve pain in childbirth and in subjection to her husband. For it is only through suffering and in pain that they will yearn for his grace and goodness. It will be in suffering and death that they will long for eternal life and salvation.

But when he promises fallen mankind suffering and pain and death, what does he promise for himself? God promises for himself suffering far greater than their suffering. For himself he promises the cross and death when the serpent will bite his heel as he crushes the serpent's head *for us and for our salvation* (cf. Ge 3:15). Indeed, while our suffering and pain may bring us to a necessary recognition of our need for him and his salvation, it is his suffering and pain that satisfies our need and accomplishes our salvation.

And it is his pain that the world would see, not his triumph and his glory. His triumph after the resurrection only a chosen few got to see. Even for those who saw him after his resurrection, the view of his glory was a fleeting one. Since his ascension, that triumph remains hidden in the Word and is seen only by the eyes of faith.

Glimpses of glory in the lives of the prophets

Even great saints like Moses did not get to see God in the fullness of his glory. He spoke to Moses, but he spoke from within a cloud so that Moses could not see or fully experience that glory (Ex 19:9; 24:15-18). Moses had the unenviable task of leading millions through the wilderness for 40 years. In the process he often saw only glimpses of God's glory. God's power and greatness were evident in the miracles that brought them out of Egypt and that sustained them in the desert. In fact, God gave Moses and the people of Israel so many glimpses of great power and majesty that the miraculous almost seemed routine. He descended in thunder and lightning, in fire and quaking on Mt. Sinai (Ex 19). But he warned the people to look on from a distance, not to come close, lest they perish in the presence of his glory. On other occasions he supported the work of Moses in very dramatic ways by sending fire to destroy (Nu 11:1-3) and by opening the ground to swallow up Moses' opponents and challengers (Nu 16:28-34).

Nevertheless, what was the result on these and on many other occasions when God demonstrated the smallest fraction of his majesty? His appearances in glory never did what we would have expected them to do. They never turned his people from sinners to saints, from stubborn, shortsighted rebels to compliant, obedient, and trusting servants of the Lord. And that should have been Moses' first clue to a fundamental reality of the way that God deals with people: his demonstrations of power may at times and for a little while provoke wonder and awe; they may even move people to a short-term dread of God's wrath. But they never create faith; they never move anyone to love and trust in God as Father and Savior; they never even cause people to obey the law outwardly, at least not for the long term.

Nevertheless, Moses wanted to see the fullness of God's glory. But God refused his request and continued to hide his glory within the cloud (Ex 33:15-23). For God's unfiltered glory, his unveiled essence in power, does not save. Quite to the contrary, it destroys, annihilates, crushes, kills. Only in lowliness, only in the proclamation of grace, only in little words whispered on a breath does God reveal and give himself to even the greatest of the saints, and that most often in the midst of suffering. Even when he showed himself in times of prosperity and when everything was going well, as when the tabernacle was finished and when the temple of Solomon was dedicated, God hid himself in a cloud (Ex 40:34,35; 1 Ki 8:10,11).

So it was also with Elijah. He was downhearted and depressed by his apparent failure. Like Moses he had had many a glimpse of God's glory. But none of the signs of power and majesty had accomplished what we would have expected. Even the fire from heaven over the sacrifice of Elijah and the downpour of rain at his prayer (1 Ki 18:36-46) had only the most fleeting effect on Ahab and the people. Perhaps the prophet thought: "If just once I see God in all of his glory, then I will know that my labor has not been in vain." But such was not to be. God hid himself, and he let the prophet "see" him only in a whisper (1 Ki 19:11-18). And then with his glory hidden in his Word, God sent the prophet on his way to finish the assignments that God intended for him. Elijah received strength not from a vision of God's glory, but from the power of God hidden in words. And that strength from God's Word conquered Elijah's despair. That strength from God's Word was sufficient for Elijah to finish the assignments that God had given him.

In the case of Moses and Elijah, as so often in the Bible, God dealt with his servants by hiding his glory. He dealt with them best and he dealt with them most effectively by hiding under the apparent weakness of his Word proclaimed in the midst of suffering. For it is to the Word proclaimed under and in the cross that God gives the power to save. That's just the way he is. That's the way he chooses to be.

Isaiah too learned that lesson at the very beginning of his prophetic service. In chapter 6 he tells us how he saw the glory of the Lord in the temple. What however did that vision stir in

Isaiah? Did it create joy or love or trust? Quite to the contrary! Isaiah was terrified. The glory of the Lord drove him to his knees in dread as he remembered his own sinfulness and that of his people. What restored him? What brought him back to life and to an eager desire to serve the Lord with all that he was, with all that he had? It was the gospel message of forgiveness that came to him in the midst of his terror! And that message came from the Word of the Lord at the hand of an angel, yes, from a burning coal on the altar. Only the Word. Only the promise. Only a mediator of grace. Only fire from the altar. That is how God deals with us, shows us grace, brings us into the possession of forgiveness, life, and salvation.

Perhaps Abraham illustrated the point best (Ge 12:1-3). God called him to leave his family when he was already 75 years old and to go someplace else. God did not even tell him where! He should go, and God would show him the destination in due course. All Abraham had to go on was the Word, the promise of God. And what of the sum and substance of that promise? God would make him a great nation, and in Abraham and his Seed the whole world would be blessed. What a promise! But that is all that it was, a promise.

Even after Abraham was outwardly successful in his new home, he possessed no land and had no son to carry forward the promise of the Savior. He was a stranger and a pilgrim. All of the outward prosperity was itself empty without that most special heir, the son through whom the Savior would come. Abraham recognized the problem most acutely in Genesis 15. After wealth, after victory over enemies, after all the glimpses of glory, Abraham had in reality nothing without that promised ancestor of the Savior. And so in the anguish of his soul he asks God in effect: "What's the point? I have no child!" God's answer? A promise! That's all. Nothing more. Even after Isaac was born, Abraham still had only promises to rely on for the ultimate benefit, namely the coming of the Savior through Isaac's descendants. How clear God made that in his call to Abraham to sacrifice Isaac, the son of the promise! God hid himself, hid his glory. He came out of hiding only in the Word of promise.

It is impossible for us to exhaust this theme. It is a central theme in the Bible and therefore in any genuine biblical Christianity. God hides. He hides his glory. He does not give himself to us or draw us to himself in majesty; he does it only in shame, not in power but only in weakness, not in victory but only in defeat, not in mighty acts but in lowly words, not in spectacular displays but in the most common of signs. And it is just in that shame, that lowliness, that weakness and apparent defeat that he saves. He comes to us hidden in the Word, just letters written and syllables spoken. He comes to us hidden in water joined to words in Baptism. He comes to us hidden in plain bread and simple wine connected to his Word in the Sacrament of the Altar.

Expressed most simply: He reveals himself and gives himself only in Christ, the crucified; for Christ is the Word made flesh, the heart of God made manifest, the sum and substance of all that God has to say to us, be for us, give to us (Jn 1). Christ is the one into whom we are baptized. Christ is the true and everlasting food of salvation in the meal on the altar. Christ is the center of the sermon and the heart and core of the liturgy. And in all of these there is lowliness that saves. In all of these our hidden God gives himself to us in that lowliness for our salvation.

Glimpses of glory in the life of Christ

Look at how Christ reveals himself. He conceals his glory, hiding it in lowliness and suffering. His two greatest miracles he hid from the world. The world did not see the Word made flesh when he entered the womb of the virgin Mary and was born in a barn. Nor did the world attend the resurrection of Christ from the dead. Those two greatest miracles and most magnificent displays of divine majesty and power were hidden. The one took place with a lowly peasant girl in a backwater of the world. The other took place early in the morning in a garden tomb outside Jerusalem; even those sent to keep watch were struck down so that they did not see him in the glory and the majesty of the resurrection.

And think of all that happened between the first great wonder—the wonder of the incarnation, and the second great wonder—the miracle of the resurrection. There were glimpses of glory on every hand. The angels served as preachers to the shepherds, and the shepherds proclaimed the mystery to anyone who would listen. But who went to worship? We have no record that anyone did. The star and the wise men from the East made

Herod and all Jerusalem wonder. But not even the priests were moved by that intimation of glory to go with the wise men to worship the One to whom the star pointed. The boy in the temple asking and answering questions caused astonishment by his outward display of wisdom. But no one asked the right question about him, the question: Could he be the One, the promised Messiah?

Or consider Jesus' miracles. In John 2 we hear of his miracle at the wedding of Cana, where he turned water into wine. John tells us that thus Jesus "revealed his glory, and his disciples put their faith in him" (v. 11). But who at that wedding was even aware of this glory? Only his mother. Only the disciples who already believed in him and saw in the miracle a visible proof of what they already knew and believed on the basis of his words and those of John the Baptist about him. Otherwise, the glory revealed remained a glory hidden. The lepers were cleansed. Thousands were fed with only a few loaves and some small fish. Even the dead were raised. Yes, evidences of power and glory on every hand. But where were all these people on Good Friday? Where were they on Pentecost Sunday? Had they been part of the crowd on Palm Sunday? If they were, where were they when he died? People today who think that the world would be converted if only we could see the miracles that Jesus once performed in Palestine should think again. That is not the way it happened then. That is not the way it would work now either. All the glimpses of glory converted no one.

God gives himself not in glimpses of glory but in lowliness and humility

That is how it always is. The greatest work of all, of bringing the spiritually dead to spiritual life, was accomplished only by the lowly Jesus giving himself in the lowly Word. Jesus testified to Nicodemus that the coming of God's kingdom is as the coming of its King, only in meekness and lowliness. It is as real as the wind is real; but where the wind comes from and where it is going, no one can say. Just so is the kingdom of God; its coming and going is hidden in the mind of God and revealed and real only in the breath of God, his Word. He told Nicodemus that he would not even *see* the kingdom of God, much less enter it, except though a birth from water and the Spirit, a birth unaided by the one born and unobserved by anyone other than its giver. And then he declared that the basis of the kingdom would be its King "lifted up" on the cross (Jn 3:1-21).

Nicodemus had expected more in the way of wonders and displays of power that would fully convince not just himself but everyone else as well. He wanted to be proud of the kingdom and its King, proud to be the companion of the King and the helper of the kingdom. That, however, is not the way God works. Only in lowliness. Only in hidden-ness. Only on the cross. That's what Jesus promised. Repeatedly he rebuked the people who were always looking for yet another sign, yet another miracle. There would be only the saving sign of his resurrection. And that great sign they would not see; they would only hear of it. Just as they did not see the rescue of Jonah after three days in the belly of the fish but only heard of it (Mt 12:38-40), so his rising is real but hidden, revealed only in its proclamation.

So Jesus starts the work of redeeming the world on the bottom rung of the social ladder. Just as prophesied (Isa 53), there is nothing noteworthy, outwardly impressive, or beautiful. It is in lowliness, in suffering on the cross that our salvation is accomplished. How unlike the heroes of the world! Abraham Lincoln is rightly admired as one who started at the bottom, in a log cabin, and through sheer willpower and effort and perseverance scratched his way to the top, to become president of his country. Who doesn't like a rags-to-riches story? Who isn't impressed with an underdog who makes good? But that is not the story of Jesus. He starts at the highest height and goes to the bottom, and then he works his way *down* from there. Paul describes it so graphically in Philippians 2:6-8:

⊕ In eternity by nature and in his essence he is God.

⊕ Equality with God, therefore, is not something he needs to grab at or put on display to prove that he has it.

⊕ He stripped away every appearance of the divine to look like a mere servant and became a man.

⊕ God concealed in man died!

✚ Nor was his death just any death. It was the death
of the worst of criminals, the death of the cross!

It is only after this total humiliation, a humiliation that was
on display for all the world to see, that God exalted him in his
human nature. But unlike the humiliation, which was on display
in the crucifixion, the exaltation is not on display until the end of
the ages. It is real and true but visible only to the eyes of faith. It
is visible only to those who believe the message. And they believe
not on the basis of seen or experienced glory but only on the basis
of the cross of Christ proclaimed in the lowly Word, "seen" in the
lowly sacrament (Ro 10:17; Jn 3:5; Ro 6:1-4).

It cannot, it must not, escape our notice how intent Jesus was
on (how else can we say it?) achieving the lowliest lowliness. Not
only did he refuse birth in the palace of a king or the house of the
high priest; he chose for his mother an unmarried peasant girl.
Were it not for his arrangement of history, that his birth took
place at the time of the great internal migration of a nation for
the sake of a tax, his mother would have been condemned by the
neighbors as a fallen woman.

Then there were the miracles. A "normal" human being, one
promoting himself, would have exercised his power very differently. Notice that in each of his miracles Jesus did enough to
demonstrate that he is indeed the Son of God with power. He did
enough to show that he is the God-man who came forth out of the
love and mercy of God. But at the same time, each miracle took
place in such a way that it would have minimum outward effect;
he did not want even the most spectacular of his miracles to
inspire a mass movement that would try to make him the God-
King of Israel. Most of the miracles took place in some out of the
way corner of Palestine. Often he sternly commanded those
whom he healed to say nothing about it, to keep it secret. When
that wasn't possible, he withdrew quickly and even separated his
disciples from the crowd, lest they become its leaders (note especially Jn 6:15; Mk 6:45,46).

It was only at the very end of his earthly ministry that he per-
mitted a fuss. Even that fuss had the ultimate goal of bringing
about his death. He raised Lazarus from the dead. He did it just
before Passover and so close to Jerusalem that the Sanhedrin

had to notice and had to act (Jn 11:42–12:11). His Palm Sunday entry into Jerusalem pushed history along to the conclusion he himself had set for it. Any self-appointed messiah would have used the entry into Jerusalem as the beginning of a coup. Anyone else would have acted quickly to consolidate power and to seize control before the opposition had a chance to regroup. But that is not at all what Jesus had in mind. He had demonstrated his power. By its very demonstration he pushed his guilty, scheming opponents into the action they had intended all along. He hid his deity. He revealed only lowliness. He marched to the cross.

As Holy Week progressed to the goal he has set for it, he humbled himself still more and then more still. What a disgrace! A disciple sold him out for the price of a slave. What humiliation! All of his friends forsook him in the middle of the night. In fact, he pushed them all away. In the Garden of Gethsemane, we catch a glimpse of how he used power only to show that he had it and then rushed to wrap himself again in lowliness. He performed three miracles in rapid succession (Jn 18:4-11; Lk 22:50,51). First, when he identified himself, the soldiers fell backward to the ground. Even in that miracle there was grace and mercy, for not one of them was killed, not one was even hurt! Then, when Peter cut off the ear of Malchus, Jesus put it back on again. Finally, and to our amazement, Jesus told those who had come to arrest him to let his disciples go, and the soldiers obeyed!—and then took Jesus away. When do arresting officers ever obey the command of the one they have come to arrest? What an astonishing business!

Indeed, if you like, you may add a fourth miracle, namely, that any of this happened at all at that particular time. For the Sanhedrin had resolved that Jesus must die but that nothing should happen during the Passover; they did not want a riot from his supporters (Jn 11:45-57; Mt 26:3-5). But it all happened at Passover, at the height of the Passover celebration; the Sanhedrin was not in control, as its members imagined.

Jesus was in control every step of the way in this "glorious" humiliation (Jn 12:20-36) by which he became the Savior of the world. Is it not an amazing thing? Jesus wanted his ultimate humiliation to take place at the time of maximum exposure, when Jerusalem was most crowded, when Jews from all over the world would see his shame and disgrace! One would have thought that he would have agreed with the conclusion of the Sanhedrin—"But not during the feast"—for at any other time of the year his humiliation would have at least been on display to fewer people. But no! Maximum disgrace! Maximum exposure! Maximum humiliation!

So, to be sure, there was power and glory evident even in the midst of deepening humiliation. All those present should at the very least have recognized the power of the one who made the soldiers fall backward and who healed Malchus. But how much faith did those acts of power, those manifestations of glory, produce? In Judas the outward demonstration of power and glory prompted despair, not repentance. In the soldiers and priests who had come to arrest Jesus it prompted no self-doubt or questioning; the soldiers took away the one whose simple question had thrown them to the ground, and the priests persisted in their unbelieving hatred. Jesus' outward display of his power did not even inspire courage in the disciples, who seized the opportunity to run away as soon as Jesus gave it to them!

Mockery, abuse, scourging, and crucifixion followed with none to help. To be sure, Simon of Cyrene helped carry the cross (Mt 27:32). But what help was that really? He was forced to help along the way to the place of execution. Assisting someone on the way to execution could hardly be called a favor. Jesus was helped by no one; he was even abandoned by his Father on the cross. It all served to make the one great central point of our salvation; it underscores and then places exclamation points behind it: Our salvation was his work and his *alone!* He fulfilled the prophecies perfectly and to the letter (e.g., Ps 22; Isa 53; 63:1-6). No one can claim the role of supporting actor on the stage of the world's redemption. No one should ever dare to say that somehow he cooperated, somehow he contributed, somehow he was Christ's coworker in the drama of salvation. It is all *tu solus, Christe!* "You alone, O Christ!"

And it was all accomplished on the cross, not one step removed from it! Not in glory, not in a magnificent display from heaven. The sun was darkened at his approaching death. The earth quaked, the dead rose, and the great temple curtain tore. But who was moved to repentance by any of it? Who was saved at these glimpses of glory in the moment of his deepest humiliation? It is at the cross, in lowliness and suffering and humiliation, that we see our salvation and not apart from it. It was in the Suffering Servant (Isa 53) that God revealed himself and gave himself for us. It takes our breath away!

Even after he won our salvation and gave himself for us in the shame of the cross, his glory remained hidden. As already noted, the resurrection was viewed by no one. Even the disciples did not see it; they only "heard" of it. His appearances to them came after the women had been sent from the empty tomb to tell them about it. And what of those post-resurrection appearances recorded in the gospels? Where was the glory? It still remained hidden. He came quickly and quietly, without the sound of trumpets, without the attending legions of angels, without so much as a halo around his head. He was in full possession and use of his glory. But still he veiled it as he pointed the disciples again and again to the Word he had spoken and would yet speak after Pentecost through the Holy Spirit (Jn 16; Lk 24; Jn 20–21). It is on that Word that they should rely, not on any outward glory or visible messianic kingdom, not even on his visible presence in their midst.

Glimpses of glory after Christ's ascension

Nor did Pentecost change his mode of operation (Acts 2). To be sure, that great day began with a demonstration of power, with a mighty rushing wind, with tongues of fire, with the miraculous ability of the disciples to speak in other languages. The noise got the outward attention of people. But who was converted by the noise of the wind? Not one. And what of the miraculous gift to the apostles, the gift of being able to speak in languages they had never studied? Some in the crowd mocked. Many were curious. Others were afraid. But the miracle of faith happened only in the midst of that mockery and abuse through the proclamation of the lowly Word and through the promise of that Word in lowly Baptism. The Word was the Word about the crucified and suffering Savior, whose shame and disgrace many of those present at Pentecost had seen. It was the Word about the Servant of the Lord, who had come in fulfillment of God's promise. The message was of the risen Savior, whose glory remains hidden, whose glory we will not see until he comes again on the Last Day.

Do you notice that even on the day of Pentecost, those who mocked and those who refused the message of the gospel are not struck down? They went their way, outwardly none the worse for their blasphemy. For the time of judgment had not yet come. The time of grace, of rescue through the preaching of the cross, had arrived. Salvation will be forced on no one through outward displays of power. It comes only in the persuasion, the gentle enticing of the Spirit working quietly in the gospel. God the Almighty remains hidden, his glory as Savior veiled in the Word, given only in its proclamation.

Even in Jesus' rare appearances after his ascension the same point is made on each occasion. The account of Saul's conversion began with an appearance of Christ in glory (Ac 9). But what of that appearance? Did Saul rejoice? Was he filled with faith and love? No! He was knocked down and struck blind. The gospel message of forgiveness came from humble Ananias and the disciples in Damascus. It came in the lowly Sacrament of Baptism. And that gospel message was accompanied not with the promise of glory but with the promise of suffering (v. 16).

Or consider Jesus' appearance to his beloved disciple, to John, some 60 or so years after the ascension (Rev 1:9-18). That appearance too began as an appearance in glory. And what did the glory of the risen Christ evoke in the beloved disciple? Dread! Horror! The sight of the glorified Savior threw him to the ground as though he were dead. What brought him back to life? What put him back on his feet and made him fit to write the final words that Jesus had to speak to his church on earth? It was the gentle touch of the Savior, a touch made gentle by his words, "Do not be afraid." Surely St. John remembered the transfiguration (Mt 17:1-9). There too Jesus appeared in glory. There too the result was fear and dread. There too quickening came alone from Jesus' gentle but powerful and effective Word: "Don't be afraid." Those same words were the recurring theme of Jesus to his disciples in his post-resurrection appearances to them. Fear and dread were natural and altogether rational reactions to his resurrection. For they had denied him and forsaken him. They were sinners and had proven it. But it is Jesus' quiet and lowly Word which quickened and restored the fallen, his word of "Do not be afraid." Not outward might, not thunder and lightning, not display and splendor; just the lowly Word and its hidden power from the risen Christ, whose glory remains yet under the veil.

Some implications that flow from the hidden-ness of God

The above should be sufficient to make the point. God hides his glory. He hides it in lowliness, in suffering, in the cross. The hidden-ness of God on the cross and in the gospel has profound implications for us in our relationship to God and in our understanding of that relationship. In fact, it is precisely because of who and what we have become as a result of sin that the hidden-ness of God is our great comfort and joy. Luther grasped those implications perhaps better than almost anyone else. He expressed them most clearly and brilliantly in the famous Heidelberg Disputation.*

It is easy enough for us here to sum up Luther's thought in the Disputation, but it takes a lifetime to learn it, even to become a beginner in appreciating it. Summed up most briefly, it is simply this: In our relationship to God, in the matter of our salvation, we are and ever remain desperate, poor, naked, starving beggars. God is everything; we are nothing. God accomplishes everything by the cross. All that we bring to him is sin and shame, death and damnation. That is true from the moment of our conception. It is true before our conversion and after it. It is no less true on our holiest day than it is on our most sinful day. And the greatest crime and sin and blasphemy of all is to imagine and think otherwise! For as his glory remains hidden on the cross, so the glory of our salvation remains hidden in our nothingness, our sin, our shame.

Even our faith, no, especially our faith, is nothing for us to boast about. To proudly declare, "Well, at least I believe!" is to miss the whole glory of Christ's work and our salvation. For the faith of which we might like to boast is a faith created and sustained entirely by the lowly promise in the lowly gospel. Its beginning, its middle, its end, its whole content from start to finish is to despair of everything in me and to trust alone in him, in

---

*Cf. *Luther's Works,* American Edition, vol. 31, Fortress Press, Philadelphia, 1957; pp. 35-70.

his cross, in his promise given in the lowly Word and sacraments. Anything else is not faith at all but damnable unbelief. Listen to how Luther puts it in a few of his theses in the Heidelberg Disputation of 1518. He declares:

> . . . the Lord humbles and frightens us by means of the law and the sight of our sins so that we seem in the eyes of men, as in our own, as nothing, foolish, and wicked, for we are in truth that. Insofar as we acknowledge and confess this, [there] is no form or beauty in us, but our life is hidden in God (i.e., in the bare confidence in his mercy), finding in ourselves nothing but sin, foolishness, death, and hell. . . . Such a man therefore is displeased with all his works; he sees no beauty, but only his ugliness. (p. 44)

Luther goes on to explain that every shred of pride in one's own works is a taking away from God the glory that belongs to him and to him alone. Pride, therefore, even in the most glistening of our works, is arrogant unbelief. Therefore, "Arrogance cannot be avoided or true hope be present unless the judgment of condemnation is feared in every work" (p. 48). Often when we think of the confession of sins, we think of it in terms of confessing guilt to this and that sin committed. And there is nothing wrong with that. We delight to hear in absolution that the this and that which we confessed is forgiven. But Luther takes us here a bit deeper. In confession we really lay our whole life and being before God, and since we are sinners, we confess that *everything* is sin, nothing is whole or holy. Our entire existence merits death and hell. Our whole being, every breath we take, is in desperate need of grace and mercy and forgiveness!

How difficult it is for us to wrap our minds around this whole concept of total humiliation before God! We just don't get it, that his humiliation is to be the pattern of our own. He humbled himself first. He humbled himself far more than we could ever humble ourselves. He did it on purpose. He did it for us. He did it in a manger and on a cross.

But we would rather not follow that example of total humiliation before the God who humbled himself for us. Instead, we want to divide our life into at least two neat categories—one containing our goodness and the other (we would like to think it a relatively smaller category) our sins and faults. And then there is the not-so-neat third category; it's a broad middle one that we might like to think is none of God's business, or anyone else's either for that matter. In that category we would put thoughts, words, and deeds that we imagine are simply the products of our own free choice and will, not good perhaps but not all that bad either. And we foolishly think that only the little bit in the second category merits confession; all the rest deserves at least a little bit of credit but certainly no blame.

No! A thousand times, No! There is only one category when it comes to goodness or merit before God, when it comes to our salvation: it's *sin,* the whole thing is *sin* and nothing but *sin.* That one category contains all that we recognize and know to be sin. It contains everything in the not-so-neat middle category, because none of it was the product of a pure love of God and a desire to serve him and our neighbor. And, yes, it includes, most of all, those things in the category we call good, if we imagine that those things somehow make us in some part worthy of God's attention, or even of his salvation. How hard that is to grasp! How much harder still to confess! The liturgy gets it right. Before we confess that we have sinned in thought, word, and deed, we confess what *we are,* that is, sinners; what we did is merely evidence and glaring proof of what we are. Before the world there may be much good and little fault and a lot in the middle. Before the judgment seat of family, friends, even of our own conscience, we may be squeaky clean, pure as driven snow. Paul, however, summed it up well: Even if he was unaware of any guilt, he would not thereby be justified before God; for by nature we are slaves—not merely occasional acquaintances—of sin, thoroughly corrupted in our nature and all that it produces (Ro 7; 1 Co 4:4).

Hidden under my outward goodness is nothingness, is sin

Again, and it is worth repeating because it is so difficult to accept, if I start to look at some things in me and in my nature that are none of God's business and certainly not deserving of hell, then I have turned my back on the First Commandment. There God declares that I should fear and love him with *all* that I am and have. And if I imagine that the best in me is somehow meritorious, is somehow at least just a little deserving of God's bother and his favor, then the best in me is even worse than what I acknowledge to be the worst in me. For the worst in me I confess; it drives me to seek for nothing but mercy and to depend on nothing but grace, namely, the always and totally *undeserved* love of God. But to think that some good in me does not need Christ and his cross is to rob Christ of his glory as the only Savior and the only One who is good; it robs him of his claim to be the One who has forgiven me *totally,* washed me by his blood *completely,* saved me from a condition that was *unconditionally hopeless and absolutely desperate!*

In fact, Luther says, since we never completely separate ourselves from this kind of arrogance that boasts in one's own accomplishment and works, we always ought to fear the condemnation of God. For it is only in such fear of his just judgment that the gospel can bring us to trust in him and in him alone for our salvation. To condemn myself in all that I am is to acknowledge that God alone is good and glorious in his essence as in his works. Luther says:

> Nor does speaking in this manner give cause for despair, but for arousing the desire to humble oneself and seek the grace of Christ. . . . They cannot be humble who do not recognize that they are damnable whose sin smells to high heaven. Sin is recognized only through the law. It is apparent that not despair, but rather hope, is preached when we are told that we are sinners. . . . Yearning for grace wells up when recognition of sin has arisen. . . . To say that we are nothing and constantly sin when we do the best we can does not mean that we cause people to despair (unless they are fools); rather, we make them concerned about the grace of our Lord Jesus Christ. (p. 51)

To be sure, St. John reminds us that perfect or complete love drives out fear (1 Jn 4:18). But where, this side of heaven, is such love? Certainly not yet in us! For we still have sin to confess, and sin is the antithesis of perfect love, as John makes so clear in the whole of the epistle. It is toward that goal of perfect love that we should strive. But it is found only in God and from him only in the gospel. We aim for it but reach it only imperfectly in this life. And so, since all remains sinful in us and in our nature apart from him, all that is apart from his gospel is, or certainly should be, filled with dread, with fear, with loathing.

Luther says:

> It is certain that man must utterly despair of his own ability before he is prepared to receive the grace of Christ.

> The law wills that man despair of his own ability, for it leads him into hell and makes him a poor man and shows him that he is a sinner in all his works. (pp. 51,52)

The theology of the cross versus the theology of glory

All of this Luther sees as the essence of the theology of the cross, a theology in which lowliness and suffering, that is, the cross, is God's true glory and ours as well. The outwardly great and glorious things in God do not save. The outwardly great and glorious things in us do not save either. As inspiring as a sunset is to a poet, as majestic as the ocean is in a storm or a mountain is capped with snow, these save no one. As brilliant as the reasoning capacity of an Aristotle or an Aquinas is, neither of them brings us one step closer to faith and salvation. As holy as the mother of the Savior or Mother Theresa may have been, neither of them could earn the smallest scrap of real estate in heaven by their virtue. As splendid as the charity of the greatest humanitarian, yes, no matter how noble is the kindness of the greatest saint, these too save no one and contribute not in the least to salvation.

That is not to say that the virtue and the good works of Christians have no value. They have no value for salvation, but otherwise their value is great, as Jesus himself testifies. The good works of Christians may prompt people to glorify God by seeking the reason for such acts (Mt 5:13-16). The true praise of God in response to the evident good works of the saints will come when those who see those works are crushed and killed by the law and then raised to life again by the gospel. And finally each and every work that is in accordance with his Word and a fruit of faith is so precious to Jesus that it is stored up and remembered by him all the way to judgment day (Mt 25:34-40).

Yes, the value of our good works as fruits of faith done out of gratitude for the gift of salvation is so great that God even promises to reward them. The promises of reward are rich indeed; just consider the blessings promised in the Sermon on the Mount, especially in the Beatitudes (Mt 5:3-12). He promises to reward such works in spite of the fact that it is his gospel alone that inspires them and gives us the strength to do them in the first place. He promises to reward them in spite of the fact that it is his rule of history, his providence, that gives us opportunities for the works and prospers them as well. He promises to reward them in spite of the fact that the fruit is wormy because of our sinful nature and condition. He promises to reward them in spite of the fact that the best of our works are far from perfect and therefore still need his grace, his mercy, his forgiveness.

But even in the carrying out of his promise to reward our works, God is careful to guard us from trusting in the works as meritorious for salvation, careful to ward off any arrogance that so easily afflicts us as soon as things go well for us. The Apology of the Augsburg Confession perhaps sums it up best:

> Moreover, we concede that works are truly meritorious, but not for the forgiveness of sins or justification. For they are not pleasing to [God] except in those who are justified on account of faith. Nor are they worthy of eternal life. For just like justification, so also being made alive takes place by faith on account of Christ. Works are meritorious for other bodily and spiritual rewards, which are bestowed both in this life and in the life to come. For *God defers most rewards until he glorifies saints after this life, because he wishes them in this life to be strengthened through mortifying the old creature* [emphasis added]. (Apology, Art. IV. Kolb, p. 171.)

But the best of our works can turn into the greatest evil and vice, if we foolishly turn to them and trust in them even a little bit for God's favor and our salvation. We should see in our good works, done out of love to God and for the benefit of our neighbor, the evidence that we have indeed begun to love God. We should see in them the fruit and the result of Christ's work for us and the

Spirit's work in us. But always and alone, the fruit is the result of the tree, not its cause. And on its best day, as already noted, it is wormy fruit, far from perfect, still needing a washing in the blood of the Savior before it can delight and please God. Always and alone, our good works are evidence of salvation received, not causes of a salvation yet incomplete. When it comes to our salvation, we are always naked, filthy, covered with shame, desperately in need of grace and mercy; we bring nothing to the table except that desperate need. Christ alone satisfies that need. His gospel alone in Word and sacraments brings us the full and complete satisfaction of our need, which he won for us by his lowliness.

Lutheran worship reflects the theology of the cross, not the theology of glory

It is this truth that all of God's glory for our salvation is hidden in the cross and all that we have to bring him is our sin and guilt that makes the liturgy so eternally relevant, so rich, so comforting. For in it we despair, since we have nothing good to bring to God as a contribution to our salvation. And in it we rejoice because God gives us everything in the cross by which he won our forgiveness.

A theology of glory is that which imagines that salvation is tied to outward greatness and success or even to outward holiness and virtue. And that is at the heart and core of Luther's anger against the Roman church, that it was drowning in a theology of glory. The works of monks and nuns looked so glorious and holy on the outside. There they were, a collection of people, dressed in drab, under the yoke of self-imposed poverty, celibacy, and obedience. They spent their whole lives in prayer, some locked away from the world completely behind their cloister walls. And with all of that they imagined (and monastic vows to this day assert the same!) that they had chosen a life closest to perfection. They claimed that their vows were of at least as much value as Baptism. They declared that not only would they help to save themselves by their works but that they even had merits left over to help save others. That Jesus never asked anyone to do such things slowed them down not a bit. That the Scriptures condemn and damn such self-righteousness likewise hindered them not in the least.

And then there was the pope himself. He called himself then and calls himself to this day the vicar of Christ on earth and the successor of St. Peter. He is considered and considers himself so close to the heart of God that he alone can interpret the Scriptures. Yes, he can even proclaim doctrines not in the Bible and doctrines contrary to the clear words of the Bible. What could be more glorious, more holy looking than that! Never mind the fact that God has made it clear that his Word alone is sufficient for all doctrine.

All of it, Luther declares, is the devil's spawn, the opposite of the gospel. For all of it turns our eyes away from Christ and his lowliness to man and his imagined glory. It robs Christ of his glory as the only Savior. It therefore destroys the Christian's only source of hope and comfort; for apart from Christ and his Word all hope and comfort is only a devilish delusion, unsure and insecure. To this day Catholicism has not rid itself of that theology of glory. With crosses everywhere and a crucifix at every turn, the priest at mass nevertheless dares to declare that he is repeating in an unbloody way the sacrifice of Christ on the cross. And the priest has been made worthy to offer such a sacrifice by his holy celibacy and his anointing from the pope or his minions. How horrible! Even the sufferings of the sick and disabled are praised as works which *complete,* or at the very least participate in, the work of Christ that saves. How monstrous!

Nor is the worship on the opposite side of the theological error spectrum any better, the worship that is designed merely to appeal to the senses—"whoopee worship." The highly emotional praise song that focuses on God's might and power, the emotion-laden sermon that whips up the crowd to bliss-filled *hallelujahs* may sound like a heaven on earth. But where is the cross? Whether it is the noise of modern-day tongue speakers, or the drama of a "miracle service" or entertainment central with a cross placed somewhere up front, they all have the one thing in common: They turn people away from the confession of the prodigal son (Lk 15:11-32) or that of the tax collector smiting on his breast in the temple (Lk 18:9-14). They turn the audience away from despair in all that we are or hope to be. They instead titillate the senses with the amusing. They challenge the soul with the trite and the trivial. They encourage a salvation that begins in man's feelings and ends with his own obedience to the law.

It is a worship that misses the depth of our sin and guilt. And missing the totality of our need, people miss as well the totality of the solution to that need in the richness of God's grace in the cross of Christ. It is a theology of glory. It is as much to be abhorred and shunned as its Roman cousin. The joy of the liturgy is the joy of hearing that sin has been forgiven, all of it, in the hidden mercy of the one who reveals himself in the Word of grace and pardon. It is the joy of the one who sees that his greatest, his only real need, is for relief from the suffering of guilt and death that only Christ could give at the cross. In the Heidelberg Disputation, Luther says:

> This is clear: He who does not know Christ does not know God hidden in suffering. Therefore he prefers works to suffering, glory to the cross, strength to weakness, wisdom to folly, and in general, good to evil. These are the people whom the apostle calls "enemies of the cross of Christ" [Phil. 3:18], for they hate the cross and suffering and love works and the glory of works. . . . God can be found only in suffering and the cross, as has already been said. Therefore, the friends of the cross say that the cross is good and works are evil, for through the cross works are destroyed and the old Adam, who is especially edified by works, is crucified. *It is impossible for a person not to be puffed up by his good works unless he has first been deflated and destroyed by suffering and evil until he knows that he is worthless and that his works are not his but God's* [emphasis added]. (*Luther's Works*, vol. 31., p. 53.)

Good works and repentance in the theology of the cross

To be sure, we see God's glory in his mighty acts. So do the heathen and they go off to damnation, worshiping the might and hoping to make personal use of it (as for example, "The Force," the god of the famous *Star Wars* movies). Certainly God is glorified in the works of Christians, which follow faith. But we rightly offer these to him in humble thanksgiving only *after* we have been found and claimed and saved by him in his lowly message of the cross in the gospel. We understand, first of all, that sin and guilt belong to us alone. All the good that we do comes from God and is the fruit of his pardon and grace. Then God alone is glorified, worshiped, and adored, as is fitting. Anything else is self-worship, robbing God, delighting in evil.

Yes, and just as important, only when we get this right will we have true and real peace with God and with our own condemning conscience. For as long as we trust in the visible, in the outward, in the works, we have only reasons for doubt and despair. For our works are never finished. They are never perfect. They are never enough. What is finished? What is perfect? What is enough? *Christ on the cross!* There he did it all. There he even said it all, when he declared it in triumph for us: *It is finished!* He was not merely speaking of his life. He was speaking of all that he came to do for us and for our salvation. That is all done; it is all hidden in the cross. It is all perfect; it is all revealed and given only in the lowliness of the gospel.

Luther expressed these same thoughts in a beautiful summary in the Smalcald Articles of 1537. There he puts it this way when speaking of genuine repentance:

> This repentance is not fragmentary or paltry—like the kind that does penance for actual sins—nor is it uncertain like that kind. It does not debate over what is a sin or what is not a sin. Instead, it simply lumps everything together and says, "Everything is pure sin with us. What would we want to spend so much time investigating, dissecting, or distinguishing?" Therefore, here as well, contrition is not uncertain, because there remains nothing that we might consider a "good" with which to pay for sin. Rather, there is plain, certain despair concerning all that we are, think, say, or do, etc.
>
> Similarly, such confession also cannot be false, uncertain, or fragmentary. All who confess that everything is pure sin with them embrace all sins, allow no exceptions, and do not forget a single one. Thus, satisfaction can never be uncertain either. For it consists not in our uncertain, sinful works but rather in the suffering and blood of the innocent "Lamb of God, who takes away the sin of the world" [John 1:29]. (Part III, 3, par. 36-38. Kolb, p. 318.)

Thus the works of the Christian do not cause faith or contribute to salvation, no, not in the least part. Rather, they are all done as a result of faith and the accomplished fact of salvation. For to return to Luther's comments in the Heidelberg Disputation: "Since Christ lives in us through faith, so he arouses us to do good works through that living *faith in his work,* for the works which he does are the fulfillment of the commands of God given us through faith [emphasis added]" (*Luther's Works,* vol. 31., pp. 56,57).

Again, it is impossible fully to express the significance and the depth of this great theme in the Bible, in Luther and in orthodox Lutheran theology. It may take us a long time to learn it, and during a lifetime it must be learned over and over again, as though for the first time. The greatest of saints may grasp it in an instant, then lose it in a moment. Mary confessed it so perfectly and beautifully in the Magnificat (Lk 1:46-55). But she had to learn it all over again when she lost Jesus in the temple (Lk 2:45-48), at the time of the first miracle in Cana (Jn 2:3-5), and most surprisingly when Jesus was at the height of his fleeting popularity (Mk 3:21,31,32). How many times did Peter have to relearn it, sometimes both grasping and losing it within just a few moments (Mt 16:16-23; 26:31-75; Gal 2:11,12).

We too are still in the flesh. We constantly bounce back and forth between arrogance and despair, both of which exaggerate our works and rob Christ of his glory as the only Savior. The fact that we are that way is what makes the liturgy always fresh and always new, and its gospel content always good news. We just never reach the point where we have it down solidly: All in us cries out for pardon; all in his cross gives it fully and freely to the faith that the message creates and sustains.

The theology of glory always fails the test

In Lutheran theology since the time of the Reformation there have been three litmus tests, so to speak, for determining if doctrine is sound. For doctrine to be sound and true it must:

- ✠ Be according to the Scriptures
- ✠ Give all glory to Christ
- ✠ Bring maximum comfort to the repentant sinner**

136

In Luther's consideration of the theology of the cross and in the consideration given to that theme so often by our orthodox Lutheran forefathers, these tests are ever prominent. The theology of glory fails those three tests miserably. The theology of glory has its center in us, in what we have done or in how we feel. The theology of the cross, however, has the Scriptures for its beginning, middle, and end. It focuses on Christ alone as Savior. And since the salvation is from him alone, there is nothing in it but comfort and peace and joy for the confessing sinner.

Following that precedent and concern, we might demonstrate the sharp contrast between the theology of the cross and the theology of glory thus:

Theology of ✝ the Cross	Theology of Glory
I am nothing and all my works are sin.	I may not be much, but at least I believe and haven't done this and that.
Christ is everything, and his work on the cross won forgiveness for *all* my works.	Christ is God whose death has made my salvation *possible*.
Since my salvation is entirely Christ's work, I am certain of my salvation already.	I will do the best I can and hope that it is enough on the day of judgment.

It could not be put any more plainly than in the words of St. Paul in Romans 5:1,2: "Therefore, since we have been justified

---

** Even a superficial reading of the Apology of the Augsburg Confession, Art. IV, should satisfy the reader that such a demonstration of sound doctrine according to this standard was at the front of the confessors' minds; most often in Art. IV, the first is assumed but nevertheless often enough mentioned; the last two are repeated over and over again. A sampler of citations that exemplify these tests for sound doctrine in the Lutheran Confessions would include: AC XX pp. 54,56; Ap XII, pp. 200,202; XV, pp. 224,225,228; XX, p. 235f.; FC SD III, p. 568; IV, p. 578; XI, pp. 564,565. There are of course many other such references; these are mentioned merely to indicate how serious the confessors were about these tests for sound doctrine.

through faith, we have peace with God through our Lord Jesus Christ, through whom we have gained access by faith into this grace in which we now stand." Notice that there is nothing tentative about it; it is not a justification merely made possible, a justification that needs to be completed by my works or even by my faith. For faith *receives* the completed work of Christ; faith does not cause it. It is justification already accomplished and a salvation made entirely ours by faith alone. Notice that God does everything and therefore receives all the glory. We do nothing but receive, and therefore what we have is certain! If anything in our justification depended on us, if the least part of our salvation had to come from us, then all would be doubt and despair. Ah, but it is all from Christ, all finished on the cross, all therefore certain and secure.

Lest anyone miss the point, the apostle repeats the same thought in Romans 8:1, as he continues his discussion of the Christian's life under the cross, the discussion he began in chapter 5. In 8:1-3 he declares to our great joy and Christ's great glory: "Therefore, there is now no condemnation for those who are in Christ Jesus. . . . For what the law was powerless to do in that it was weakened by the sinful nature, God did by sending his own Son in the likeness of sinful man to be a sin offering." The Bible says it and, therefore, we believe it: Our salvation is entirely the work of Christ on the cross, given to us through faith alone.

God saves only through the hidden glory of the cross

Notice as well that for the one pursuing a theology of glory, there is ultimately no comfort at all. It seems so comforting on the surface; for it gives some sense of respectability to fallen man, some pride left over from his sins. But it is all an illusion manufactured by the serpent, idolatry of the worst kind, and unbelief from beginning to end. For faith has its roots and its entire content in the Word. The theology of glory turns its back on the Word and prefers sight or reason or the feeling of the moment. Faith that comes from the Word loves nothing more than to extol Christ. Real faith does not "navel gaze," does not look to or inside of itself for hope and comfort. It looks outside of self, to Christ, to his cross, to his merit, to grace, to the promise of the gospel. The theology of glory insists on at least some credit for fallen self. But what genuine comfort for the sinner can there be if he clings to his own works for his certainty? For he can never know if he has done enough, has completed what Christ could merely begin.

The theology of glory is a recipe for despair when it is realistic, for arrogance when it is not; neither despair nor arrogance have anything to do with faith; neither gives glory to Christ; neither brings real consolation to the sinner. But faith draws all its comfort from Christ, from his work and his Word; therefore, the comfort is real, sure, certain, and secure! For Christ and his Word never lie and never fail. And this faith, which receives everything from the cross in the Word, delights in nothing more than to give all glory to Christ on the cross for the salvation that flows perfectly and forever from the cross.

So let God remain as he will, with his glory hidden on the cross. Let him do as it pleases him, reveal and give himself in the lowliness of the manger, of the cross, of the Word, of the sacraments. For what it has pleased him to do and reveal and give in his hidden-ness on the cross is our salvation, our faith, our peace, our joy, our life, and our life eternal. We would not want it to be any other way. To him we most gladly say, *Amen!*

So God really has two very different kinds of glory. There is the glory that is his in his mighty acts in nature. There is glory that is his in the wisdom of the world, which even the heathen possess to some extent and which is certainly useful for our life here on earth. There is the glory that is his even in the works which men do out of kindness or compassion or love for one another; without such works, family life and society itself would doubtless collapse. In point of fact, all humanly devised religions have their whole attention fixed on this outward glory, the glory of God in nature, in reason, in human works and achievements, or at least in human potential and possibility. But God does not give himself, does not save, through any of these.

And thank God for it! If he saved only through his mighty acts in nature we would with good reason forever flee from him in terror and so not be saved at all or ever. If he saved through the genius of human reason, where would that leave the child, the slow-witted, and the not-so-brilliant ones among us? Indeed, who could approach him at all in the brilliance of his all-encompassing mind? No one would be saved. If he saved through the goodness of man, what would there be for any of us but despair? For whose goodness can approach the goodness that is God in his essence?

So he saves us through his other kind of glory, the glory that is hidden. He reveals himself and gives himself and saves through the baby in the manger. No one will run away from *him* in terror. He saves us through the man of sorrows on the cross. No one will dread so weak and helpless a God. He saves through words of the gospel in the Bible, through the gospel in the water of Baptism, through the gospel with the bread and wine in the Supper of his body and blood. Who is afraid of those means by which God reveals himself, gives himself, saves? And he saves so completely that he forgives everything in us and gives us everything in himself. So no one need fear that he has not done his part; for our part is to receive. No one need fear that his works are not enough, for it is only *Christ's* work that saves. No one need fear that his sin is too great; for God's sacrifice is greater than the sin of the whole world. No one need fear that his faith is too small, for the sigh of despair in self and *Amen* to him is the faith that saves; that faith is not a quantity to be measured but a gift received in the promise of the God who would not lie to us.

It is not too much to say that the hidden glory is so great that it *must* be hidden. For in our fallen state, we could not endure that surpassing glory of God in all its fullness. That is at least in part what St. Paul has in mind in 2 Corinthians 3. The glory of God in the Law of Moses was visible. It was so glorious that Moses had to hide his face after he spoke with God, lest the people run away in terror. If that glory was glorious, a glory that brought not only terror but even death, then how much more glorious is the glory that brings life and salvation? Such is the glory of the gospel!

Those who proclaim that gospel share in its glory. But it is a glory that is veiled in lowly words of the Bible and the lowly acts of the sacraments. It is veiled in the lowly men who stand for him at his altar and proclaim for him in his pulpit. It is veiled in the simple Christian witness of husband, wife, child, friend, and neighbor. Veiled, we receive it. Veiled, we receive its saving benefit. Veiled, we pass it on.

6

The Hidden God in the Christian

God hid his glory in the Christ who lay in the lowly manger. He hid it in the Christ who suffered on the cross. He only reveals himself and gives himself in the Christ whose glory is hidden. And it is in the giving of the Christ with hidden glory that he saves us. It all happens by means of the gospel in the lowly Word and in the lowly sacraments. When the hidden God reveals himself to us in the gospel, he gives himself by means of the gospel. And where God gives himself to us, he also gives his glory, the glory that is still hidden under the cross. The glory of the Christian is just as real as the glory of Christ—and just as hidden.

Think for a moment again of the sharp contrast in Christ, the contrast between what is and what is seen. From the moment of his conception, Christ is the God-man, almighty, all-knowing, present everywhere, without any limits imposed on him by time or space. But he hides all that in a body that looks so ordinary, so limited, capable even of death.

What then of the Christian? What is real but hidden, and what is seen? The list of things real but hidden is a long and mind-boggling one. But so deeply are the real things hidden that we are often unaware of them and never appropriately grateful for them or joyful in their possession. And why is that? It is precisely because they are hidden in weakness and lowliness under the cross. When we look at Christ, we see the cross. His glory is hidden. When we look at ourselves, we see the cross. The glory is hidden. In this chapter we will examine the realities and the cross that hides them.

The reality of who we are

Consider first the reality. We can begin where St. Paul begins in most of his epistles. How does he address those to whom he is writing? He starts out with words like these: "To all in Rome who are loved by God and called to be saints" (Ro 1:7); "To the church of God in Corinth, to those sanctified in Christ Jesus and called to be holy" (1 Co 1:2); "To the church of God in Corinth, together with all the saints throughout Achaia" (2 Co 1:1); "To the saints in Ephesus, the faithful in Christ Jesus" (Eph 1:1); "To all the saints in Christ Jesus at Philippi" (Php 1:1); "To the holy and faithful brothers in Christ at Colosse" (Col 1:1); "To the church of the Thessalonians in God the Father and the Lord Jesus Christ" (1 Th 1:1).

What is the one great reality that ties all of these addresses together? It is this fundamental reality that he is writing to *saints!* That is what the believers are, saints. They are holy people. The root meaning of the word *saint* is "holy"; saints are holy ones. Their sins have been forgiven, so that from God's standpoint they are perfect because of Christ and the forgiveness he has given them in the gospel, given them by faith. By Baptism they have been washed clean (Ro 6:1-4; Eph 5:25-27, et al.), so that in his eyes each believer is spotless, blameless, clothed with the righteousness of Christ himself, buried with him, risen with him. For Christ's sake each one is God's dearly loved child, an heir and joint heir with Christ of eternal life and blessedness. Yes, even now Christ rules all things in heaven and on earth for their benefit. As far as God is concerned, each and every one of the elect already lives forever and rules with Christ in heavenly places. For Christ has not abandoned his church. Where the head is, there the body must be. He lives! He reigns! And he does it all for the benefit of the saints who are washed clean in his blood (Eph 1, esp. also 2:6,7; Ro 8:37-39). That is the reality. That is how God sees us. That is how things actually are with us.

The implications of that reality on our attitude toward ourselves

The reality of our status as saints and children of God has or should have profound implications for our lives here on earth. First of all, it should have profound implications for how we think about ourselves as individuals. Whether young or old, rich or poor, healthy and active or sick and bedridden, no Christian has reason to be arrogant and self-righteous. And no Christian has any reason either to be depressed and despairing.*

How can we possibly be arrogant and self-righteous when we see ourselves as God sees us, when we recognize the reality? That we are saints, holy people, is entirely his gift in Christ, given us by faith through the Word and the sacraments. St. Paul reminds us that there is no room for boasting when everything that we are and have and hope to be for time and for eternity is a gracious gift of a gracious God, purchased by the blood of Christ alone (Ro 3:27; 1 Co 1:26-31; cf. also 1 Pe 4:10,11).

Likewise how could we be depressed or despairing? *We are saints, children of God, heirs of eternal life, those for whose bene-fit Christ rules over all things*—that is the reality. What is there to be depressed about? Our experience, our reason, our emotions may have only the slightest grasp of this reality, may at times have difficulty in perceiving it at all. But God does not lie. Seen or not, understood or not, felt or not, our only real problems have all been solved for us; sin is forgiven, death is swallowed up in victory, hell is vanquished. So again, what is there to be depressed about? Any other problems, whether the result of my own sins or the sins of someone else, will in due course also be

---

*We are not speaking here of those who are diagnosed as clinically depressed, depressed as the result of some apparent imbalance in the chemistry of their bodies that affects the balance in their minds.

solved for my benefit and Christ's glory. That's his promise (Ro 8; Mt 28:18-20; Jn 14–15).

And as for despair over past sin, what possible reason could there be for that? All of our sins were paid for on Good Friday and washed away in Baptism. Or do we really want to imagine that our sin could be greater than Christ and his merit? Far be it from anyone to think so foolishly! Far be it from anyone to think so ungratefully! If Christ conquered death and the devil, and he did, then when he tells me that he triumphed even over *my* sin, I will simply trust him and his Word and be most grateful that God never lies.

Instead of arrogance or self-righteousness, instead of depression or despair, the Christian has reason to rejoice beyond all measure because of the reality of his status. The Christian is a saint and child of God, a brother or sister of Christ and an heir of everlasting life. That a Christian would think of his life as meaningless or insignificant or in any way trivial is ruled out by the status that Christ won and that the Holy Spirit gives in Word and sacraments. It cannot be emphasized too strongly. That status is the reality. It is not a status yet to be earned or achieved. It is not a status that is merely potential, a possibility only gained by the best of us and not real until we get to heaven. No, it is ours by faith in him who loved us and gave himself for us. It is ours right now!

The implications of that reality on our lives with one another

That reality has implications as well for our attitude toward and our lives with one another. For what is real in my status is just as real in fellow believers. Even though I am not able to see the faith of others, to see therefore their sainthood perfectly, I can hear their confession of faith. And I take them at their word. If they are not living in open sin and defending their sin, I look at my fellow confessing Christians the way that God looks at all of his believers. And then what kind of relationship will we have with one another? We are brothers and sisters in Christ. We are one in him, since Christ lives in each of us, lives in each not as a percentage or a fragment but wholly and entirely. You are one for whom Christ died and rose again and so am I. For you, no less than for me, he rules all things in heaven and on earth.

If I can just keep that reality in mind, what respect, what dignity, what honor you have in my eyes! To use you or take advantage of you for my own ends should never even occur to me. I wouldn't dream of hurting or harming you. I cannot imagine speaking ill of you or insulting you. My fondest ambition is only this, to love and serve you. For in loving and serving you, I love and serve Christ, who lives in you (Mt 25:40). If you are sad or depressed, I want to cheer you up by reminding you of the reality of your status and of the reality of my love for you and my eagerness to serve you. If you are in need, it is an honor for me to be able to help you in any way that I can; for in helping you, I come as close as I can to giving the infant Jesus a blanket against the cold Judean night. In serving you, I wipe his tortured brow on the way to the cross. Even if you are in error, have fallen into sin or even into self-righteousness, I can only ache until I have done all that I can to call you back to the love and grace and mercy of Christ.

And what of those who are not in the household of faith? They too have a real status in the eyes of God. They are lost. They are condemned. They are damned. They are heirs of death and hell. That is the tragic reality because of their rejection of his grace, his Christ, his cross. But at the same time, God loves them. At the same time, it is also true that Christ died for them. Since I know both realities, I live in a constant awareness of their need and the possibility that I could help them in that need. I can be a mirror of the love of Christ, with the prayer that they may be drawn to his Word by what they see in me (Mt 5:13-16; Gal 6:1-10). I can look for opportunities to share the good news of salvation with them, so that the Holy Spirit will have the opportunity to work in them as he has worked in me. I may not be able to do that as often as I would like. I may be successful or may not be. I may not be bold enough or perceptive enough or sharp enough to say all that I know or would like to say. I may at times be capable of nothing else than to be like Philip when he began to share the Savior with Nathaniel; Philip merely said, "Come and see" (Jn 1:46). Be that as it may, the reality of my status as a redeemed saint and child of God shapes my life with them. My awareness of the reality of their desperate need shapes my ultimate goal in life with them.

The bottom line of these realities is that as a Christian my goal is to present my whole life to God as a living sacrifice, confident of his mercy and grace, joyful in service to him and my neighbor (Ro 12; 1 Co 12–13; Php 4:4-7). My heart rejoices, and my life reflects that joy. Greed is a stranger. For how can one who possesses everything be greedy for anything? Plotting revenge against someone who hurt me does not come to mind. For how can one whose brother Christ rules the world be bothered with petty revenge? Fear finds no home in my heart. For God has given me heaven in Christ and governs all things to bring me to that blood-bought goal. Petty backbiting and gossip never find a launching pad on my tongue. For that is the tongue I use to praise God and share his salvation; far be it from me that I should use it for malice and wickedness (Jas 3:9-12).

The reality is hidden under the cross

What glorious realities! They are just as real as is the glory of Christ in eternity and as real as his glory was even when hidden in the lowliness of the manger and the shame of the cross. Ah, and there we come to it again: As Christ's glory is hidden in lowliness and on the cross, so too this glory of the Christian, real as it is, remains hidden in lowliness and under the cross.

And that is how God has arranged and willed it. St. Paul gives us an excellent example of both the glory and its hidden-ness in the Corinthian epistles. At the same time he shows us the why of that hidden-ness. The Corinthian Christians did not appreciate the hidden-ness of God, the hidden-ness of his glory under the lowly cross. They wanted glory, glory that could be seen and experienced and felt outwardly. Looking for an outwardly glorious gospel, many of them had begun to look down on Paul, such a lowly looking apostle. They wanted a glorious apostle. He seemed too weak, too frail, too limited to be worthy of much attention. They would have preferred someone more impressive in appearance or in his presentation of the gospel.

Paul answers them with the message that the glory of God is hidden, hidden not only in Christ on the cross but hidden as well in the lowliness of the church under the cross. It is hidden in the lowliness of its messengers and then in the lowliness of its members. Read the Corinthian epistles. Paul says it in a dozen different ways. He reminds them, and us, that the message on the surface is foolishness (1 Co 1) and that human wisdom can do nothing but laugh at it. For how could God become a man and then suffer and die on a cross? How could there be anything there but weakness? The preaching of salvation by faith in the crucified would seem to be nonsense. Nevertheless, that is the only preaching which has the power of God to save.

Still, on their best day the divinely called messengers carry the glory and the power and the salvation of the gospel in themselves as in frail, breakable, inherently weak and worthless clay jars (2 Co 4). All of their worth is hidden within. All of their glory and the salvation they bring are likewise hidden within and under that weakness, that frailty, that outward appearance of worthlessness.

What of those to whom the foolishness of the cross is preached? What do they have, but sin and shame, before they hear it? They know nothing of salvation apart from that message and the Spirit who makes it wisdom and salvation in the hearer (1 Co 2). But even after they hear and receive the message and its benefit, there remains an enormous gulf fixed between their confession of faith and their life of faith; there remains so much weakness and frailty on every side in even the best of saints.

Because the glory both of God and of his church is hidden, whatever looks splendid on the outside, so holy and so God-like, should make me at once suspicious. Luther has a recurring theme in the Heidelberg Disputation, as we have already noted. The splendor of the papacy, of monks and nuns, the glory of Rome—it all looks so holy on the outside. The great monasteries and convents dedicated to the saints and martyrs all seem to say: *That's where God is, where God is to be found!* But it all is devilish, a lie, deception, when seen as man's merit before God, as the proof that the doctrine is sound because the life looks so holy on the outside.

Luther said the same thing about the *Schwärmer,* the *Rottengeister.* They were the fanatics of his day who despised the written Word of God in favor of their own dreams and their supposed direct pipeline to the Holy Spirit through their meditations and prayers. They were all emotion. They were all enthusiasm. But people like that sort of thing. It looks so holy. It looks so "Spirit filled." But the emotions and the enthusiasm took the place of love for the written Word; it put man instead of Christ again at the center just as much as man was at the center in the papacy. In fact, Luther said that the pope is the worst *Schwärmer* of all, since he claims to have all truth hidden within the shrine of his own heart.**

Whether he was speaking of the papacy or of the self-appointed new prophets, he said they all had this in common: On the outside they all seemed so holy, so filled with the Spirit, so godly. But they also had this in common: They shunned the cross in favor of glory on the outside; they were not as interested in Christ's work for us as they were in their work for Christ. And so with zeal and a sincerity separated from the cross, they denied the heart and core of the gospel. They brought people to trust in their own works, in their own holiness, yes, in the apparent glory accomplished by the fallen *self.* Indeed, over them should fall the condemnation voiced by St. Paul in Galatians 1:8, "But even if we or an angel from heaven should preach a gospel other than the one we preached to you, let him be eternally condemned!"

The reason why the Christian's glory must remain hidden

But why does it have to be that God's glory is hidden under weakness and lowliness, under the cross? Why does it have to be that way, not only for Christ but also for his church, for each and every Christian? Paul uses himself as an example in his epistles. He shows us the point with special brilliance in 2 Corinthians 10–12. There he contrasts most sharply the hidden reality with

---

** For those whose German may be a bit rusty: a *Schwärmer* is someone who is all emotion, all enthusiasm, but with little substance underneath; the word comes from the verb *schwärmen,* which is the buzzing of the bees in a swarm, who seem to have nothing but energy and enthusiasm, with no goal or direction. The *Rottengeister* were people with a mob spirit, with emotions whipped into frenzy, driven even to violence, without any sense or reason, because they imagined that the Spirit was moving them.

what is seen. What was the reality for Paul? He was an apostle, chosen by Christ the risen Lord. He was given a gospel message that had worked powerfully in thousands who came to faith through his preaching and teaching. He was, and he knew it, an especially chosen vessel of God's grace and mercy to a fallen world. He was taught by the risen Christ himself (Gal 1:12). Even this blessing he had, that he was caught up into heaven while still alive here on earth (2 Co 12:1-4). Could a man have greater honor than the honor Paul had?

But with all that honor and glory there was also a potential problem. What if the glory got so stuck in Paul's head that he would become proud? What if he started to think that the gifts and glory received were not for his comfort in all his troubles and for service but rather were proofs of his own personal superiority? Yes, and what if he was blessed outwardly with such eloquence, such worldly wisdom, such charm and personal appeal that people came to the gospel because Paul himself seemed so great? What then? Where would be the glory of God? Where would be the praise of Christ? Where would be the power, the miraculous power of the gospel to create faith, if faith seemed so reasonable and its preachers so irresistible?

Precisely to thwart such temptations and devilish possibilities Paul received, *as a gift of grace,* a thorn in the flesh to torment him (2 Co 12:7-9)! As already noted in chapter 2, we do not know and do not need to know what the thorn was. The point is that it was a constant and a painful reminder to Paul that all glory belongs to God and none to Paul. It was a constant and painful reminder that every success was the success of the gospel, not of Paul personally. It was a constant and effective tool to beat back the sinful flesh that always wants outward glory and always wants to take credit for anything positive and wants nothing more than to delight in *self* alone.

But it was also for the benefit of the Corinthians that Paul's cross, his weakness and lowliness, should be seen. In that, Paul was an imitator of Christ, whose weakness was on display for all to see and whose glory was hidden on the cross. Moreover, since Paul's weakness was so obvious, no one would be able to say that the faith of the Corinthians was the logical result of so powerful, so effective, so charming and personable a preacher as Paul. No, their faith could only have been the result of the message of Christ crucified! To Christ and to his Word alone belongs the glory! None of it belongs to man—not to the pastor, not even to the apostle! None of it belongs to the one who believes it either. It is all the miraculous working of the Holy Spirit through the lowly Word. It is a Word of the crucified. It is a Word proclaimed by frail and altogether unspectacular men. It is a Word received and believed by fallen and often broken vessels of clay.

Thus in grace, in love, in mercy, Christ hides his glory in the church, hides it under weakness and lowliness in both the preacher and the hearer, hides it under the cross. For were it otherwise, the sinful flesh would take advantage and boast. The flesh would think it had reason to trust in *self* and go right back to the worship of *self*. So on every hand, on every side, what do we see? The saints have flaws and faults all their own. They have fears and doubts not yet overcome by the gospel. They have temptations and sins that torment them and pose an obstacle and a stumbling block both to themselves and to those who expect Christians to be better than they are. It's all cross. It's all weakness. It's all glory that is as hidden as was the glory of Christ in the manger and the glory of Christ on Good Friday.

So the two realities exist side by side. On the one hand, there is the glory that we are already children of God, heirs with Christ, saints. On the other hand, that reality is hidden under weakness and frailty, under the cross that is both in us and all around us. Constant temptations and the recurring temptations obscure and blot out the halo around my head. The sins and failings of the saints around me hide from my eyes their glory as forgiven heirs of eternal light and life.

We prove our own weakness by comparisons

Yes, and it is all too tempting for me to focus on the failings of those around me. My own flesh does not want to deny *self,* and it certainly does not want to deny *self* in favor of the likes of these fallen brothers and sisters around me. If I focus only on what I see, I can even convince myself that I am better than they are. And since I am better and more saintlike than they, it makes all the sense in the world that they should serve me, little or no sense that I should serve them!

Once I have convinced myself that I am really better than they are, it is only a short step away to convince myself as well that my sins need no repentance. And since my sins are not all that bad anyway, why even struggle against them. After all, I'm a saint underneath; I have the pure gospel. Let those whose failings and sins are so obviously great repent and struggle. That's not something I need to bother with, at least not now. C. F. W. Walther makes the point with his own special eloquence. He says:

> Indeed, the more purely and correctly and richly the gospel of Christ and his grace is preached, so much the more secure, careless, and bold do many become in their sins. . . . Either they think that they could still stand in grace with all the sins that still rule over them, since they still believe in Christ, or they think that when death one day will knock on the door, then they will want to sigh quickly for grace, and then God will certainly receive them to grace as he received the thief on the cross. (Sermon for the Ninth Sunday after Trinity on the text, 1 Cor. 10:6-13, *Epistel Postille,* p. 330.)

Such thoughts surely are not strangers to any Christian. Their very presence should be all the evidence we need that we are still a long way from a perfect *self* denial. They likewise prove that our only real need is the constant and desperate need for the gospel of mercy and grace in Christ.

The balance between hidden reality and the obvious cross

There can be no doubt about it: The reality is hidden very deeply indeed, the reality that we are saints, joint heirs with Christ, dear children of the holy God, who has made us holy by his blood. But what is seen and all too apparent is weakness and sin, failure and struggle, in a word—the cross. So apparent, so glaring is the cross that the glory hidden deep inside may easily be forgotten. And that can be a problem. For when the glory hidden within is forgotten, the purposes of the cross will likewise be lost. There has to be a balance between the two—the hidden glory and the obvious cross.

151

God uses the two realities, that of hidden glory and that of evident and obvious weakness, to accomplish his purposes with us and in us. In his Word he reminds us repeatedly of the reality of our glorious status. For the constant reminder of our status keeps us from despair. That status of children, of heirs, of saints is sure and certain since Christ alone has won it for us.

But were we to focus only on that status, we could fall prey to pride. And so the obvious weakness that we see and feel, our temptations, our recurring guilt, and even our doubts are set on the other side; they help us to do battle against pride and arrogance. They drive us again and again to our knees. They cause day after day the sigh of *Lord, have mercy!* to well up from deep within our heart and soul.

Luther summed up that balance between our status as saints under the cross in that single phrase: *Simul justus et peccator!* "At the same time saint and sinner!" That is, saint—as far as God is concerned by virtue of Christ's merit and the forgiveness given fully and freely in Word and sacraments—and sinner—as far as I can see in my daily experience, my daily struggle against the devil, the world, and my own sinful flesh, which always seem on the brink of winning the battle and driving me into despair, sin, shame, and vice.

The Word is the key for striking the right balance

Because of the need for this balance between the hidden glory in our status before God and the obvious cross in our daily experience, the Word must be our indispensable and constant companion. For it is in the Word that the reality is pressed to our bosom. It is the Word that assures and convinces us of our blessed status. And it is in the Word that the strength to triumph under the cross is given to us in rich measure. To separate ourselves from the Word, therefore, is spiritual suicide. Yes, to the extent that we do not let the Word be our constant companion, to that extent we forget the glory of our status; to that extent as well, we cut ourselves off from the only source of strength that we have for bearing the cross the way that God wants us to bear it. It is not a surprise that so many fall by the wayside when their contact with the Word is spotty and sporadic. That's exactly what Jesus warned would happen in the great parable of the sower and the seed (Mk 4) and in so many other parables that center on the Word as the source of life in the kingdom of God.

We share the hidden and the obvious
with all the saints of old

Our experience as both saints and sinners kept alive and in the kingdom of God only through the power of the Word is the common experience of all the saint-sinners who have gone before us. The writer of the epistle to the Hebrews holds before us the example of the great saints of the Old Testament. After describing their faith in the midst of suffering (chapter 11), he writes: "Therefore, since we are surrounded *by such a great cloud of witnesses,* let us throw off everything that hinders and the sin that so easily entangles, and let us run with perseverance the race marked out for us" (12:1). God hid his glory in the cloud during the exodus. He hid it in those great appearances of his at the dedication of the tabernacle and then of the temple. And he hid his glory as well in that great cloud of witnesses. Think for a moment about that great cloud whose best exemplars the writer lists in chapter 11. Their glory is hidden as in a cloud.

So often those great saints looked like losers. The Bible leaves us with the record not only of their saintliness but also of their apparent failures and the sins that showed their need for the Savior. Noah was a great saint. For 120 years he preached God's Word and did not despair even though almost no one paid any attention to him. But Noah was a sinner too. After God had kept his promise to save the church by sending the flood, Noah got drunk (Ge 9). Abraham was a great saint who left everything, trusting only in the promise of the Savior. He was willing even to sacrifice the son of promise, confident that God could raise him up again. But he was also the sinner who passed his wife off as his sister because he was afraid and did not trust the promise of God to protect him and his family. That happened twice (Ge 12, 20)! Did he learn nothing from the first time it happened? Moses was a great saint. Trusting in the promises of God, he led his people for 40 years through the wilderness. But he was also a sinner who in anger disobeyed the Word of the

Lord and so was prevented from entering into the Promised Land (Nu 20).

The list goes on and on. Each one in the great cloud of witnesses is both saint and sinner. Each demonstrated his joy in the status he had with God by faith. Each showed as well how necessary it was for that status to come entirely as a gift of grace. Each lived by faith in the promise of God's Word, not by the sight of his own perfection. Thus each lived under the cross. They seem so often on the brink of destruction. Their glory as heirs of salvation and even ancestors of God's own Son is hidden under weakness and pain, under one calamity after another, and finally under death itself.

What happens when the glory becomes obvious and the cross hidden?

So it remains as ever it has been. The church in general and even each individual Christian often appears to be on the brink of destruction. The reality of glory is altogether hidden. And so it must be, so that Christ and his Word receive all the glory for the preservation of the church in general and the faith of each Christian in particular. Indeed, when everything goes well for the church, when it appears altogether glorious and appealing on the outside, it has ceased to be the church, as Jesus reminds us (Lk 6:26). At the very least, it is on the way to corruption and decay. Look at the example of the church after the building of Solomon's temple. Everything was so good that it became bad. Look at the Christian church at the end of the persecutions and the beginning of the legalization of Christianity under Constantine in the 4th century. Everything was so good that it became bad. And the point could be repeated for every age of the church.

The same sad parallel exists with individuals. When things go so very well, they are easily tempted to fall into spiritual laziness, corruption, and decay. And why is that? Why is it for the church? Why is it that way for the individual? Because in our fallen state with our still corrupted nature, we all too easily pass from grateful worshipers of the Giver to idolatrous worshipers of the outward gifts and material evidences of God's kindness and generosity.

It is the cross of loss that reminds the church collectively and each of us individually that we remain always in desperate need of mercy. It is the cross of temptation that reminds the church collectively and each of us individually that, come what may, we have reason to rejoice and give thanks to God for his incomparable goodness. He sends us things that make us glad instantly and does it out of love for us. He sends us sorrow and loss, which in the moment cause tears, but that too is only and alone out of love for us, to deepen in us gratitude for and trust in the promise of the glory that is found and given only under the cross. For even the last enemy, death, has been defeated for us by his death. Even in the pain and the ugliness of dying, we remain children of God, heirs of glory with Christ, saints.

Another reason why the glory is hidden under the cross

The Bible gives us still another good reason for why God hides his glory in us under the cross. Paul speaks about it in 2 Corinthians. The one whose life is untroubled and always free from temptation or pain may fall into the devil's trap of imagining that what he has is really his to do with as he pleases. He will miss the point that God's blessings are given, including the blessing of the cross, so that we can be useful and of service to one another. Listen to Paul, the apostle who had it all but had it hidden under the cross. Listen to Paul's description of the reason behind God's gifts of both the days of gladness and the times of sadness:

> Praise be to the God and Father of our Lord Jesus Christ, the Father of compassion and the God of all comfort, who comforts us in all our troubles, *so that we can comfort those in any trouble* with the comfort we ourselves have received from God. For just as the sufferings of Christ flow over into our lives, so also through Christ our comfort overflows. If we are distressed, it is for your comfort and salvation; *if we are comforted, it is for your comfort, which produces in you patient endurance of the same sufferings we suffer.* And our hope for you is firm, because we know that *just as you share in our sufferings, so also you share in our comfort.*

We do not want you to be uninformed, brothers, about the hardships we suffered in the province of Asia. We were under great pressure, far beyond our ability to endure, so that we despaired even of life. Indeed, in our hearts we felt the sentence of death. *But this happened that we might not rely on ourselves but on God,* who raises the dead. He has delivered us from such a deadly peril, and *he will deliver us. On him we have set our hope that he will continue to deliver us, as you help us by your prayers. Then many will give thanks on our behalf for the gracious favor granted us in answer to the prayers of many* [emphasis added]. (2 Co 1:3-11)

It is certainly clear that Paul says none of these things from some ivory tower, isolated in a cloister from any real life, from any real pain or suffering. Luke, Paul's companion on some of his journeys, tells us in the book of Acts about many of Paul's troubles as a missionary. Paul himself tells us too of his physical and spiritual struggles in some detail in 2 Corinthians 7 and 11 and elsewhere in less detail. The point is that his was a hard life indeed. But he saw in all of the weakness, in all of the struggles, in all of the suffering, the kind and generous hand of the Savior; for through such experiences he learned how to comfort those who were tempted and those who were suffering. Comforting the sorrowing and encouraging the tempted was not just theory for the apostle. He knew what comforted him in his weakness and struggle. And he knew that the same would comfort and strengthen those whom he served. Yes, and he wanted them to know as well: You also suffer, not only so that you can be comforted but so that in your turn you also may comfort and support those around you on whom the cross is pressing hard.

The suffering that we experience comes from the hands of a loving God, who teaches us by it to rely on him alone for rescue. And once we have learned that, he lets us also taste his kindness and his generosity in pleasant experiences and in a measure of outward peace and prosperity. Then he takes that peace and prosperity away again or lets something come that disturbs it. And why does he do that? So that having enjoyed his outward generosity and also having suffered from its loss, we may rely on him for our rescue *and* have a heart of compassion for our brothers and sisters who suffer. God designs our loss and our rescue to form in us hearts of compassion for others who suffer. Nor is that compassion merely passive. We long both to see the sufferers rescued *and* to be ourselves God's instruments for their rescue. That's why we suffer under the cross. It is so that we may be first grateful for God's rescue and then eager to help those still waiting for deliverance.

We hear at times of those who have "made it" in this life. We hear them say that now that they have been so successful, they want to "give something back." And in such a spirit they may show themselves very generous indeed. But the world's idea of giving something back is a long way from the attitude that God seeks to form in us by his generosity. The worldling who is just giving something back usually sees his wealth and his success as his own to do with as he pleases. He may congratulate himself, and we may congratulate him too, that he is moved to be generous with a part of what he has. But look at how far that is from Paul's attitude. The whole church is under the cross. All suffer, now this one more and that one less. And when it is my turn to suffer less and to enjoy a measure of peace or prosperity, the whole reason for it is that I might praise God and be of service to those under the heavier cross of the moment. "Give something back"? It all belongs to God, the pleasant days and experiences and the days of loss or sorrow. It all belongs to God, and I have it all from him on loan, or as a gracious gift, to be used to his glory and for my neighbor's good. We are but stewards of his manifold goodness, of his goodness in days of joy and in days of sadness no less.

Does that mean that we do not enjoy, or should feel guilty if we do enjoy, the success and prosperity that God may grant us? Of course not! We give thanks and praise to God for all such times, as especially the psalms encourage us to do (e.g., Ps 103–108, 111–113, 116–118). Thus to enjoy God's gifts is certainly a good thing; but the primary reason for such days of gladness is this, that they give yet another reason to praise and thank God for his kindness. Then they spur us on in the desire to serve God in serving those around us, especially when God's kindness is hidden under the pain of a cross. But in all of it, in days that are pleasant and days that are not, the goal remains the same. Paul summed it up well when he wrote to the church at Rome: "If we live, we live to the Lord; and if we die, we die to the Lord. So, whether we live or die, we belong to the Lord" (Ro 14:8). And again: "So whether you eat or drink or whatever you do, do it all for the glory of God" (1 Co 10:31).

So then there is a grand and glorious procession under the cross. Today I am weak and poor, struggling and needy. My status as a saint and a king and a priest, one for whom Christ rules the world, is not evident. My glory is hidden under the suffering of the cross. And another comes to me, another saint, another heir with me of eternal life. He sees my pain or I tell him of my suffering. He shares the comfort of the gospel with me. He reminds me of the glory hidden under the cross. If possible, he helps me in some tangible way. And lo and behold! The message has its divinely intended effect. My spirit revives. The circumstance may be unchanged. But encouraged by the Word, strengthened by the promise of Christ's gracious presence, I get up and go on. I press forward under the cross to await relief and deliverance in this life or in the next life, if that should be the Savior's will.

Tomorrow the one who comforted and strengthened me with the message may need to be comforted and strengthened. And if not that one, then someone else will be weighed down under the cross. Like Paul, I will not blush to share the comfort of the Savior's promises. For I know from experience: The gospel works! Even though outwardly it is only words, words that at the time may sound like a cliché, even sound foolish. Nevertheless, Christ accompanies his Word. Nevertheless, the Holy Spirit moves the heart to embrace the promise of Christ, no matter how weak that promise may seem on the surface. Ask any pastor. He will tell you how one suffering in the hospital smiled in the midst of pain and said, "Thank you, Pastor!" after hearing the pastor's devotion from the Word of God. Was there any flash of light from heaven? No. Was there the whirring of angel wings in the room? No. Was there at least a little shaking of the bed to indicate the Spirit's presence? No, not that either. There was just the assurance that Jesus loved us enough to come down from heaven and die on the cross; with a love like that, so full, so perfect, so great, we can be sure that he will never forget about us or leave us. No, he will remain with us in sickness, in pain, in suffering, in death itself.

Nor should we fear that our pain is a punishment for sin, though at times some of our suffering may indeed be the consequence of sin. The repentant gambler does not get his money back. The restored adulterer may have permanently lost his family. But those consequences of sin, painful and, yes, necessary as they may be, are not punishments for sin. All the punishment Jesus carried on the cross. It is rather the gracious hand of the Lord, drawing us ever closer to himself by his Word and sacraments. He lets us suffer the consequences of our sins so that we may be warned against continuing in them. He lets us experience the chastening hand so that we may treasure all the more the forgiving hand. That's what he has promised, and he would not lie to us.

The words are simple but so powerful. Only one who has suffered shares them with confidence. For such a one knows that they will bring the strength of Christ to a brother or sister under the cross. He knows that those words raise up the fallen and the crushed so that they can carry their cross until Christ is pleased to grant relief.

Again, Jesus' glory is hidden under the cross. It is hidden under his cross, and it is hidden under our cross too. It is under the cross that he reveals himself in the words we share with one another. And it is under the cross that we share with one another the strength that he gives there for cross bearing. Without the cross we would not know the blessed fellowship that comes from Christ through fellow Christians who share him with one another, prompted by comfort received and comfort now needed.

So for us, this side of heaven, the cross must ever be! His cross saves us. Our cross comes from his saving hand and without it we would be lost (Ro 6). For without it we would fall into arrogance and self-centeredness and self-righteousness under which the hidden glory of the status of saint would drown and die.

Mary put it all so beautifully in the Magnificat (Lk 1:46-55), which the Holy Spirit gave her at the time of her greatest exaltation—she was to be the mother of God. He gave it to her at the time of her greatest humiliation—she was an unmarried, poor peasant girl. And what does she sing?

"My soul glorifies the Lord and my spirit rejoices in God my Savior."—In the constant changes of life, today pressed down by the cross, then crowned with rescue and even outward blessing, what else is there that is constant and what other reason for real and lasting joy than this sublime truth that God is my Savior?

"For he has been mindful of the humble state of his servant. From now on all generations will call me blessed, for the Mighty One has done great things for me—holy is his name."—He alone is holy; I am as lowly as can be, a sinner from conception and birth. But his holiness he has given me in the Savior's merit and in his promise. She is blessed; so are we, and for the same reason!

"His mercy extends to those who fear him, from generation to generation."—Therefore (as Luther said in the Heidelberg Disputation cited above), I will fear him in all my works and rejoice in his alone, because it is in his works as Savior that mercy is perfect, full, complete.

"He has performed mighty deeds with his arm; he has scattered those who are proud in their inmost thoughts."—Pride puts my works alongside his and imagines that between the two of us we accomplish something, even salvation; but it is his mighty deeds on the cross that accomplished everything. Therefore, pride is chopped up in little tiny pieces and thrown like dust into the wind.

"He has brought down rulers from their thrones but has lifted up the humble."—The thrones of the proud are nothing to him, as history shows. One after another fail and fade into nothing. Those who vainly imagine that they are lords over their own lives, he tosses into the dust. But the humble, those who under the cross despair of themselves and live alone by faith in his promise, he raises up. They are saints; they are kings and priests for whose benefit he rules over all things.

"He has filled the hungry with good things but has sent the rich away empty."—Therefore, I will boast that I am

ever starving when it comes to righteousness, so that he may fill me up day after day with his own righteousness.

"He has helped his servant Israel, remembering to be merciful to Abraham and his descendants forever, even as he said to our fathers."—He keeps his word forever. He will keep his promise also to me. He kept it already on his cross. He keeps it no less in mine!

7

Crosses—A Sampler

We have considered the absolute and constant necessity of Christ's cross for our redemption. We have discussed the necessity of the cross that comes as the result of our own sinful nature, on the one hand, and from his grace and goodness, on the other hand. We have looked at obstacles to cross bearing that we encounter both in ourselves and from those around us. We have pondered the glory of God that is hidden under and in his cross, and ours as well, and reasons why that glory is and must ever be a hidden one. And we have given thought to the benefits that come to us and to others as a result of this cross bearing. It should be evident that all of the Christian's life is connected to the cross and embraced by the theology of the cross. It is under the cross that we are in a grand procession on the way to the crown already won and reserved for us in heaven.

To bring the whole matter to a close, it will be useful for us to spend a few pages on some typical and very specific crosses that can be found in the household of faith. The cross changes its outward appearance often in the life of the church and of the individual. But no cross is unique and borne only by one in all of history, except of course for the cross of the Redeemer. St. Paul reminds us, "No temptation has seized you except what is common to man. And God is faithful; he will not let you be tempted beyond what you can bear. But when you are tempted, he will also provide a way out so that you can stand up under it" (1 Co 10:13).

It is useful for us to keep this in mind: those who have gone before us and our brothers and sisters in the faith even now have gone and are going through the same things that we endure. Blessed is that one who in union with the church follows after Christ beneath the cross, trusting in him alone to save. Blessed is that one who wants nothing more than to be nourished by the Word and sacraments along the way; for thus nourished, the Christian has the strength Christ gives to stand and to continue his pilgrimage journey when bowed down under the weight of the cross. Blessed is that one who in the company of his fellow saints draws strength from their sharing of the gospel with him, so that he may also be God's instrument in strengthening them in the hour of trial!

We will divide crosses of temptation and testing into different types somewhat in the way that Luther does in his comments on the Sixth Petition of the Lord's Prayer in the Large Catechism (Kolb, p. 454, par. 107,108). Some temptations and struggles are most common to the young, others to the adults and older people, and still others to stronger Christians, to leaders or pastors and teachers in the church. Luther's list and this sampler are, of course, by no means complete. We simply want to look at crosses that are rather typical in the interest of strengthening the one who imagines that he is all alone under his cross. We also hope to provide, in some small measure, the balm of the gospel that heals and strengthens those under the crosses listed and those under crosses in some way related to the ones listed.

The special crosses of the young

The temptations common to the young are often the most obvious. There is nothing subtle about passion that wants to run wild or the desire to rebel. So blatant can the temptations and sins be and so painful their memory that David much later in life prayed, "Remember not the sins of my youth and my rebellious ways" (Ps 25:7). The sinful flesh these days finds more incentive and incitement for the passions of youth than could have been imagined in times past. Styles of clothing are often deliberately provocative. The entertainment offered by much that is popular in music, movies, and on television easily excites the easily excitable. To make such entertainment even more tempting, the underlying message is almost always the damnable notion that there is no such thing as sin or any such thing as a consequence for sin. Modesty and shame in matters carnal would seem to be things of the past.

Even common decency has been eliminated in favor of the principle that good is whatever I want simply because "I have a right to be happy!" The premise remains unexamined. Who gave such a "right to be happy"? At whose expense should the imagined right be exercised? If everyone else has that right, might they exercise it at my expense? The premise remains unexamined because the imagined right collapses into nonsense as soon as it is examined. What after all is happiness? In what does this chimera, this impossible dream, of happiness consist? Is it the virtuous life attained by strict self-discipline? That's what Aristotle thought, but his definition seems far removed from the modern idea of happiness. Is it just feeling good? There are millions of drug addicts, alcoholics, gamblers, adulterers, and the like who have thought so. Now that they are sick, bankrupt, dying, destitute, disgraced, or in prison, they may be wondering why the gods of happiness have dealt so cruelly with them.

But never mind the philosophical problem of the imagined *right to be happy*. There is a still more evil assumption in the assertion. That is the assumption that happiness is only to be found in the casting off of any yoke, of any limitations, of any regulation of my life. In a word: The assumption is that happiness is to be found in *sin!* To a considerable degree it is the sin of self-gratification, the opposite of self-denial. It is the sin of idolatry that happiness is to be found in the unlimited service of *self.* It is, of course, a lie that happiness is to be found in sin. That lie, however, has become a bedrock assumption and a governing principle for millions even long after they've left youth behind. It is a very appealing lie to the sinful flesh. The devil and the world are only too happy to preach it. The flesh is only too eager to embrace it.

The message has been made all the more appealing in our day by the advent of the Internet. Who can count the millions of young people (and not just young people!) who have been seduced to their destruction, both physically and spiritually, by the poison of easily accessible filth? Vile miscreants are only too ready to take them into the lowest gutters of depravity, vice, disease, and ultimately even death.

And why not? After all, if we owe our existence to a mindless evolution, if we are nothing essentially different from an animal, accountable to no one, with no guide in heaven and nothing after the grave, then why not behave accordingly. As the Epicureans of Paul's day taught: Let us eat, drink, and be merry; for tomorrow we die.

Coupled with and aiding these obvious spurs for the flesh is the desire common in most young people for each to find his or her own identity. A young person reaches an age when he or she does not want to be merely the bottom sheet under a piece of carbon paper on which parents or traditions or the dominant culture of church and state have stamped their own images. Each wants to be an individual, distinct and unique. That search for individuality, for uniqueness, easily finds expression in rebellion against what little authority is left in the lives of the young. It may be rebellion against the authority of parents or of government in school and on the street or of the church.

It is interesting to watch how this process of trying to become an individual unfolds. Characteristically, a child experiments and pushes boundaries more out of curiosity than anything else. A small child mostly wants to see if he or she can get away with something; the child just wants to know where the boundaries are. But the body of the small child needs all the energy it can muster just to grow. When the day is done and the young child goes to bed, it sleeps the sleep of the exhausted if not the altogether innocent.

Then, sometime during the late teens, the major physical growth stops. The body, however, continues to produce the energy needed earlier just to grow. The result is restlessness. The result is a nagging feeling of frustration. The thought starts to form in the mind that the days are coming when the almost adult young person will be expected to settle down, get married, get a job. The days of something always new and different, always exciting will be replaced by decades of routine. The word *routine* is a synonym for the word *boring* in the mind of the young. That is the one dirty word in the vocabulary of most: *boring!* They will become their parents, whose lives they consider uninteresting and tedious. And so the rebellion begins. Two mutually exclusive demands dominate. One is spoken; the other, acted out. The spoken demand is "Stop treating me like a child!" The acted out one is "I don't want to grow up; I want to stay a child but with growing freedom, no responsibilities, everything always new and different and exciting!"

That is a very dangerous time for a child on the way to becoming an adult. Again, it is a time of restlessness and frustration. What makes it so dangerous is that the young person at such time is looking for an escape from that restlessness and frustration. Sadly, the ways of escape are all too many and all too readily available. In earlier days, the boy or girl may have experimented with vices and evil and quickly forgotten their effects. But now they are looking for an escape from reality, from frustration, from fear of the future, from loneliness in their *angst*. The experiments become a deadly and addictive form of self-medication for the pain of growing up. Some will try to escape into the fog of alcohol or other drugs. Some will look for solace in sex, mindless or otherwise. Some will stave off any possibility of thinking about their condition or their future by endless entertainment and noise that make thinking impossible. The more healthy and the ones more likely to survive may still try to lose themselves, albeit in more socially acceptable ways, in sports or academics. Many may bounce from one of these hoped-for solutions to another, all in the search for . . . for what? For happiness? For identity? For forgetfulness? For relief from the pain of growing up?

Sadly, no one seems to be telling them that their restlessness is temporary, that it will pass with maturing of body and mind. No one tells them that the day will come sooner than they think when the chaos of youth and the desire for constant change and excitement will pass. It will be replaced by a desire for calm, for things and people that are reliable, for islands of stability in a world that is a sea of confusion and a quicksand of unreliability.

In point of fact, for most it is necessary to go through this time of restlessness and confusion in order to reach maturity. If a young person succeeds in escaping through some of the ways just mentioned, he will only postpone growing up. And the longer he postpones it, the less likely it is to happen; he may remain an immature child his whole life long. Who doesn't know people like that?

Such temptations to one degree or another afflict almost all of the young at one time or another, and they certainly do not leave the young Christian untouched or unscarred. Beneath the surface of these temptations and difficulties that are common to most young people, there are crosses that young Christians bear, no matter the degree to which these temptations plague them. There are some questions during this time of life that press hard as crosses.

✛ How can God possibly love me when all I do is lash out at people who are just trying to help me?

✛ How can God possibly love me when I have fallen into this or that sin and cannot seem to escape it?

✛ If God really cared about me, why does he let me be plagued with temptations that I just cannot resist?

✛ If God really cared about me, why does he let me suffer so all alone in the world, with no one who understands me or really cares about me?

✛ Why should God love me, when I find it so hard even to stand myself?

✛ What's the point in resisting sins that I know I'm going to commit anyway? Why not just give up instead of tormenting myself with a struggle that I will lose anyway?

✛ If I don't do what everybody else does, then I won't have any friends. Worse yet, they will discover what I am working so hard to keep a secret: *I'm weird!* Why does God leave me so alone?

✠ If I don't join in abusing and picking on so and so, then everyone will think that I am as strange as he or she is. Why does God make helping someone so difficult, so expensive?

Some assumptions common to the young (and maybe to most others as well in our culture) aggravate all of these problems, temptations, and crosses. The assumptions are adopted unconsciously from the television habit. On television all problems can be solved quickly and easily within a half-hour or an hour, with time out to get a sandwich or go to the bathroom. The notion that life at times can be very difficult, and for some difficult all the time, occurs to almost no one. The thought that some problems take months or even years to solve, and that other problems have no solution but can only be endured, finds no room in the mind.

Thus if my life is difficult and my problems have no quick and easy solution, then there must be something fundamentally wrong with me. *I'm weird!* Most teenagers, even if popular and running in a pack, have such thoughts at times. Thus, again even when popular and running in a pack, a teenager may feel very alone, understood by no one, with only the goal of keeping those around him from finding out how really weird he is. That is one of the ironies of youth: It is a time when they are seldom alone and yet is for many the loneliest time of their lives.

Closely related to these problems in the lives of young people is the problem of self-centeredness. It is an obvious and easy problem to understand. A child simply assumes that the people around him are there primarily for his benefit. Parents are there to provide for and take care of him. The school exists to serve him. Friends are supposed to like him and share their toys with him. The reverse never enters his mind—the idea that he exists to serve and that everything done for him has that as a goal, that he should be equipped to serve, to become a useful and productive member of society. But as parents and others start to expect him to shoulder responsibilities, it becomes increasingly difficult for him to cling to the assumption that he is the center of his universe. Confusion starts to replace that illusion. And that confusion fosters the nagging sense that there is something wrong, that he must be weird. What if people find that out about him? Each one imagines, to put it another way, that everyone is always watching him, ready to pounce on him, laugh at him, and call him weird. That's the curse of the self-centered. It just never occurs to him that most of those around him are going through exactly the same things he is. It does not occur to him that they are much too busy worrying that someone will find them out to be concerned with his potential fall.

If only parents, teachers, and pastors would remember that there was a time when these were also their questions, fears, and worries! If we remembered or admitted to ourselves that we were once just as confused as our young people are today, we might be of more use to them. And that is the point: We want to be of use to them; we want to comfort and strengthen them. They badly need our help to bear up under the pressures of their own sinful flesh and the world in which they live—under the weight of the cross. Without such help they will certainly stumble and fall more than they would have otherwise. Without such help the pain of their existence will only increase and the happiness they are seeking will become ever more distant. Real happiness found only in the arms of the Savior, real fulfillment found only in self-denial that serves may seem so far away as to be unreachable to them.

But they never listen! is the excuse that we too readily offer for not offering help. It will help if *we* listen first. Too easily we compare their problems to our own adult problems. We consider our problems real, their problems just temporary and trivial. We forget that God has broadened our shoulders to bear the weight of heavier crosses by granting grace earlier to bear, or at least to survive, the lighter ones. Yes, and those lighter ones on narrower shoulders are not all that light—they were not so light for us either 10 or 20 or more years ago!

In point of fact, they do listen to one who has listened, even sometimes to one who has not. They may not let on that they are listening. They may not even want to listen. But they do listen. To hear words of understanding and encouragement from a parent, an interested teacher, a concerned pastor means much more than the young person can express.

Sometimes we think that they are not listening just because they cannot express in words what they are thinking and feeling. But we can! We've been there. We can say, "I know what it feels like to . . . ," or even simply offer, "Being young is a lot tougher than people want to admit." Or "I remember how lonely I was when I was your age." Or "I remember thinking that there must really be something wrong with me, because no one else seemed to have my problems and no one else seemed to have problems that lasted so long." Or "If there is one thing I've learned over the years it's that the best way to triumph in my own struggles and fears is to help someone else with theirs. In taking care of other people's needs instead of always worrying about my own, I have learned that God finds ways of satisfying my needs too." Just as we need to hear obvious truths expressed repeatedly, so too do our youth need to hear these things more than once.

Again, it is worth keeping in mind that a teenager assumes that he is all alone and that no one is going through what he is. He does not know that all his friends are going through the same thing in one way or another. And it certainly does not occur to him that his parents, his teachers, or his pastor also went through the same things when they were his age. Just a glimmer of understanding from a Christian parent, teacher, or pastor can be a tremendous help to the young Christian pressed down under the cross. It can serve as the beginning of a conversation, lay the groundwork for a future conversation, or give some credibility to other things that the adult may have to say later on by way of encouragement.

What a cross it is if the problem or temptation threatens the one enduring it with despair! To teach the young to bear the cross, to willingly deny *self* and follow the Savior, is a great and high responsibility. And it will never be easy, not for the teacher, not for the learner either. For a mother to embrace with patience the rebel son who is unlovable especially to himself is a Christlike thing if ever there was one; he will never forget it. For a father to find time to sit with the drama-queen daughter, whose head seems to hold nothing but gum and gossip, and listen to her is vastly more important than the daily sport scores; she will remember it her whole life long. Let the son see his father pray and his mother quietly reading her Bible. Let the daughter see her father gently hold his wife's hand and let her see her mother yield to her husband's headship. Let our children hear their parents discuss the Sunday sermon at the Sunday dinner table, discuss it with reverence and respect. Let them share some of the problems their parents have. Then let them hear how their parents try to solve the problems in the light of God's Word and how they rely on the mercy of God to get them through their problems. Yes, let them hear sometimes their parents' confessions to one another and the forgiveness they share with each other and then with their children too.

We make the crosses of our children heavier than they need to be when we let them assume that we do not care and could never understand. We live to serve. Who better to serve with time, with patience, with love than our own children? It doesn't take a certificate of genius to do it either. Mostly it requires just a little bit of a good memory and the desire in all things to serve Christ in serving those he has given us. Let's not forget that he was busy with the work of redeeming the world, but he was not too busy to pick up little children in his arms and bless them. Or are we busier than he was?

Perhaps one of the simplest but most useful things that a parent can do is to remember the opening words of the Lord's Prayer: "Our Father!" Luther tells us in the Small Catechism that this address encourages us to approach God with boldness and confidence, since he is our loving and dear Father. How sad for that parent whose child cannot understand what Luther means because he would never dream of approaching his earthly father at all, much less with boldness or confidence! Blessed be that father and mother whose children grasp at once what Luther means in the catechism, for they see their parents as Christians who love them with both kindness and discipline, just as God loves them. There is nothing heroic about such modeling. It should be as natural for a Christian as breathing. That it is so difficult for so many is a further indication of how far we still have to go in our own denial of *self* and faithful following after Christ under the cross. But what greater work could there be than the work of helping the young become faithful followers of Christ under the cross? And what more rewarding mission than when that work is with our very own children, the children that God himself has entrusted to our care?

When a young person is in pain and suffering from a guilty conscience, especially then do they need the message of the law and the gospel put into proper balance and perspective. While there must be consequences for sin so that we do not become bold to embrace our sins, there must also be the assurance of the love of God in the gospel. When the consequences for sin sharpen the sense of guilt, the beauty of the gospel may shine all the more brightly. Just something as simple as this may make the guilty aware of the gospel in a way that they never were before: "Just think; when Jesus was hanging on the cross, and all around him said, 'Come down!' he refused. And why? Because he thought of you at this very moment in your life. Thinking of you, he refused to come down. He insisted that he would stay and bear all the guilt that is yours and its eternal punishment. That's how much he loved you! He didn't suffer hell and die for a nameless, faceless blob of humanity. He suffered hell and died thinking of you!"

The simple fact of the matter is that I remain a self-righteous Pharisee until I recognize Jesus on the cross just for me. We remain people who imagine that at least in a little bit we deserve him and his passion. But once our guilt has crushed us, we are ready for the real meaning of grace and of all that he is for us in the gospel. The first real glimmer that we are utterly depraved and in desperate need of grace usually comes when we are teenagers. What a gift of God if you can be the one who brings that flicker to a flame in the life of a young person under the cross! What a blessing to be the one who brings this candle into the dark night of despair: "So you think that God cannot love or forgive you? Consider this: He ruled over all of history so that you would be baptized and he adopted you there in baptism. He promised to be your dear Father because of Christ, even though he knew what you would do. He has ruled over all of history so that you would hear the message of forgiveness and, yes, even eat and drink the price of forgiveness in the Sacrament of the Altar. Isn't that more than enough evidence and proof that he loves you, even you, even now? No one will ever love you more than he has or than he does!"

Does it seem impossible to help the young mature? Does it seem out of the question to strengthen them under their particular crosses, so that they rise up to carry them and then grow up to carry adult crosses? May it never be that a Christian parent, pastor, or teacher would give up on the noble work of serving the young. For to do so is to give up on the promises of God and on the power of the gospel. Remember that faith and the Christian life are always miracles. They are always gifts from God that are a surprise, which we would never even have expected were it not for his promise and the gospel's power in our own lives. Will we always be successful? You will find the answer to the question by looking in the mirror. Because of our own sinful flesh, the gospel does not always get the fruit it should in us either! The Spirit of God works through the gospel when and where it pleases him (Jn 3:5-7). Sometimes it takes a long time for the seed that was sown to germinate and grow. Sometimes others will see the fruit of the seed we sow and enjoy it. Our task and honor is to be faithful; ultimate success is God's work. Be content with the honor God has given and trust his promise that our labors are not in vain (Gal 6:9,10).

Just what are the special blessings that come with the difficult and special crosses born by the young? Perhaps the simplest and most obvious is that their special crosses are often God's way of getting their attention. Until these trials hit, most young people are blissfully ignorant of their need of a Savior and of his constant grace and mercy. To be sure, they may have memorized the truths of the gospel especially in confirmation class. But those truths for many remain as vibrant and significant in daily life as the history of the Civil War. As indispensable and necessary as the learning of the facts is, it takes the cross to bring them to life! And God can use the crosses of the young very effectively to get their attention. But it takes Christian parents and Christian pastors and teachers to show the young the eternal and saving value of the gospel message, a message that they knew before but now can come to grasp in a much more personal way. All Christians live much of their lives on the swing that goes back and forth from self-righteousness to despair. Perhaps those swings are nowhere quite as dramatic and obvious as they are in the lives of teenagers; certainly there is no higher calling for an adult than that of helping the young people in our lives to find their center at the foot of the cross of Christ!

The special crosses of those in the middle

The crosses that come into the lives of adults during their most productive years are no less heavy than those left behind in their teens. In one particular way they are much more difficult: The crosses of adults are often so subtle that they go unrecognized. That is the special danger adults face from, let us say, their 20s to sometime in their 60s. The passions of youth, so fiery and so insistent, are replaced by ambition and the struggle to survive in a highly competitive, risky, and predatory world.

What could possibly be wrong with the ambition to succeed in that kind of a world? After all, we are working for our families. We are working because the alternative is a life devoid of the things that mark one as a *somebody*. We are working out of love for our children, so that we can give them an even better life/education/things than we had when we were children. We are working so that in our golden years we will not be left at the mercy of the state or of our children for our survival. Isn't it interesting? The very life that seemed so intimidating or so boring to us when we were 15 can consume us by the time we are 30!

Perhaps one word can sum up the special difficulty of the Christian's life in the middle; it is *priorities*. The business of making a living, of getting ahead, of accomplishing goals, or even of just surviving from day to day and year to year in our fallen world, can turn our eyes away from the cross of Christ and his saving benefit. Our priorities can become altogether worldly, fixed on the temporal and the temporary. For the problems and possibilities of the moment are insistent and demanding: "Do it *now!* Tomorrow may be too late! Hurry up! This opportunity only comes along once!" The demands of the moment can become the priorities of one grabbing for a handful of dust that he imagines to be gold. Indeed, exactly those and only those are the priorities of most of those around us. They seem so normal, so natural, so altogether appropriate. After all, aren't we supposed to work diligently? Isn't it a sin to waste time? Even the Bible tells us that (2 Th 3:6-12). God doesn't drop manna out of heaven anymore. Who will provide for me and mine if I don't?

175

What will become of us in our old age if we have not "squirreled way ample nuts" for the future?

All of these concerns have a ring of validity to them. That's what makes the temptations so subtle that we may easily miss the danger. Think of it this way: *In establishing our priorities we too easily confuse means and ends.* Work, the acquiring of respect, the gaining of things for now and for tomorrow are not the *ends,* are not the goals of life. They are the *means* for reaching other and better ends and goals.

If we confuse the means and the ends, we load on ourselves one heavy burden after another. The devil tempts us to make the exchange, to reverse means and ends; he promises us the world if we will just fall down and worship him. "Just for a moment," he says, "put Jesus and the Word on hold; you can get back to them later. For now, for the moment, worship at the altar of success and all your needs and even your wants will be assured to you." But he is a liar from the beginning. If we heed his siren call only this can be guaranteed: We will fail! We will never achieve the corrupt goal/end we sought.

Work is good and God-pleasing, but not as the goal of life. What the devil promises is the whole world if we make work the goal of life. What does he really give? Ruined health, a family in decay because of neglect, and a worship life that is a shambles because it gets in the way of work. Work as an end, rather than a means to a better and higher end, is a cruel slave driver indeed.

Respect and honor are good things, but when respect and honor become the end, the goal of life, what happens? We twist in the wind of human opinion for fear of losing someone's respect. What happens then to the absolutes of the Word of God? Do they fall by the wayside in the interest of winning the respect of people who have no use for the Word of God? What becomes of the opportunities God gives to share the gospel with those who do not have it? Do we dare to do it, or do we withhold the life-giving gospel from one on the way to eternal suffering because we don't want to risk hurting his feelings?

Saving for the future so that we do not become a burden to the state or to our children is certainly a good thing. But if it becomes the end and goal of life, there will be no peace in this life and maybe none in the next either. Gold becomes god. And there is never enough of it. Fear of the future, fear of lack, fear of possible suffering, fear of the loss of wealth are like a dark cloud that hides the promises of Christ to never leave or forsake us. The assurance of God's Word that God's providence never fails gets drowned out by the wailing of "Yes, but what if . . . ?" The goal of savings has actually turned into an attempt to make trust in the providence of God unnecessary. If we have enough from our own efforts and from our saving, we will not need God's mercy and help; we will have provided for ourselves without him!

The problem is that all we are and have apart from him is uncertain and insecure—and deep down inside we know it. Thus when we put our trust in ourselves, in the uncertain and the insecure, we have no peace. We have only fear. We turn into squirrels chasing our own tails with neither satisfaction in the chase nor any hope of gaining our goal. Again, we load on ourselves suffering of our own making and then, just as foolishly, cut ourselves off from the only real source of peace and security in the arms of him who loved us and gave himself for us.

If work, the acquiring of respect, the gaining of things for now and for tomorrow become ends instead of means, what happens to our Christianity? The Savior becomes an interruption in our gaining or our enjoying of temporal and temporary things. On Sunday morning, God may have an hour or so, but real confession and absolution are not the center of life. The time during the week for reading the Bible and for private prayer just disappears like the dew of the morning: "I've got to get the kids ready for school. I've got to hurry to get to work." In the evening, "I'm just too tired from the rigors of the day. It's time for television. It's time for the game." It would be far better if with the setting of the sun, we called to mind the ancient Latin proverb, *Sic transit gloria mundi*—"So passes the glory of the world!" And since it all passes, where should I fix my eyes? Obviously on that which does not pass with the setting of the sun, on Jesus and his Word, which no darkness can hide!

But instead, Jesus and his Word become an ever smaller cubbyhole in life. He and his Word even become distractions to what is *really* important. Means have become ends. Even the common table prayer before meals has the taint of "Hurry up with it so that we can eat!" It's the eating that has become all important, not the God who gave the meal and who sustains us through it.

The descent has begun. That descent is a steep and slippery slope and has damaging effects on every aspect of our life. As our life in Christ is damaged and our walk with him strays into swamps and ditches, we can expect to get bogged down and lost. Yes, we will hurt those we most wanted to help along the way. Having less and less time to really love and serve them, we end up causing them to trip and get bogged down with us. For to the extent that we have misplaced priorities, to the extent that we have turned means into ends, to that extent all those will suffer whom God has given to us so that we could serve them. Our help won't be there. Our counsel will be warped by our misplaced priorities. Our example will be that of the heathen.

First the marriage suffers. "I am busy with getting this and that done" leaves less and less room for the "we" in the marriage. The husband forgets those lines that won him his wife's love. The wife forgets those buttons that she pushed to win her husband's devotion. The husband marries his work and his toys in his quest for significance. The wife marries her children or her own work and her connections with other women in her search for some meaning or for someone who will pay attention to her. Neither the husband nor the wife lives any more to serve the other; each lives a life increasingly separated from the other. Instead of deepening, the love grows cold, old, and indifferent. She asks him what he wants for supper, and he does not grasp that this is her way of telling him that she loves him and wants to please him. So instead of answering her with appreciation, he dismisses her with a grunt, ignores her, tells her not to bother him or that he doesn't really care. It's that last phrase that she hears—that he doesn't really care.

The husband, on the other hand, comes home from his work to his wife each night. She does not understand that to him this is an important way of telling her that he is devoted to her, that he loves her. For he has given up a male's most valued possession in her favor; he prefers her to his freedom. Not listening to this unspoken expression of devotion, she grumbles that he never tells her that he loves her anymore and never shows it either.

Neither listens to the signals of the other, they stop appreciating each other. They stop living to serve each other. Old age comes, work is set aside, and the children are grown and gone. Then husband and wife stare at each other as though they were strangers. She thinks he is uncaring and in the way. He calls her a nag and a nuisance.

No one starts marriage that way. But when we leave Christ and his cross behind and make something else the goal and end of life—even if it is the family—marriage and the family suffer. As each one turns means into ends, a couple can expect the marriage to take such a course. Little wonder that so many marriages end in divorce. Tragic wonder that in our congregations the percentage is not all that much better! Sad wonder that a significant percentage of marriages that do not end in divorce nevertheless settle into a pathetic indifference of husband and wife to each other. Such marriages long ago left behind the "one flesh" that God intended the marriage to be (Ge 2:23,24) and the mirror image of Christ's marriage to the church that a Christian marriage should be (Eph 5:22-33).

The rest of the family, of course, also suffers when husbands make their work or their pleasure goals/ends in their lives. The whole family suffers as well when wives make personal fulfillment their goal, with children or their own careers or other associations the means for reaching that goal. Children grow up without good models when it is time for them to seek a spouse. Left without models, they take the path of least resistance and let the passions of youth rule their choices and decisions. Confident that their passions will never cool, they plunge headlong into marriages that are all but doomed to repeat the marriages of their parents—a fate the offspring thought impossible for themselves during courtship and on their wedding day.

Nor is the life of the church unaffected. Parents and their children stray further and further from the Savior and his Word. The children were baptized and then dumped into the parish school, the Sunday school, or into confirmation class. But they have learned from the example of their parents that what they hear in church really has more in common with Santa Claus and the Easter bunny than it does with the meaning and the purpose of life. As Santa Claus and the Easter bunny are left behind, so too are the vows made at confirmation. Christmas is cute; Easter is nice; *repentance* and *Jesus only* are just words. And where is the sign of the cross received on the forehead and upon the breast in Baptism? Where are the words stamped on the heart: "If anyone would come after me, he must deny himself and take up his cross and follow me" (Mk 8:34)? Where is the answer of the soul: "Here am I. Send me!" (Isa 6:8)? Where is the answer of the man of God: "Speak, for your servant is listening" (1 Sa 3:10)? Where is the answer of the handmaid of the Lord: "May it be to me as you have said" (Lk 1:38)?

So pastors struggle to do mission work among members who think they already know everything and need no further repentance. When the marriage or the children are in trouble, the church may be the last (and cheapest!) resort for counseling. But the counsel they get that calls for repentance and a life directed by the Word of God is not the counsel that they want. What they want is for the pastor to bless their sinful choices or for him to take sides in a battle that has already been lost by all concerned.

At the same time, the witness of these members to their unchurched neighbors, friends, and relatives is a tragic one. The unchurched person sees in the lives of these churchgoers nothing appealing, nothing better than what he has in his own life apart from the gospel. Why then should he bother with the church? It seems to him that the church is just after growth for its own sake and probably only wants him for his money.

In so many ways this sorry tale in so many marriages is really little more than a playing out of the same problems that we have seen in the teenager. Each one assumes that he or she is the center of the universe for whose sake the other one exists. Each then becomes sullen and withdraws from the other as soon as the reality sets in that the other expected the same single-minded focus. It's a bit more subtle than the self-absorption of a teenager. But in its essence, it is the same thing. It plays itself out more gradually, less dramatically. And that makes it all the more difficult to spot and nip in the bud or to reverse once the malady has become habit. In the marriage, one spouse taking the other for granted leads to disappointment in each other's lack of devotion. That lack of devotion leads to indifference, then to coldness, then to the collapse of so much or all of what God intended to give through marriage and the family.

It all starts, as noted, with the matter of *priorities,* with turning means into ends. When anything other than Christ and his Word are turned into the goal of life—whether it is work or respect or saving or even family and children—crosses are sure to follow for the Christian.

✠ Greed or ambition for its own sake begets disappointment, since neither greed nor ambition can ever be fully satisfied. Then comes the temptation either to complain that God blesses others more than he blesses me or to push God still further to the fringes of life in the vain struggle to satisfy insatiable greed and ambition.

✠ God himself may send frustration and failure and loss in his loving attempt to call us back to himself. Since we have wrong goals, what he sends is a heavy burden. The devil wants to use that burden to drag us still further away from God by arguing that our loss proves that he doesn't love us or really care about us.

✠ The growing indifference to God or doubt about his grace makes every problem in life more difficult to bear, for we see ourselves as carrying the load alone, without either God's help or God's good intentions, without even the understanding of those who are supposed to love us most.

✠ Physical sickness may come also from God's gracious hand as a way of bringing us to a reordering of our priorities. But the devil will try to use it as still further evidence of God's indifference or, alternately, to drive us to despair with the thought that we are finally getting what we deserve for our idolatrous lifestyle.

✠ Disappointment in spouse, in children, in fair-weather friends who are just as self-centered as we have been, tempts us to withdraw still further into self and self-service.

181

All these difficulties that come into our lives and attack our faith are, of course, our own fault. But when God either sends or permits such things to come into our lives, he is calling us with them and reminding us: "If anyone would come after me, he must deny himself and take up his cross and follow me." The unhappy consequences that come from our confused priorities and our reversing of means and ends are God's not-so-gentle taps on the shoulder to get our attention. For what we thought would make us "happy" or "successful" or "fulfilled" has turned out to be a cup filled with bitter herbs of disappointment and frustration. Perhaps we should look elsewhere for "happiness," for "fulfillment." Maybe it's time to rearrange the furniture in the soul, to clean the house of the heart.

What's the solution? It is a return to the basics. It is a return to the Word, which we thought we knew so well that we could ignore it in favor of other things. It is going back again to precisely what this book has been all about from its first page. "If anyone would come after me, he must deny himself and take up his cross and follow me." Indeed, when we consider all of the pain we bring on ourselves when we forget or refuse that cross, we get a new insight into Jesus' promise, "Come to me, all you who are weary and burdened, and I will give you rest. Take my yoke upon you and learn from me, for I am gentle and humble in heart, and you will find rest for your souls. For my yoke is easy and my burden is light" (Mt 11:28-30). It all goes back to the beginning and to the prayer of St. Augustine: "Thou, O Lord, hast made us for thyself and our soul is restless until it finds its rest in thee." And that prayer is but the echo of the psalmist who sighed when all in life seemed futile and empty, "Whom have I in heaven but you? And earth has nothing I desire besides you. My flesh and my heart may fail, but God is the strength of my heart and my portion forever" (Ps 73:25,26).

It's all really so simple. Why does it take us such a long time to learn the lesson, and why do we have to learn it over and over again? Is it not a testimony to the depth of our own perversity? And is it not a witness to the faithful love and grace of God? He takes us again and again into the schoolroom of his merciful heart in the Word and sacraments. There he repeats the lessons again and again as needed in order to win and re-win us. It should be abundantly clear: The cry of the church, "Lord, have mercy; Christ, have mercy; Lord, have mercy!" is never old or unnecessary for any of us, and it should never be mere vain repetition.

Likewise, his answer to our cries for mercy, the answer he gives in the gospel promise, remains our single greatest need in life. His answer of free and faithful grace prompts us to join with Jeremiah as he sat in the rubble of Jerusalem. The city was destroyed in God's judgment on the impenitent. Jeremiah prayed in the ruined heap when he had lost everything, and we join him in his prayer when the painful consequences of our own sins, our own wrong priorities, have hurt or crushed us: "Because of the LORD's great love we are not consumed, for his compassions never fail. They are new every morning; great is your faithfulness. I say to myself, 'The LORD is my portion; therefore I will wait for him'" (Lam 3:22-24).

Once we have gotten back to the basics of the law and the gospel, to confession and absolution, we can reexamine this whole matter of priorities, this business of ends and means. It is a reexamination that may have to be carried out often during our adult years. For the devil, the world, and our own sinful flesh never give up in their attempts to distort our priorities; no day goes by when they do not conspire to turn means into ends.

Jesus summed up most succinctly the end, the goal of life, when he said, "Do not worry about your life, what you will eat or drink; or about your body, what you will wear. . . . But seek first his kingdom and his righteousness, and all these things will be given to you as well" (Mt 6:25,33). What a treasure trove of instruction and wisdom on the matter of priorities, on the business of distinguishing ends and means! The end, that is the purpose and the goal of life, is to seek the kingdom of God and his righteousness. The kingdom of God is by definition his gracious rule in our hearts and lives by means of his Word. It is the enthronement of Christ in the what and the why of our existence. *He* is the center. *He* is the focus. *He* is the goal. Whatever does not have Christ and service to him in his kingdom at the center is sin. To whatever extent he and his rule are not the center, there is a corruption of priorities, a reversal of means and ends.

If service to Christ in his kingdom is a goal of life, then it is all important that his righteousness be the first and foremost goal of life. For service in his kingdom is not possible and will never be possible apart from his righteousness. And where will we find his righteousness? Again, we have returned to the basics of our faith. His righteousness is found in the gospel alone. His righteousness is the white robe of innocence that he wraps around us when God declares us forgiven because of Jesus' holy cross and passion. For the opposite of righteousness is guilt. When guilt is removed, there is righteousness—there is no third possibility. Yes, and it is by this righteousness given in the gospel that his kingdom comes to us and is preserved in us. Where his righteousness is not, there his kingdom is not; where his righteousness is, there his kingdom is, and there we will be in service to him and to all around us.

Thus the kingdom of God and his righteousness are the ends, the goals of life. The gospel in Word and sacraments is the means by which God gives us his righteousness and establishes his kingdom in us. What then becomes of work, of family, of the struggle to survive, of accomplishments, and even of pleasures in this life? Do they mean nothing when we establish priorities and sort out ends and means?

Jesus does not say that hard work or ambition or respect and honor or planning for the future are bad things in and of themselves. Indeed, often the Scriptures urge us to work hard, to have a good name in the world, and even to plan to some extent for the future. Indeed, God warns us often in his Word that lazy indifference to work and responsibility in the world is a mark of unbelief (e.g., 1 Th 4:11,12; 2 Th 3:6-13; 1 Ti 5:8). The question is not whether such things are good or bad in themselves. The question is this: Are these things *ends* or *means*? Jesus dealt with the problem of ambition that had become a misplaced priority even in his disciples. They quarreled about which one of them was most important. Jesus showed them that their ambition to be first was good only if it was a means to another end and not an end in itself. What was the end, the goal, that ambition should have? *Service* (Mt 5:14-16; Mk 10:42-45; Ro 13; 1 Pe 3:13-18)! That's the one-word goal of hard work, of respect, of planning: *service!* It is service that is done in submission to the Word of God and in accord with his commandments. It is service that seeks the good and the benefit of the family, the church, and society in general. It is service that always has in mind the honor of God and the benefit of my neighbor. It is service which is useful in displaying to the perishing world the peace and joy of the one whose life is hidden in Christ.

Thus, though work, respect, and honor, and the things of the world are not the goals and ends of life, they are important as *means.* They are not means for *finding* or *gaining* the kingdom of God and his righteousness, but they are means for demonstrating that we *have* the kingdom of God and his righteousness. For those in the kingdom of God who already possess his righteousness given freely in the gospel also have and use the things of this world. Jesus says as much at the end of the verse—"all these things will be given to you as well" (Mt 6:33). If these things were of no importance, Jesus would not have promised to give them to us. Food and clothing, friends and family, respect and honor, health and wealth, and the abilities to attain and keep them—all these too are gifts of our most generous God. They are gifts given not as the ends or goals of life but gifts given for us to use in service. They are means to that end, to the end of service to him. We can list ways in which all these things are means to an end, rather than ends in themselves. God's gifts of earthly things are:

✠ *Means* that move us to the *end* of thanksgiving to God for his gracious and abundant generosity (e.g., Ps 105, 106, 107).

✠ *Means* through which God even gives us leisure and enjoyment to the *end* that we may have energy and zeal for further work in his service. Consider, for example, his Old Testament institution of the Sabbath as a day of rest from work to prepare one for work. Think of his arrangement of day and night, so that we may rest from work in order to be fit for work.

✠ *Means* to the *end* of service to our family, of service to the church in the work of proclaiming the gospel, of service to those in need in the world.

Is it not clear that *priorities,* this whole matter of *means* and *ends,* is upside down in the world, outside of the kingdom of God and his righteousness? For those outside of the kingdom of God and his righteousness, all these *means* have become *ends.* Whether we are thinking of health and wealth, friends and family, food and drink, or work and pleasure, to those outside of the kingdom any and all these are the reasons for living and the goals of life. That one should have and enjoy them is what life is all about. Without them life is bitter and meaningless. Indeed, even with them life may be bitter if those around me do not grasp that the real reason for their existence is my pleasure! And how many will ever grasp that they exist primarily for my use and pleasure? The result? Again, disappointment, frustration, and an ever deeper sinking into the abyss of futility in the worship of the dead gods of greed and ambition.

Yes, we cannot help but call to mind again Jesus' words when he presents us in Mark 8 with the imagined alternative to bearing the cross: "What good is it for a man to gain the whole world, yet forfeit his soul? Or what can a man give in exchange for his soul?" (Mk 8:36,37). Confused priorities. A reversal of ends and means. It all comes down to a fool's bargain. Even if the whole world could be gained, it still would be a fool's bargain. On the other hand, the kingdom of God and his righteousness are free! They bring with them and have as their very essence the forgiveness of sins, life, and salvation.

What better incentive could there be than that for a continual examination and reexamination of our priorities to make sure that we have means and ends in their proper places? God gives us all so that we are free to serve all. Having all things from him, we labor to use all things for him. Friends and family are there as his gifts for me to enjoy with thanksgiving and, more important, to serve. Health and wealth I enjoy for a time so that I may serve with them those whom God has given to me to serve. Even the gospel itself is a gift given so that I may give it away, first of all to those nearest and dearest, then through the work of the church and my own Christian witness in word and deed to those near and far.

Where priorities are out of order and means have become ends, disappointment and frustration will never be far away. Where the kingdom of God and his righteousness are first, everything else that we need (as distinguished from everything else that the flesh may want) comes from the hand of God in due course. That's the promise of the one who does not lie! There may be times when the truth of this passage is difficult to see. Just at such times the Lord in his mercy is calling us to readjust our priorities; he is calling us to take another look and to see if we have allowed means and ends to be reversed. Sometimes we do not realize the extent to which means have become ends until we lose some of those things that we have come to value too highly as ends in themselves. As noted earlier, at times the extent to which we grieve excessively over a loss is the extent to which we had become too attached to it. Loss then can indeed be *das liebe Kreuz,* the *dear* cross, through which a loving and merciful God calls us back to himself.

We have but scratched the surface of the special temptations and crosses of the middle years of life. But many if not most of the other special temptations and consequent crosses will fit into this general scheme of things: Where priorities are confused, where means and ends are reversed, there we can expect to bring needless pain, frustration, disappointment, and suffering on ourselves and those around us. These can all become crosses that the Lord sends to bring us back to himself. As well, they can all be tools in the devil's toolbox to drive us still further away from Christ and his cross. Which will they be for you and me? The question is never an idle one. Its God-pleasing answer is found in the cross and not apart from it. It is found in his cross of redemption. It is found in our own humble and patient, yes, joyful embrace and bearing of the crosses he sends us in our lifetime. The simple fact that during these years we have so many and important distractions should serve to make us all the more watchful. Sheer default and carelessness have shipwrecked more souls than any one sudden outbreak of wickedness.

Indeed, carelessness and indifference are usually the parents of wickedness.

Special crosses in the golden years

If the most prominent spark for the cross in youth is unruly passion, if the hallmark that presages the cross in the middle years is a confusion of priorities and the reversal of means and

187

ends, then the most common source of the cross in the golden years may well be *calluses on the soul.*

By the time we reach old age, we have seen and come through many battles. We have lived through the passions of youth. We have perhaps often tasted the heady wine of ambition and then choked on the bitter dregs of disappointment. We have learned painful lessons about the perversity of human nature—not just our own but the perversity found in so many whom we have loved or respected or served. Friends may leave without a thought. Children go away and do not look back, at least not as much as we think they should. The workplace sends us away and pushes us aside and would rather that we did not keep popping up, as though life couldn't go on without us.

All these are intimations of old age. When it arrives in full bore, still greater indignities may await us. We don't tell people what to do anymore; they tell us what to do, often in tones reminiscent of the tones we used years ago when speaking to children. The respect to which we thought we were entitled degenerates into impatience with our slowness. The people in a hurry, the people who really matter because they are young and active, look at us as though we were just in the way, just wasting space. Add to all of this the weaknesses and the illnesses and all sorts of infirmities that may assault the body and the mind in advanced years, and the picture is reasonably complete: We always imagined that we were in control; now it is all too clear that we are not. It's a painful, bitter pill to swallow!

The result? Calluses on the soul! A man may sink into mindless grumpiness. He has been bruised and wounded too often. Now he lets no one in to his mind or his soul. He lived for his work, and now others do it. He got respect for his skills and had friends with whom he shared his interests. But now all that is going or gone. He long ago traded interest in his wife for his work or his hobbies or the friends with whom he shared work and hobbies. As all these leave, he can no longer relate to the wife of his youth, who in turn long ago gave up any expectation that he really cared about her, her wants, or her needs.

His wife, in fact, has also found herself in a world of disappointment that leaves her too with calluses on the soul. She can no longer find fulfillment by managing the lives of her children; they are grown up and gone. So she looks for meaning in manipulation. Brushing her indifferent husband aside, she finds ways to keep the lives of others in constant turmoil; that's how she makes it clear to all and sundry that she is still important and a force to be reckoned with. If from time to time she suspects that the objects of her manipulation resent her more than love her, she does not change her behavior. She just becomes more bitter and more resentful, more calloused.

When disease or just the frailty that attends advancing years finally makes it impossible for us to control much of anything in our lives, the calluses on the soul can display their full ugliness. Others have to take care of us. We are dependent on them. But that care does not always beget gratitude. Quite to the contrary, the pain of both body and mind make us all the more grumpy and impatient, all the more irritable and demanding. Surely there must be a special place in heaven for those Christian souls who take care of us when we are like that and who do it with grace, with gentleness, with kindness, even with respect for what little is left of our dignity!

How everything changes only to stay the same! If we think about it, the condition just described is the perfectly logical outcome for those who lost battles against passion in youth and the struggle against twisted priorities in the middle years. For the grumpy old man and the manipulating old woman have both given way to the rule of emotion and to behavior that has *self* and the moment at its center. It is the behavior of those who have begun to see the futility of their greed and ambition, their desire to get their own way and to control things. Vain and futile though it be, it is all that they know and they will not give it up. But now it is a hopeless struggle carried on in obvious bitterness, a sort of vain raging against the winds and the fates.

How do we deal with the calluses on the soul? How do we see in the special circumstances of old age the cross of Christ and our own cross? We want to embrace both of them as gifts that have come to us from the God of all grace and mercy. Perhaps never in our lifetime are the alternatives as clear as they should be for us in old age.

✠ With advancing years, ambition has to be replaced with a certain resignation that the years of gain and upward mobility are over. We can become bitter about the loss and let that callus cover our soul. Or we can give thanks to God that the silliness and vanity of so much of our life is finally over and done with so that we can see more clearly that only one thing is needed; that one thing is everything that we have fully and freely in Jesus and in his Word.

✠ The body is losing its ability to bounce back from sickness; sight and hearing are failing; organs that always worked before now hurt more than they work. We can get angry and bore everyone to death with our endless complaints of aches and pains; we can even shake an occasional fist at God for letting us suffer thus. Or we can look to the cross of Christ and say: "You embraced this pain that I feel and so much more because you loved me and desired only my salvation. I was your priority, not your own comfort and ease! Now in my pain I marvel still more at your love for me." We can recognize in the loss of strength and vitality God's hand, as he sweeps away all the distractions and the noise of life, so that we can focus on that one thing needful.

✠ We are becoming ever more dependent on those around us for help and care. Our loss of control over our lives and bodies can make us bitter and resentful; it can become an excuse to unleash our anger at those who have taken control away from us. Or with our glory as sons and daughters of God hidden securely in Christ, it can become our goal to make the work of those who care for us as pleasant for them as possible. That is, after all, a service that we can still perform. Given the difficulty of their task, that's no small service. It is no small virtue to know how to accept service from others with gratitude rather than grumbling. We rejoiced in our day to serve; now it is time to rejoice in the service of others, to let them know that we appreciate their help and that we pray for them and thank God for them.

✠ The specter of death draws ever closer. Friends and loved ones die every year. Our own frailty together with the death of loved ones makes it harder and harder to pretend that death only happens to other people. The devil grabs us by the throat in the middle of the night to whisper in our ear, "And you too must die!" He, as Luther reminds us so often, likes nothing better than in these last days of our life to dredge up all our failures, all our sins, and throw them in a heap on our head and in our face. The memory of past sins, of things done to hurt others, of things left undone that could have helped another, these are heavy burdens indeed. It may drive us to the point of despair. Or under the weight of the cross, we can run to the gospel, run to the sacraments, run to the promises of Jesus. When we are too enfeebled to run anywhere else, where better could there be for us still to run! In his promises and at his cross, we can find sure and certain refuge from the storms that swirl around us during the last great battle for our souls.

So much in life and in death is a matter of attitude. We can let the calluses on our souls become rock hard and ugly by making our failing and dying selves the center of our attention. Or we can in every ache and pain, in every loss and disappointment, look up as the disciples did on the Mount of Transfiguration (Mt 17:8) and see no one except Jesus. With every ache and pain, in every loss and disappointment, he is cutting the cords that bind us to this life and the shackles that have for so long chained us to the world. He is getting us ready to rejoice on the great day of our homecoming to him and to his Father's house. He is magnifying in our souls his own love for us that moved him to suffer all pain and sorrow, even the torments of hell, to bring us to where we shall see him as he is.

After all is said and done, our loss of control in our old age merely makes more obvious what has been true all along: We never were really in control, even on our strongest and most successful day. The only difference between the times of frailty in old age and the vigor of youth is that in old age we recognize the reality much more readily—and with the end of the vain struggles of life, we have much more reason to give thanks for that reality. The reality is that God has kept his promises. He has not forsaken us. He has remained our strength and stay every step of the way. And in the last and fearsome struggle he will not change his promises or his saving habits toward us.

St. Paul's attitude puts the whole matter into beautiful focus. He was in prison. He expected that his life would end soon in martyrdom. Many were the crosses he had already borne. Many were the burdens and trials and afflictions. But now they were all coming to an end. And this is what he says as that day draws nearer: "The time has come for my departure. I have fought the good fight, I have finished the race, I have kept the faith. Now there is in store for me the crown of righteousness, which the Lord, the righteous Judge, will award to me on that day—and not only to me, but also to all who have longed for his appearing" (2 Ti 4:6-8).

Did you notice it? No calluses! His life had been an exhausting race. His epistles bear witness to it, that his work gave him one fight after another. And many of those battles, doubtless the most difficult and painful ones, were with members of the congregations that he had founded and served so faithfully. But there is no trace of bitterness in his tone. There is only gratitude for the time he had served, and yes, gratitude for the fact that that time was now passed. What a model for us! We had the honor to serve; now we have the honor to lay down the burdens of service and fill our hearts and souls with what lies ahead: a crown of righteousness placed on our heads by him who is our righteousness. What lies ahead is Jesus! What is there for us to complain about?

So there are but two tasks to focus on as the end draws near: Ever more to see Jesus only and, as much as possible, to serve still by making the work of those around as easy for them as possible, as we pray for them and give thanks for them. In the process by word and deed, we make a good confession; we let those near and dear and those who serve us know that our confidence, our hope, our peace is all in Christ. With him we died in Baptism and were raised again to life. With him we are ready to pass through the valley of the shadow of death and on into an eternity of triumph in heaven. Because of him we will soon pass from imitating him in his humiliation to sharing with him his exaltation. *Wer so stirbt, stirbt wohl!* "He who dies thus dies well!"

8

The Special Crosses of Pastors and the Visible Church

Now this was John's testimony when the Jews of Jerusalem sent priests and Levites to ask him who he was. He did not fail to confess, but confessed freely, "I am not the Christ." They asked him, "Then who are you? Are you Elijah?" He said, "I am not." "Are you the Prophet?" He answered, "No." Finally they said, "Who are you? Give us an answer to take back to those who sent us. What do you say about yourself?" John replied in the words of Isaiah the prophet, "I am the voice of one calling in the desert, 'Make straight the way for the Lord.'" . . . "He is the one who comes after me, the thongs of whose sandals I am not worthy to untie." . . . The next day John saw Jesus coming toward him and said, "Look, the Lamb of God, who takes away the sin of the world! This is the one I meant when I said, 'A man who comes after me has surpassed me because he was before me.'" . . . The next day John was there again with two of his disciples. When he saw Jesus passing by, he said, "Look, the Lamb of God!" (Jn 1:19-35)

When asked about Jesus, whose following was increasing at John's expense, John replied, "A man can receive only what is given him from heaven. You yourselves can testify that I said, 'I am not the Christ but am sent ahead of him.' The bride belongs to the bridegroom. The friend who attends the bridegroom waits and listens for him, and is full of joy when he hears the bridegroom's voice. That joy is mine, and it is now complete. *He must become greater; I must become less*" (Jn 3:27-30).

John the Baptist remains for us the best exemplar of both the glory and the cross that belongs to the church and its pastors. These verses sum it all up. So too do the favorite depictions of St. John in painting and in sculpture; he is portrayed with a lamb at his feet and a cross in his hand. Hanging around the cross is a banner inscribed with the words *Ecce Angus Dei!* "Behold the Lamb of God!" That is the whole work of the church and, therefore, the pastor's whole occupation, to proclaim to the lambs at his feet the work of the Lamb, who takes away the sin of the world by his suffering and death on the cross. The only thing missing that would make the depiction still more fitting would be the addition of the last words from the verses cited above: *"He must become greater; I must become less."*

And faithful pastors do this in the context of Jesus' promise to his disciples, "I tell you the truth, anyone who has faith in me will do what I have been doing. He will do even greater things than these, because I am going to the Father" (Jn 14:12). Just think of it! The master promises that his servants will do greater works than cleansing lepers, feeding thousands, raising the dead! And that while they strive to become less and less, so that by the works they do he may become greater and greater! It boggles the mind! And his Word is true. Greater works than these, works that match his best, we do. For day in and day out, year after year, Jesus uses us to proclaim his salvation in all the world. And that message, just as he promised, calls in and saves the elect out of every land and language.

Those of us who are pastors might do well if we would set aside June 24 (the Feast of the Nativity of St. John the Baptist) and June 25 (the Feast of the Presentation of the Augsburg Confession) to consider anew what our service is really all about, both its glory and its unique crosses. The dates are especially appropriate since for most pastors they fall so close to the anniversary dates of ordination into the holy office of the ministry. As well, they fall close to the great festival days of Ascension and Pentecost, days that close in triumph our yearly pilgrimage through the Half Year of Our Lord. We have just concluded our annual journey with our *Lord of the Cross* in the preaching and teaching of all that he has done for us and for our salvation. June 24 and 25 fall also at the close of the busiest times of the year for pastors; school is out and most of the organizational activity in a parish tends to fall into low gear.

What better or more convenient time could there be for us to refocus or to sharpen our focus on our high calling under the cross of Christ and in imitation of our great forebear, St. John the Baptist? No mere mortal ever showed us the way better than he. It's all about Christ, not about me. It's all about pointing to Christ, the sacrifice for sinners of whom I am chief, as that other great model for the ministry put it. Yes, it's all about getting lambs to think more and more about Christ and less and less about me. Even in his death St. John carried out his great theme of "He must become greater; I must become less." For no martyr ever died more shamefully; St. John died, not as a great hero making a bold confession like St. Stephen but at the whim of a drunkard following the lead of a bimbo.

If every Christian individually must bear the cross, then it would be surprising indeed if the servants of the church did not also have crosses to bear. The crosses of pastors are like those of everyone else and yet different enough to merit some separate attention. When Christians, as we have already noted, fail to carry the cross, they do great damage to themselves and to others. But when pastors fail to carry their crosses, the damage is even greater. They should be patterns of submission and humble obedience to the Word, patterns who draw the sheep and lambs ever closer to Christ. Theirs is a great and holy calling. If they instead become patterns of self-service in ambition, in greed, in an unholy doctrine or a disgraceful life, then the sheep more easily stray and fall prey to the wolf because of it.

The Bible motivates us with its abundant testimony to the holiness of the pastor's calling both in its blessings for the pastor himself and in its blessings for those he serves. John the Baptist considered it nothing but joy to see Christ his Savior and to bear witness to Christ's saving work to all who would listen. St. Paul counted everything trash and loss in comparison to the glory of having Christ and proclaiming Christ (Php 3:7,8). In the pastoral epistles Paul repeatedly urges pastors to embrace Christ and the cross because of the benefit both to themselves and to those they serve. Indeed there is no greater joy in the world than to spend one's life in the heart of God; that is exactly where we are when we are studying the Scriptures and proclaiming their sacred and saving truths in preaching and teaching and in the administration of the blessed sacraments.

But as great as the blessings are for us and those we serve, just so great is the desire of the devil to rob us and our hearers of those blessings. Therefore, the warnings of the law directed at pastors are more urgent and ominous than they are for anyone else. If they despise their holy office by neglect or indifference, if they fail to deny *self* and to faithfully carry the cross when faithfulness is costly, the judgment and wrath of God will not miss its mark. Listing passages of warning would fill the page. Warnings fill the books of Jeremiah and Ezekiel in particular. We will be content to note just a couple of examples. Moses, the greatest of the prophets, failed just once as far as we know. The failure at first glance seems so small, especially when compared to the frequent and blatant failures of his people. He struck a rock when God had told him only to speak to it (Nu 20:1-12). But that was disobedience. It set a bad example. It failed in the presence of the people to honor God with obedience. For that one seemingly or relatively insignificant act, Moses lost the honor of entering the Promised Land.

Then we have the example of the prophet sent by God to rebuke Jeroboam in 1 Kings 13. God told the prophet to deliver the message and return home without stopping to eat or to drink. The prophet faithfully, even heroically and at great risk, delivered the message. But then he let himself be deceived by another; he turned aside for a meal on his way home. That disobedience seems so small compared to the disobedience of Jeroboam and the other idol worshipers. Yet they all lived; the prophet was killed by a lion. Jesus said it all: "From everyone who has been given much, much will be demanded; and from the one who has been entrusted with much, much more will be asked" (Lk 12:48).

Let us therefore embrace the cross with the strength given in the gospel and the encouragement offered so richly for the work of our holy office. Let us rejoice in the promise and presence of the Savior and the gracious companionship of the Holy Spirit, as he watches over and blesses our work with his precious means of grace. And let us take to heart the warnings against self-service and use the examples of unfaithfulness as clubs to the sinful flesh. For the devil will never give up inciting the flesh to shun the cross and to go again to the worship of *self.* If both the encouragement and the warning are necessary for all Christians, they are most certainly necessary for the servants of the gospel!

The cross of the young pastor

Let us consider the crosses of the leaders of the church, its pastors. In some interesting ways they run along parallel lines with the crosses of everyone else in the three stages of life already discussed. At the same time, the pastor's vocation lends some unique characteristics to the shape that the cross takes.

The young graduate from the seminary comes to his first parish full of passion in a good sense of the word. He has spent four years in seminary training, in addition to the years of college and perhaps of high school in courses designed to prepare him for service to the church. He is dedicated. He is eager. He is highly qualified for the work ahead of him. He has studied the Scriptures in the original languages and learned how to use those languages in that study for the rest of his life. He knows that his training in the Scriptures will enrich him and countless souls entrusted to his care for the rest of his life.

He has ambition that is focused on the kingdom of God and his righteousness. He has seen from church history long past and from history that he has viewed close up how much damage a pastor or teacher can do to the kingdom of God. He is determined not to make the mistakes of those who have gone before him. He will be the best pastor that he can be. Since he is not going to make the mistakes that he has seen others make, he is confident that he will succeed where they have failed! At the same time he knows in his head that he should not be arrogant and should not worship at the shrine of outward glory and success. He knows that he should embrace the cross and follow Christ under it, and that is certainly what he wants to do.

Although he was taught the theology of the cross at the seminary, he has not yet discovered that the theology of the cross also has to be caught as much as taught. That is, God teaches it in his Word and shows us what it is really all about in life. And so our young pastor arrives at his first parish. After his years of training, he thinks himself ready to answer all the tough questions that his people might put to him. After his experience as a vicar or a parish assistant, he expects that he is ready to go forth to feed the lambs, to strengthen the sheep, and to win the heathen for Christ. After his many years in the classroom at the feet of good and perhaps also some not-so-good teachers, he thinks that he knows what to do and what to avoid in teaching others. He thinks he knows how to teach so that children and adults will hang on his every word and then do just what he has told them that Jesus wants them to do. Our new pastor may be only dimly aware that he has thoughts such as these or that his thinking verges on arrogance. But most experienced pastors will chuckle with the wisdom that comes from age and experience at reading these words: Yes, deep down inside, that is what I thought back then!

Then life happens. Then Jesus begins to teach him the theology of the cross all over again. The cross comes. The pastor shouldn't be surprised, since that is what Christ promised. But he is surprised and taken aback by it. Lo and behold, not everyone listens. They all promised at his ordination to support him when he correctly applied the Word of Truth. But when he refuses to bury someone whose confession is that of an unbeliever, the relatives get angry with him. When he wouldn't marry the couple who insisted on a service that blatantly contradicted the Word of God, some people left the church. When he refuses to give Holy Communion to someone's visiting relative who is not a member of a church in fellowship with us, still more people get upset. Last Sunday he noticed that someone slept through the whole sermon! Two weeks ago children in confirmation class didn't bother to do their homework—yes, and angry mothers called when he rebuked the children for their unfaithfulness. As for his Bible class, well, he is doing the best he can, but interest in it is still slight.

Then there are the evangelism calls and the delinquent calls. That's real mission work. But he is astonished at how many people are in no hurry to get to heaven and at how little they care about their souls' salvation. They promise to come but then do not come. Others are rude in their rejection of the invitation to the banquet of heaven and eternal life. Still others come for a little while but then get upset over one thing and another; they go away more fixed in their rejection of the gospel than they were before.

Then there is the problem of time management; he needs time to prepare, time to get out from behind his desk, time for counseling people, time for evangelism and delinquent calls, time for visiting members and getting to know them and their needs better, time for sick calls and shut-in calls, time for his family, time to think and time to pray. But there are only 24 hours in a day. After six months or a year, our young pastor is already beginning to feel old and certainly overwhelmed.

To be sure, some gladly hear the Word. Someone came out of church last Sunday morning and whispered in a small voice, "Thank you, Pastor! How did you know that that is exactly what I needed to hear?" There are some ushers and some members of the council and some others who faithfully and gladly do all that they can to help the pastor and the church. There are some who stick it out in an adult instruction course; either in the class or privately, the pastor does at times get to see the Holy Spirit work when the light goes on in someone's eyes at the message: Yes, Jesus died for you too!

But the number of those who help, who listen, who appreciate the pastor's efforts in their behalf and in Jesus' name seems so small. And their encouragement seems small too next to the frustration that comes from dealing with the indifference and the aggravation that is piled on by those who are never satisfied. There should be more help and fewer excuses, more listening and less indifference to the Word, more appreciation and less complaining, less nit-picking!

The pastor may have expected so much more, yes so much more than what Christ promised. He may have expected more glory and less cross. He may have expected, not to decrease but to increase. Indeed, his members may have expected that too. Many a congregation welcomes a young graduate with the expectation that he is young but possesses the wisdom that comes with 40 years of experience! With his youth he can do everything, and with the imagined 40 years of experience, he can do it all quickly and perfectly. Their disappointment that he is not more successful than he is only compounds his own disappointment.

The pastor is at a crossroad. How will he deal with his own weariness and frustration and disappointment? To put it another way, what will he do with the cross? The road with Jesus in the lead goes straight ahead, but it is strewn with rocks and thorns and thistles, watered often by tears. Numerous side paths with Jesus only in sight but not in the lead, turn off in other directions. At first it is easy to see Jesus on those paths, and the side paths have the allure that they do seem less bumpy, less strewn with thorns and thistles. But watch out! The farther along one goes on them, the more distant Jesus becomes until he is altogether out of sight. Those on such pathways may remember Jesus, but he has ceased to be the priority. "He must become greater, and I must become less" long ago became an empty slogan.

What is there that tempts the young pastor to turn aside from the way of the cross? What is on those side roads that is so appealing?

The central and most compelling temptation is that which is common to us all when we are young. We focus way too much on self. The passion of youth, including a passion for good and noble things, is often, whether consciously or unconsciously, *self* centered, rather than *Christ* centered. And so:

✛ If *I* don't get this mission to grow, everybody will blame *me* when it fails or closes.

✛ If *I* were a better preacher, people would listen and come; *I* must be doing something wrong or *I* would be more successful. How come they don't like *me*?

✠ Maybe it will work if *I* tell more funny stories in the sermon; maybe then they will like *me* and listen to *me;* perhaps less about repentance and more about—well, about anything else will work.

✠ Maybe if *I* am not so strict in doctrine and practice, maybe if *I* give a little here and a little there, *I* will grow this church faster; we can get around to the "tough stuff" later when they are more mature and like *me* well enough to listen to it.

✠ Yes, maybe if *I* don't ruffle too many feathers, the officials of the district and the synod will see what a fine pastor *I* am, and *I* will finally get a call to a place that will really appreciate *me.*

Oh, how clever the devil is! As he plants these weeds in the pastor's soul, he throws dust in his eyes, so that our young curate still imagines that his heart is pure and his goals are noble. What, however, is the reality? The one who succumbs to thoughts such as these has started to forget the basics of his ministry. He is forgetting the promise of Christ, that many are invited, but few are chosen (Mt 22:14). He is forgetting that Jesus did not call him to be successful or popular but to be faithful—consider the examples of John the Baptist, of all the prophets, of St. Paul.

To put it another way, he is forgetting that there is only one means of grace—the gospel in Word and sacraments—and there is only one Savior of the world. The pastor is not the means of grace; he is the trumpet, not the tune. It is the sound of the gospel that converts and preserves faith. As important as the trumpet is, it is the tune of the gospel that accomplishes everything. He is not a second messiah either, as though it were his responsibility to save the world by his efforts, his eloquence, his personality, his charisma. There is but one Redeemer of the world, one Savior of each individual whom God has elected. Each of the elect will hear the tune played by the Holy Spirit in the gospel; in the Spirit's own good time (not the pastor's!) they will believe it and be saved by it. That we are the trumpet and not the tune, the messengers of salvation and not the Messiah, is both our great comfort and our highest honor.

If the pastor begins to think that success is his to achieve and salvation his to provide by his own skill and cleverness, then he has started down a perilous path indeed. He has laid aside the cross. Having discovered that talk of the cross turns people off, he stops calling others to bear it as well. He may now become more popular, more outwardly successful. But he is not preparing Christ's flock for his return. On judgment day such a pastor may hear with his unprepared members the dread words "I tell you the truth, I don't know you" (Mt 25:12).

That is not to say that the pastor should be indifferent to the quality of his work with the Word and with God's people. Not at all! He should strive, as St. Paul urged Timothy (1 Ti 4), to be diligent and zealous in his teaching and preaching and in his daily life as well. But the diligence is directed to faithfulness to the Word and to service. It is all done out of love for Jesus and out of love for those who will be saved by Jesus alone through the Word alone. No one was ever saved by false doctrine or compromises with false doctrine. Nor was anyone ever delivered from the devil's snares because his pastor was nothing more than popular and pleasant. What needs to be kept in mind here is that at first the line may be a very thin one between zeal for Jesus and his Word and love for his flock, on the one hand, and a growing preoccupation with self and one's own welfare and popularity, on the other.

So what is the cure? The pastor in whose heart these temptations take root has almost certainly abandoned a private devotional life. He is busy, so busy. He has looked for ways of saving time so that he can get more work done in the service of the Lord. The first corner to cut is in the time that he spends alone with Jesus in his private devotions. After all, does he really need that? He is always "in the Word" isn't he? He is studying the text for his next sermon. He is preparing for Bible class. He has a devotion in mind for his next round of hospital and shut-in calls. He even conducts family devotions with his wife and children. Why does he need more than that for himself?

He needs more than that for himself because of the special temptations that the devil has just for pastors, namely, those temptations already described. Just as Jesus so often in the gospels took the disciples aside to talk to them privately, so Jesus wants to take his pastor aside and speak to him about the temptations unique to his holy office. He wants to call him away from temptations to arrogance when things go well and temptations to despair when they do not. He wants to call him away from the siren summons to success. He wants to call him away from contempt for the ungrateful and the stubborn, the indifferent and the careless. He wants to call him to repentance for his own sins first. He wants him to see the patience that Jesus still has even for his pastor. He wants to catch him again and again with the net of his grace and mercy. He wants the pastor ever and again to be lost in wonder and awe at the love and patience of Christ for the lost, the erring, the foolish, the perverse, the love and patience of Christ—in a word—for him!

Yes, Jesus wants to call his pastor to the cross! He wants his pastor to see how special the love of God is for his church: the Lord gives it his best gifts in the apostles and prophets, in faithful pastors and teachers. He gives it those gifts to be used and used up for his own glory. And in the process he gives to those he has called to serve a rich and over-rich abundance of grace and blessing for his ministry, for his own soul first and for his special bearing of his cross. And he does that as he takes his pastor aside day after day and speaks to him in his faithful Word. He does it in fulfillment of his promise, just as he did it for the apostles and prophets of old; he loved them too—and most of them according to tradition suffered a martyr's death as evidence of their love for him and loyalty to his Word. In the ancient church the martyr's crown was highly prized as an evidence of God's special love, for as God gave his dearly beloved Son on the cross as a gift to his church, so in love he gives still his best gifts, even unto death, out of love for the church! What honor to be loved by God that much, that we should be used and used up for his church!

And what will the pastor discover if he refuses the shortcut of abandoning his own devotional life? What will he find if day after day he buries himself in the heart of God, as he listens to his voice in the Word?

✠ Little by little, more and more, he will marvel at the mercy of God, not just for his members but especially

205

for himself. For no one has less excuse for his sins than a pastor. But Jesus still loves pastors too!

✠ Little by little, more and more, he will marvel at the ways in which God stirs the soup of human experience. He will notice it in the lives of members, as God strives to get their attention with his special mix of pleasant things and suffering. And then he will notice it in his own life; he will see how just when he thought that all was lost, God arranged some little blessing, some little success, some little kindness from an unexpected quarter to assure his pastor that his work was not in vain—just as God promised that it would not be in vain.

✠ Little by little, more and more, he will come to appreciate and give thanks for the miracles of grace that God used him to accomplish. God could have picked someone else to baptize that baby, someone else to usher that dying member into heaven, someone else to bring salvation to that lost soul, someone else to help rescue that one failing marriage. But he didn't. God picked him! What a wonder! What a gift! What grace! Yes, Sunday after Sunday, holy day after holy day, some are still there to hear the message that God gave him to proclaim from his Word. They could be somewhere else, doing something else or nothing else, but they are here. What an honor God has bestowed on him that he should be counted worthy to speak to them in his name! What an honor these people have shown him that they have come to hear God speak through him! "Who is equal to such a task? . . . Our competence comes from God" (2 Cor. 2:16; 3:5).

✠ Little by little, more and more, he may come at the end of his devotions to pray the prayer that Luther learned to love in the monastery. In the face of weariness and frustration and disappointments, he may look into the face of God and say, *Benedictus Deus in omnibus donis suis!* "Blessed be God in all his gifts!" That is such a great pastor's prayer, especially at the beginning of the day. As he faces challenges and more to do than can get done, the pastor does well to begin the worship of the day with thanksgiving for all that God has done and still will do, even through his own ever-faltering efforts!

✠ In sum, little by little, more and more, he may discover that the means of grace, the gospel, really does work! No matter what the outward evidence in the moment, God sustains his pastor's faith and, yes, his joy, through the gospel promises. Thus strengthened and reminded of his baptism, the pastor can go forth refreshed and renewed; the old man has again been drowned and the new man has come forth to serve and to serve and, then again, to serve.

Yes, maybe we pastors should set aside June 24 or 25 to go and find a cave somewhere where we could just sit for a while and think on these things. It certainly would be very worthwhile from time to time just to go back again to Mark 8:34: "If anyone would come after me, he must deny himself and take up his cross and follow me." The pastor's cross is that, for the sake of the gospel, he will endure opposition, not just from the world but most painfully also at times from some of his own members when he is faithful to the Savior. But even more, the pastor's cross is the struggle against himself; it is the struggle to put Jesus and his Word first, followed by the souls entrusted to his care and those who may yet be entrusted to his care through his faithful proclamation of the gospel.

Even more important, however, than a yearly examination of ourselves and our motives in the light of God's Word is this that we do not abandon our daily private hours with Jesus. Through those precious hours spent with him, we will grow in knowledge and in grace, sustained and strengthened by his Word. That is his promise; it is a promise we share with our people and a promise we should be the first to trust!

Will our private devotional life make every pathway smooth? Will it end our frustrations and our weariness? Of course not. For Jesus never promised that our pathway should be smooth and our labor without frustration or weariness. What he did promise

was that he would give us strength for the day and that ultimately our labor would not be in vain. He will show us that when
and where it pleases him. And when he does not show it, it will
nevertheless remain true, because he said so. Apart from that
Word, there is only the prospect of temptations that defeat us
and crush us and make us unfit in doctrine, in life, or in both for
the holy and noble calling he has given us.

There are, of course, times when God does show the success of
his gospel in the hearts of those we serve with it. There are times
when congregations flourish and grow even beyond our fondest
expectations. There are times when a parish is at peace and when
members are not shy in expressing their thanks to their pastors.
When that happens we are on our knees in adoration and thanksgiving for *his* success. For if we are busy congratulating ourselves
instead of thanking him, then we will need to blame ourselves as
well when things do not go so well. The point is, that in good days
and bad no one has a better reason to give thanks to God for all
his grace and blessing than a pastor. And no one has more reason
to be grateful for his calling in life than one whose vocation it is to
always become less, so that Jesus may become greater!

The cross of the mature pastor

All that has just been said with reference to a young pastor
applies, of course, to a pastor of any age or experience. Nevertheless, there is a new cross and struggle that comes to a pastor of
some experience. It is the cross of a kind of professional*ism*. To
be sure it should be expected of a mature pastor that he is and
acts in a professional manner. That is, he knows the difference
between being warm and personable, on the one hand, and care-
lessly chummy, on the other. He knows how to be dignified without being stuffy. He knows how to present himself as one whose
authority comes from Christ for service as opposed to acting like
the lord and master of Christ's flock. He knows that he is where
he is to serve, not to be served or to "do his own thing."

But in knowing all these and related things there is a temptation. The temptation is that he sees himself as, or begins to act
like, nothing more than a religious professional. The heart sur-
geon who has performed one thousand bypass operations no
longer thinks of doing a heart bypass the way he did when he

performed his first ten such operations. To a considerable extent this amazing surgery may become routine for him. The pastor can fall into that kind of thinking as well; he can fall into professionalism. If he gave up on his private devotional life when he was younger, it would be very easy indeed for him to slip into the attitude of the professional religious person. He knows how to smile when he should. He knows how to look caring and concerned when he should. He knows how to be available for some people and some problems and how to be too busy for some other people and some other problems.

In short, his vocation has degenerated into a business like any other; it has become little more than an occupation. He has about as much love for his people as the grocer might have for the customer in the aisle. Members have become customers; they are a means to an end, the end of providing him with a living. He does not want to be part of their lives, to carry their burdens with them, and to share their joys. The picture of Jesus as the Good Shepherd and the good pastor, who gives his life for the sheep, has long ago faded from his image of his own calling. The examples of St. John the Baptist, of St. Paul, and the exhortations of the pastoral epistles no longer inspire him. If anything, they only give him a slightly guilty conscience. When the telephone rings, he secretly sighs within: *Now what?*

As for his sermons, well, what can we say? If he gave up on a private devotional life in order to save time, there is a good possibility that the second thing he gave up in order to save time was a thorough study of the text for his sermons. Soon he will forget what he was trying so hard to save time for. But whether remembered or not, his preaching has started to take a long and sad downhill slide. He doesn't really preach the text anymore; he preaches about the text. His sermons have begun to sound all the same. He thinks that no one notices. He thinks that it doesn't make any difference. That no one says anything to him about it convinces him that no one really cares anyway. It becomes his habit to drone on in general terms about the text with trivial stories on the side and applications that will neither inspire nor bother anyone.

Luther has some scathing words for such pastors. He says that they are more fit to be swineherds than pastors and that they should be driven out of town and pelted with dung as they go (Large Catechism, Preface; Kolb, pp. 379-383)!

How sad! Since the Word is powerful, since the Holy Spirit is always present with the gospel in Word and sacraments, the faith of his members may still survive. It won't be as healthy or as joyous a faith because of the indifference of the pastor to careful preaching and teaching and application of the Scriptures to their lives. But they may survive. At any rate the elect will hear the Savior's voice and follow him into eternal life, just as Jesus promised. The tune that the Holy Spirit played was sweet enough to overcome the fact that the trumpet was tin. But still, how sad!

The solution? It is the same as that already indicated. It is the motto of that greatest of Lutheran theologians, Martin Chemnitz: *Ad fontes!* "Back to the source!" As any entrenched habit is difficult to overcome, so too is the habit of indifference to souls who may wear us out but who are still the blood-bought of the Lamb. If a pastor finds that he has drifted into a kind of professional-*ism,* he may indeed find it difficult to rekindle the ardor that he knew, that good passion that was his when he graduated from the seminary. He may come to the sad conclusion that a certain torpor has overtaken his soul in his Bible reading and in his prayers, so that he no longer feels the presence of God in the gospel or the urging of the Spirit in his prayers. The Formula of Concord has an interesting comment on such a state:

> For the presence, effectiveness, and gift of the Holy Spirit should not and cannot always be assessed *ex sensu,* as a person feels it in the heart. Instead, because the Holy Spirit's activity is often hidden under the cover of great weakness, we should be certain, on the basis of and according to the promise, that the Word of God, when preached and heard, is a function and work of the Holy Spirit, through which he is certainly present in our hearts and exercises his power there (2 Corinthians 2 [1 Cor. 2:11ff. or 2 Cor. 3:5-6]). (Formula of Concord, Solid Declaration, Art. II, par. 56; Kolb, p. 554.)

The solution to such a condition of weakness is not the one that the devil suggests. He urges that we just give it up and sink still deeper into our own perceived deadness. The solution offered by the Formula of Concord, by the apostles and prophets, by our Lord himself is the opposite. They urge us with one voice to trust the promise, yes, to immerse ourselves in it. For the Spirit is active whether felt or not. And when he wants us to feel it a bit more, we will. Indeed, he wants to test us, to train us to trust in his promises, not just in our perceptions, our feelings.

A pastor who wants to climb out of the swamp, out of the muck and mire of professional*ism,* might do well to take himself back to kindergarten. A great kindergarten of the soul is the gospel of Mark. A pastor might go back and reread it as though he were reading it for the very first time. He might take just a few verses, certainly not more than a chapter in a day, and imagine that he had never heard the story before. He might ask himself with each little section: "If I or any other mere mortal were writing the story, how would it turn out?" He might ask himself each day, "What in this story is a surprise and a turning of everything upside down from what we would expect by our own reasoning?" He might ask further, "What does this story or these verses teach about God and about me that no other story teaches quite so clearly?" In this last question, the mature pastor will have an advantage over a younger one, for by this time he knows the Bible very well and should be able to make comparisons and contrasts more easily than the novice.

As he reads he can pray without ceasing for the blessing of God on his Word. He can storm the gates of God's heart with the cross of God's Son, pleading with him to keep his promise to bless the Word where and whenever it is heard. He can beg anew for grace, which is always undeserved, and for mercy on his own wretched soul.

As he rises from his knees, he may want from time to time to go to a real kindergarten, whether in the parish school or the Sunday school. He may want to sit down with a little child and ask the child to tell him the story of Jesus. He will no doubt be awestruck by the Holy Spirit's ability to bring Jesus so beautifully and clearly into the heart and the mouth of a little child. If that isn't reason enough to get back to the noble work that is his as the instrument of the Holy Spirit, it is hard to imagine what would be enough. Let him go and visit a dying member and ask, "Are you ready to go and see Jesus?" If he listens to the answer, he will not soon again conclude that his holy office is just a business. For the answer will either inspire him with the faith of the dying or it will show him that he has holy work to do in getting this soul dressed for eternity with the robe of Jesus' blood and righteousness.

If he finds that he has just been droning through the liturgy on Sunday morning, he might do well to restudy it. He might go back and map out all of the great doctrines presented there in their proper order. He might remember that the purpose of the salutations in the liturgy is a solemn and holy one, to hold before himself and God's people the great work they are engaged in: They are about to call on the Almighty and on the King of grace! He might ask himself what purpose the blessings have before the sermon and after it and at the close of the service. He might call to mind that in the blessings as in the readings he is coming from the heart of God with blessings for his people, not just with churchy *hellos* and *good-byes*. He might impress it again on his heart and soul, that those sitting in front of him have a desperate need for what he has to say to them. They may not always know that, but he certainly should both know and appreciate that he is the one God has called to satisfy their desperate need.

As with our young pastor, the chief cross is not the problems that others make for us. The chief cross is our reluctance to deny *self* and follow in the footsteps of him who has loved us and given himself for us.

The cross of the elderly pastor

There really is not much to say here that is different from what was said in the last chapter about the cross of the elderly in general. The temptation for the pastor too is the temptation presented by *calluses on the soul.* Having come through the passions of youth and the struggles to stay fresh and committed in the middle years, the time comes for laying down the burdens of office. New problems arise in the congregation and in the church at large, and he no longer feels up to the challenge. Both the agility of the mind and the energy of the soul begin to wane.

If the pastor has lost the earlier battles, he will have a harder time winning the battle against the calluses on the soul. He will be irritated that the younger men do not seem to be interested in his advice based on how he did things in his day. If he is perceptive, he may start to notice that they are a bit bemused when he starts to offer it too freely or unasked. If he is a bit more perceptive, he may remember how he smirked 40-or-so years ago when some elderly sage thought he was giving the wisdom of the ages when he said, "Of course, when we still had German services, we didn't have these problems!"—or something maybe equally true but also equally irrelevant.

The cross of the elderly pastor can be a heavy one indeed if he has to fight against resentment that his time has passed and that he must either move to the side or be pushed there. But it doesn't have to be that way. He can create this misery for his declining years or triumph over it.

The triumph, not surprisingly, is found in the promises of God. Only now the elderly pastor has the luxury of looking back over years of service and noting with growing thanksgiving how God has kept his Word. The church has survived. People have heard the Word from him, have grown in grace, have died in saving faith. Doubtless he will even see proofs of it; each year he will receive cards and letters from people whom he has served. Especially those whom he helped get through some particularly difficult times in their lives may express to him their gratitude that the Lord sent him to help them. They don't send cards and letters to their good plumber or their wonderful grocer, or perhaps even to their good doctor; they send them to their pastor with a recognition that his service to them was for time and, more important, for eternity. What a delight! What a joy to look back on years thus spent in the service of the one who made us his own in Baptism and then still could not give us enough; he granted us the holy office of the ministry for such a time as we had it and he could make use of us in it.

If in spite of all that, we still are tempted to grumble at becoming irrelevant, we might do well to call to mind the example of David and Solomon. And we do well to take heed to the example of Paul with Timothy and Titus in the pastoral epistles and with the elders of the church at Ephesus (Ac 20).

In the case of David and Solomon one has to wonder: Did David imagine that he could preserve the church from the grave? What care David took to provide everything that was necessary for the building of the temple after his death. No detail was too small for his concern. No provision too costly for his generosity. Did he perhaps think that with all of his devoted and dedicated service to the next generation, he was assuring the orthodoxy and devotion of the next generation? The simple fact is, that no matter what we do in our time and with our faithfulness, each generation has to win the battle for the faith again and anew (Jude 3). If we thought that we could do it for the ages to come, then we were arrogant and foolish.

Paul shows us the proper attitude in his exhortations to Timothy and Titus in the pastoral epistles and to the elders at Ephesus in Acts 20:13-35. Those who follow will have new problems, new opponents, new challenges and threats and opportunities. The best that Paul could do, and the best that we can do, is to be a pattern of love for Jesus and his people and an example of unswerving loyalty to his Word. If the next generation sees in us patterns of sound doctrine and a godly life worth following, they may well be encouraged to follow it. And in following, God will show them in his Word how to meet the challenges of their age— challenges that we no longer are best equipped to face. Nor will we be lax in our unceasing prayers before the chief Shepherd and bishop of our souls, that he would preserve his church in faithfulness and his pastors in purity of doctrine and life to the glory of his own most holy and saving name!

We will find a beautiful summary of the whole matter if occasionally we attend a graduation or a call service at the seminary and then a funeral service for a pastor. Go to those two kinds of services and notice how alike they are. From beginning to end, both kinds of service are heartfelt and often tear-filled hours of adoration and thanks to God for his free and faithful grace. There is nothing better; there is nothing else. We would not want to have it any other way. Then reread for imitation 2 Timothy and Titus and 1 Peter to rekindle or refresh the gratitude that should be ours above all others for God's great goodness to us. Such should be a good cure for calluses on the soul.

The church under the cross

The church in its essence is glorious as Christ is glorious. He is the Bridegroom and the church is the bride. All that he does, he does for her. All that has, he gives to her. She is holy because he has washed her in the waters of Baptism, so that all her sins are gone in that precious flood. And, yes, she is holy because she carries out the only works in the world that are holy; she listens to her Bridegroom's voice and gladly submits to his will. Then she hastens into every nook and cranny of the world to share the glad tidings of the salvation that he has wrought. She tenderly nurses her children with the pure milk of the Word. She washes them with the water that washed her. She feeds them with the bread of life in Word and sacrament by which alone she is sustained.

She is imperishable because the Lord of heaven and earth is her protector, her shield, her fortress, and her strength. He rules over all of history for her benefit. She will never be destroyed because his Word can never be destroyed. Her very existence in the world proclaims in every age her Bridegroom's resurrection and ascension. For in every age, if the world had gotten its way, she would have perished. She could not have preserved herself; only the Almighty, whose love for her is as boundless as his power, could preserve her.

So she stands to the end of days as a city set on a hill, which alone has the light of the gospel that saves for time and for eternity. For it is still true and will always be true: *Extra ecclesia nullus salus!* "Outside of the church there is no salvation!" Yes, outside of the church, life is not worth living and death is only the beginning of eternal terror. But in her warm embrace there is nothing that cannot be endured in this life and endured even with peace and joy; for there awaits the eternal banquet of the bride and Bridegroom, where her children will be forever with the Lord. There they will share in his glory, see him as he is, and nevermore wish that they were anywhere else or doing anything else than what he wishes and wills.

Were it not for her presence in the world, it is the world that would perish. It continues only because she is in it; it continues because the work that the Bridegroom has given her to do is not yet finished. So nations come and go. People strut across the stage of history and then disappear. Political systems, business enterprises, unions of people for cultural or social or even religious purposes all seem so important when they first make their appearance and come to prominence. But they all perish and their great heroes die, some remembered, most not. Only the church endures with her lamps brightly burning, waiting for her Lord's return. There are not enough superlatives in the language to adequately describe her glory and her beauty.

But the church lives under the cross. And she dare never forget it. Indeed, how could she forget it? All of her sons and daughters march under the sign of the cross. Not one of them lives without it as long as their pilgrimage lasts in the church militant on earth. Our confessions have a number of crystal clear expression of this truth that the glory of the church is hidden under the cross. They echo the theme previously cited from the Heidelberg Disputations. In the Large Catechism, Luther reminds us that the cross is not optional for the church any more than it is optional for the individual believer. Indeed, it is always a wonder that the church survives and a miracle of the gospel that anyone would ever be attracted to her, given the cross under which she lives and loves and labors. How utterly unattractive she is in Luther's description of her:

> Wherever there are upright preachers and Christians, they must endure having the world call them heretics, apostates, even seditious and desperate scoundrels. Moreover, the Word of God must undergo the most shameful and spiteful persecution and blasphemy; it is contradicted, perverted, misused, and misinterpreted. But let this pass; it is the blind world's nature to condemn and persecute the truth and the children of God and yet consider this no sin. (Luther's comments on the Eight Commandment in the Large Catechism, Part I, par. 262; Kolb, p. 421.)

The Apology likewise portrays the church under the cross, with her glory real but altogether hidden from the eyes of the world and even from the eyes of those who should know her best:

> . . . because the kingdom of Christ has not yet been revealed, they [the ungodly] intermingle with the church and hold offices in the church. Just because the revelation has not yet taken place does not make the ungodly the

church. For the kingdom of Christ is always that which he makes alive by his Spirit, whether it has been revealed or is hidden under the cross, just as Christ is the same, whether now glorified or previously afflicted. . . . Thus he [Christ] teaches that the church has been hidden under a crowd of wicked people in order that this stumbling block may not offend the faithful, and so that we might know that the Word and sacrament are efficacious even when they are administered by wicked people. (Apology, Art. VII & VIII, par. 17-19; Kolb, pp. 176,177.)*

The easiest part of the theology of the cross as it applies to the church is this that she suffers opposition and persecution from open foes outside of her and hidden foes within. And who can count the damage that such foes have done? Tyrants in every age have seen her as a threat to their own power and mercilessly worked to crush her. Cain started it with his murder of Abel. Ahab and Jezebel wanted to kill all the faithful prophets. Herod murdered St. John the Baptist. How many Christians were killed by the Jews before and after the conversion of Paul? How many died in the local and universal persecutions of the emperors before the conversion of Constantine and then later during the reign of Julian the Apostate? In the 20th century the number of Christians slaughtered by Hitler and Stalin alone no doubt exceeded the total number of martyrs in every earlier age.

Then there is the even worse damage done inside the church by false teachers and their adherents. Thousands of the faithful have been put to death by others who called themselves Christians and insisted that they were the church. The Smalcaldic War and the Thirty Years' War in Germany were in part crusades aimed at destroying orthodox Lutheranism. That meant, of course, killing orthodox Lutherans while burning their churches

---

*For an excellent summary consideration of the history of the theology of the cross as applied to the church, the reader may wish to consult "Luther's Theology of the Cross," by Hermann Sasse. It was originally Letter 18 in his *Briefe an lutherische Pastoren*. An English translation by Arnold Koelpin can be found in the online essay file of Wisconsin Lutheran Seminary Library, www.welsessays.net. I have attempted to summarize Sasse's letter in Appendix 1.

and libraries and closing their schools. And it was all done in the name of Christianity, with the salvation of souls as the excuse and the justification for it.

But the damage done by tyrants on the outside and by heretics and hypocrites within is only the beginning of the church's woes and crosses. Even the faithful pastors, teachers, and members of the church who want nothing but the best for her may do her harm, in spite of their best intentions. They impose on the visible church the very crosses they themselves struggle with as individuals. In the church as an institution, as a congregation or a school, as a synod or a denomination, what will we always find? Each in his turn has to struggle against unruly passion sometimes, wrong priorities at other times, calluses on the souls at still other times! Unruly passion can infect the church as an institution. A certain professional*ism* can tempt her officials. Calluses on the soul of organizations can embitter and alienate those who otherwise would cheerfully support her.

Passion may want growth for its own sake. That can lead to a proliferation of programs that are little more than gimmicks. And woe betide the pastor who gets tired of ever-new programs from above that promise to be the solution to organizational stagnation! Or passion for the salvation of souls can lead to the founding of ever more churches and mission fields, when there are not enough resources to support the ones already in existence. The fields are white for harvest and the opportunities always seem greater than our abilities to seize them. So old fields, perhaps not so ripe anymore, may be starved in the interest of new ones that on the outside at least seem more appealing. Indeed, the visible church too can develop a messiah complex; it can imagine that this single organization is the one and only hope for saving the world. So somehow we have to do it all. In the attempt, the message becomes ever more shallow because it is just too expensive and time-consuming for it to be otherwise—we have to hurry on to the next thing.

Those charged with the responsibility of deciding what to open and what to close have a heavy burden indeed. The appeal of a new field is so urgent and hope for its success so compelling. The cry of the old field, that precious souls not be abandoned, is heart wrenching. No matter what the decision, the critics will be shrill in their denunciation. Thus enters the temptation to professional*ism*. Those who have to make decisions that they know are going to be upsetting to well-intentioned pastors and members whose appeals were turned aside can develop tin ears. They only pretend to listen. They are tempted to feel contempt and scorn for the herd that just doesn't understand or want to understand. Their one concern is to "spin" what was decided, to declare it to be the will of God, and to bludgeon the gainsayers into quiet (and consequently embittered) acquiescence. Those thus pummeled into silence will likewise have their battles to face. They may yield in the struggles against resentment and the temptation to a hostile refusal to listen to any voice other than their own or to offer of any kind of future support or cooperation.

So calluses grow on the souls of both leaders and led, to the detriment of the work and joy in the work. Only the devil is happy. The outward unity of the church is threatened and the inward unity of the church in doctrine and practice is imperiled. For when the day comes that false doctrine invades the organization, pastors and officials alike will be too busy with "their own thing" to act with any kind of resolve against it. And that day will surely come! It has come to every visible Christian church in the past. Only the arrogant can think that such a day will never come to their own church. Indeed, the assumption that we can never fall is already the beginning of the fall. For it is born in sinful pride and begets careless indifference to the Lord's repeated exhortation to watch and pray, lest we fall.

Jesus says, "If anyone would come after me, he must deny himself and take up his cross and follow me." His words apply to all of us. Each in his place, each in his call, needs to go back to Jesus' call again and again. Each day is, as Luther also reminds us in the first of his Ninety-five Theses, a day for repentance. The repentance that we preach always needs to start with us. If it is not a deeply ingrained cry from the heart of the church and its leaders in offices and in the pulpit, it will probably be but a hollow call when they issue it to others. Without such an earnest cry for mercy and a gospel-worked eagerness to take up the cross, to deny self and to follow him, talk of repentance, insistence on purity in doctrine and practice, yes, the call to the cross, all end up being pushed to the "rear of the bus."

We need to recognize and admit that the flesh, our flesh and that of our members and prospects, never wants to hear about the repentance that the Bible and the Lutheran Confessions talk about. That is a repentance which consists of horror and terror in the presence of the wrath of God proclaimed in the law. It is a horror and a terror that can only be stilled by the voice of Christ in absolution, in the gospel in Word and sacraments. All of Article XII of the Apology deals with a repentance that is earnest and serious and sincere. Where such repentance is not worked by the faithful use of the law and the gospel, the Apology warns that "hearts that do not feel the wrath of God loathe consolation in their smugness." And then a few lines later, "For these are the two chief works of God in human beings, to terrify and to justify the terrified or make them alive" (Apology, Art. 12, par. 51,53; Kolb, p. 195). What the Apology affirms is nothing more than what the Bible says in every book and the penitential psalms and so many of Jesus' parables say most dramatically.

Gimmicks may amuse and entertain and give a moment of outward popularity to their masters. But they will not provoke the terror of sin that only the Holy Spirit can work through the law, and they will not give glory to Christ as the absolutely necessary and only possible Savior from sin and guilt for time and for eternity. Only the Holy Spirit can do that through the proclamation of the gospel. The joy that comes from gimmicks which entertain will consequently and more likely be a merely superficial sentiment in the flesh. The true joy of the soul is the gift of the Holy Spirit in the proclamation of the gospel to the sin-sick heart. Again Article XII of the Apology cites one of the famous sermons of St. Bernard to make the point about as well as it can be made:

> It is a faithless trust, containing only a curse, when we sin in hope [i.e., sin with the thought that it doesn't really matter since it will be forgiven anyway]. However, such should not be called trust, but an insensibility and a pernicious deception. For what is trust to one who does not pay attention to the danger? Or what remedy is there for fear where neither fear nor its actual basis is felt? Trust is consolation. However, those who rejoice when they have

done wrong and exult in the worst things have no use for consolation. Therefore, let us ask, brothers, that we be told how great are our iniquities and sins, and let us desire that our crimes and offenses be shown to us. Let us search our ways and with earnest attention examine all our pursuits and dangers. Let everyone say in his anxiety: "I will go to the gates of hell," so that now we may take courage in no other way than in God's mercy alone. This is the true trust of a person who forsakes self and relies on the Lord. (Apology, Art. XII, par. 58; Kolb, p. 196.)

This kind of repentance will never be popular with the mass of humanity. Our own flesh doesn't like it either! As in the days of the prophets, as in the days of Jesus and the apostles, as in the days of Luther and the confessors, most run away from repentance as fast they can. Most will run away even when the promise of real and lasting and eternal joy invites to earnest repentance (as in the invitations in the liturgy before the confession of sins). In fact, those won first by gimmicks (and thus not really won at all!) will also run away if the one who won them ever gets around to the matter of true repentance and the joy of the gospel that comes to those who despair of ever saving themselves.

The biblical and confessional call to repentance needs to be impressed on everyone each day. Each day is another opportunity to turn aside and listen to the voice of the Savior, as with law and gospel he calls us to listen to him and to serve him alone. That listening and serving requires ever and anew the drowning of the old man in Baptism. That listening and serving requires an attitude of humility which stoops before the cross of him who died and rises before his empty tomb with one ambition: to serve. We serve the Christ in those we serve. We serve in the recognition that not a one of us is infallible. We serve with the understanding that our own flesh is the chief obstacle to service and the flesh of those we serve the second obstacle.

But in it all we make it our aim and endeavor to be faithful to him and to his Word. He will yet keep his promise to gather in the elect through the pure proclamation of that Word. Yes, and he will as well keep his promise to give us enough crosses of frustration and seeming failure, so that we learn anew to depend on him and not on ourselves. He will yet teach us that faith is always a miracle and the exception. He will yet teach us that in every age the church should have perished; it was preserved only by his providence in history and his effectiveness in the gospel. When we have done all, we will rejoice to confess that we were indeed unworthy instruments of his grace but instruments nonetheless. And finally when he comes, we will have an eternity to sing with wonder and amazement: Thanks be to God, who has given us the victory through our Lord Jesus Christ!

Appendix 1

A summary of Hermann Sasse's "Luther's Theology of the Cross," originally Letter 18 of *Briefe an lutherische Pastoren,* October, 1951.

For Luther the cross of the Crucified is central to everything. It is the cross that gives the incarnation meaning; Easter is the resurrection of *the Crucified.* The theology of glory, on the other hand, finds a different center, a center in Easter or in the incarnation without reference to the cross. But it is the theology of the cross by which the church stands or falls. Anselm's *Cur Deus Homo?* (Why did God become a man?) makes the incarnation central as the actual event of our salvation. Irenaeus in *Against Heresies,* V, Preface, says, "On account of his infinite love God became what we are, in order that we might become what he is." For the Eastern church the cross is hidden in the miracle of Christmas and in the miracle of Easter. The darkness of Good Friday vanishes in the splendor of these festivals. The cross is outshone by the divine glory of Christ incarnate and the risen Lord. To the extent that the cross is present, it is not the cross of the suffering Christ but of the triumphant and not-suffering Christ, the Christ of *"In hoc signo vinces"* (by this sign you will conquer). The reason for this theology of glory in the East is that for the East the idea of the total depravity of man remained repugnant; the East saw sin only as a sickness to be healed, not as a crime to be paid for, as in the West.

But even in the Western church, the cross is more a sign of the theology of glory than of the theology of the cross. It or its relics appear as that powerful sign before which the enemies fall. In it, God's power becomes visible and real in the world.

It is not until the middle and the late Middle Ages that the cross becomes not a sign of Christ victorious but of the suffering Christ, the man of sorrows. It is Anselm in his *Cur Deus Homo?* who, in spite of his rationalizing, first fully developed the doctrine of the vicarious atonement. His expression of vicarious satisfaction is the only doctrine to come out the Middle Ages that ultimately found universal expression in all of western Christianity. Lutheran, Catholic and Reformed all have some expression of the doctrine that Christ's suffering made satisfaction for the sin of all. Even in Catholicism, *sola gratia* remains a possibility; it is in the canon of the mass, in the *Agnus Dei,* in the *Tu solus sanctus,* in the *Rex temenda* of the mass for the dead, in the baptismal formula; sadly it is only one possibility of many.

Thus Luther did not discover the theology of the cross, or even that it always must be superior to theology of glory; that was already there in the Middle Ages. What he did see is its depth, that man, like Moses (Ex 33), always wants to see God's glory but cannot. To search for God in philosophy, in the natural world, and in mystical experience is all a quest for a theology of glory, the theology of the heathen; then (in his comments on Ps 65:17) we talk about God like a shoemaker talking about his leather, so skilled have we become with Aristotle. God is reduced to an object (cf. also Heidelberg Thesis 29). Luther does not deny that God's attributes are manifest in the world; he just denies that knowing such is of any ultimate value. For the theology of glory can never save anyone. It is only in the foolishness of preaching, the preaching of the cross, that we are saved (1 Co 1:18).

By the theology of glory, seeking God in nature, we perceive the invisible God by his visible works, his power and majesty and glory; but God himself remains invisible. It is in the cross—God's shame, his humility, his weakness, his suffering and death—that God lets us see himself. Here God becomes visible who in the works of creation remains invisible. That means: God becomes visible as far as he can possibly become visible to mortal men, as he became visible to Moses when Moses was allowed to look after him to see the *posteriora Dei* (the back of God).

Thus the cross is *the* revelation of God. A revelation by definition is the coming forward out of hidden-ness, out of secrecy. In his essence he is hidden in light which no man can approach (1 Ti 6:16), in thick darkness (1 Ki 8:12), hidden (Isa 45:15), whose face cannot be seen (Ex 33:20; Jn 1:18; 1 Jn. 4:12). Only in heaven does he become visible to our eyes (1 Jn 3:2; 1 Co 13:12; Rev 22:4). Only in Christ do we see him now; he is the incarnate Word, and we behold his glory in the incarnation, in the word/ Word made flesh; he comes forward from his secrecy. No *Deus nudus* (God as he really is) for anyone who wants to live; only in Christ does *Deus absconditus* (God hidden) become *Deus revelatus* (God revealed). But even then he remains hidden; for we do not see his glory except in the suffering in the human nature. So even in revealing himself in Christ, God is hidden, as in Gethsemane and in the fifth word from the cross. Even in the miracles his glory is hidden: at Cana it was his disciples who believed in him, not the crowd at the wedding; nor the five thousand fed; nor even necessarily the sick whom he healed or the dead he raised. It is only to faith (created by the Word!) that his glory is evident under the veil of humility and the cross.

And thus is the church likewise hidden, apparent only by faith and to faith (Apology VII, VIII:18). Indeed, all objects of faith are hidden, as even the Word of God is hidden in letters and grammar. The cross demands faith *against the evidence.* And thus it contradicts reason at every level: under flesh and on the cross God is the atonement for the sins of the whole world, the very real wrath of God really assuaged, and all human efforts to that end are therefore the ultimate evil. Doing nothing alone is good.

Likewise in man, good fortune, good health, wealth, worldly peace, all these may in the theology of glory be good, but in God's economy hurtful, so that in love he withholds them and gives their opposites to our salutary frustration and despair. It is at the foot of the cross that man learns that God's way is to kill in order to make alive. Think of the example of Abraham and his sacrifice of his son; even in God's words, his command, God appears as the enemy, as coldhearted and cruel beyond measure; faith clings to him in spite of the evidence that God himself gives against himself! Anything else is a damnable theology of glory, the glory of reason, of man at the center of everything, of man as god.

Appendix 2

Behold the Hidden Glory of the Cross!
A Sermon Series for Lent and Holy Week

Sermon 1: Ash Wednesday
It Is Hidden in the Savior's Solitude

Text: Luke 18:31-34

I. It is our greatest sorrow that we cannot help him.
   A. We would like to help him a little or perhaps at least rewrite the script.
   B. Not only can we not help him; we caused all of his sorrow in the first place.
   C. The greatest crime of all is imagining that we either could help or even have helped him in his passion.

II. It is our greatest joy that we cannot help him.
   A. He relieves our sorrow by willingly doing it all.
   B. That he alone has carried his cross is our whole comfort and confidence.

Our Lenten journey this year begins as did the Lenten journey of Jesus and his disciples so many years ago. We hear Jesus' call to go with him up to Jerusalem and up to the cross of the first Lent in Luke 18:31-34:

> Jesus took the Twelve aside and told them, "We are going up to Jerusalem, and everything that is written by the prophets about the Son of Man will be fulfilled. He will be handed over to the Gentiles. They will mock him, insult him, spit on him, flog him and kill him. On the third day he will rise again." The disciples did not understand any of this. Its meaning was hidden from them, and they did not know what he was talking about.

I.

In Jesus' call to us on Ash Wednesday, he gives us a bloodcurdling preview of what we are about to see in this great drama of Lent. It is horrible in the extreme. And it is shocking. The Creator of the universe will be mocked and insulted? How can that be? The one who gave us breath at birth will be beaten within an inch of his life? Is that possible? He who is the author of every good and perfect gift that we have ever had since we were born, he will be cruelly tormented and then shamefully executed? His glory is hidden, hidden completely in the cross.

Do you perhaps wish that you had been there? Does this thought spring to mind: "Ah, Lord Jesus, if only you could have taken me along! Maybe I could have helped you. Maybe I could have wiped your face with a cool towel. Maybe I could have yelled to the crowds that all you were doing was for their salvation. Maybe I could have been at least one defense witness for you at the court of the high priest or at your trial before Pontius Pilate. Maybe I could have done something, just some little thing, to lighten your burden, to show my love and gratitude for what you were doing for me, even for me." Don't you want to say that to him as he begins again his journey to the cross in Lent?

Jesus takes us aside with the Twelve and announces to us, "We are going up to Jerusalem." And we want to heed his call. We want to respond by following after him as he marches to the cross. And it is our greatest sorrow that we cannot help him in all that he is about to do for us and for our salvation. The Twelve could not help him either. But exactly that is the glory hidden in the coming cross. Jesus makes that clear already in his call to the disciples to join him on his final journey to the holy city. For he tells them, "We are going up to Jerusalem." But after that one little word, *we,* the subject of the sentence changes. He does not say, "We are going up, and we will suffer." No. We are going up. But it is Jesus alone who will suffer there in the way that he describes. The Son of Man will fulfill the Scriptures. The Son of Man will be mocked, will be insulted, will be spit upon and flogged and killed. All who follow him to the cross, his first disciples and we along with them, can therefore only be spectators at this great drama that is about to unfold. His glory is that he alone is the Savior. His glory hidden in the horrible solitude of all he suffered is that our salvation should be entirely the gift that comes through his cross and his alone.

We go up to Jerusalem. But Jesus will suffer there, and he will suffer alone. But still, don't you want to be like Peter and at least take him aside to rewrite the script? Don't you want to say to him on Ash Wednesday, "No, Lord Jesus! That's not the way it should be! If we cannot help you, at least let us see you go up there in triumph. Let us see you as you were on the Mount of Transfiguration. Let us see you with your robes as white as snow and your face shining like the sun. Let us see you talking with the holy prophets of old. But not this way! Not in shame and disgrace. If you must suffer, then let the suffering at least be hidden from view. For no one wants their shame and disgrace put on public display. We should hide that from view. How can we endure to see you that way: covered with spit, black and blue with bruises, washed in blood? No, no, that will never do. Let us see you in glory and in triumph. At the very least, let us and all the world be spectators at the triumph of your resurrection."

But if we said that to Jesus, he would surely turn and sharply rebuke us, as he did with Peter when he expressed similar sentiments. This is the way it must be, Jesus would tell us. For he is going to fulfill the Scriptures, to fulfill all that was written about him in the Old Testament. Nothing will soften the blows. Nothing will relieve the pain. No one will help him. And it all has to be done in broad daylight, in public, so that all will see the shame and disgrace. We would have hidden the shame of his passion and put the glory of his resurrection on display.

But Jesus will have none of that. All will see his shame. No one will view the glory of the resurrection. That will be hidden and made known not by sight but by his Word and his presence in the Word and the testimony of the few who saw him after that glorious event.

Oh, what sadness that we cannot help him whom we love and adore! Yes, what a disgrace for the whole human race that no one helped him bear the burden of the whole world's sin, not his mother, not the Twelve, not the church or the state; no one helped him. To be sure, the angels served him for a moment. They served him in Gethsemane. But while he is enduring what he told us would happen during his trial and execution, even the angels are nowhere to be told. After Gethsemane they do not appear again until Easter Sunday.

But there is more. Jesus refuses Peter's advice and our suggestions that the script should be rewritten. And he arranges things in such a way that the Twelve cannot help him in his suffering, and we cannot either. But there is still more to it than that. We not only do not help him in his agony. We caused it all in the first place. From beginning to end, all that he has said that he will do on this journey he is doing in our place, in our stead, on our behalf. Was he despised and rejected? We should have been. Was he left alone with no help in the hour of pain and sorrow? We should be. Did even his Father abandon him at the crucial moment on the cross so that in the midst of life he was suffering the torments of the damned in hell? That was our lot. We were conceived and born deserving that. We have turned aside from his Word and sinned every day so that we deserve his suffering for all time and for eternity too. And truth be told, we didn't even care that our sins would bring him to such suffering, such abuse, such a death. How many times in a day do we turn aside from him without even thinking and refuse even to go up with him to Jerusalem? We have better things to do. We have our minds and hearts fixed not on him but on our own pleasure and convenience. It is easier to watch television than to pray. It is more convenient to love gossip or the lusts of the flesh than his cross. For family bickering, there is always time. For his Word and a family devotion, well, perhaps later. It is time now for the sports page, not for a page in the Bible.

And it gets worse still. We imagine in our total wickedness and depravity that we are not totally wicked and depraved. We think that we really don't deserve what he endured; and we yawn or are maybe even irritated when someone points it out, especially during Lent. We vainly assume that somehow or other there is at least a scrap of merit in us for which we should not have to suffer and for which he should therefore not have had to suffer either. So foolish are we, to put it another way, that we imagine there is some good in us that does not require his journey to the cross. It's just another way of saying that deep down inside we think we have actually helped him somehow, at least once in a while, at least sometime or other. That's the greatest sin of all and the one we are least likely to recognize, much less confess. It is the sin of arrogance. It is the sin of thinking that at least a little bit in us needs no forgiveness and, yes, is even deserving of some eternal reward.

But in Jerusalem Jesus suffered for everything that we are and have been when we did not perfectly love God and serve him with all of our hearts, all of our minds, all of our strength. And when was that? Every moment of our lives!

II.

So our sorrow deepens. For we go up to Jerusalem, up to the cross with him in Lent. But don't follow too closely, as if you were going to somehow be of help to him in his sorrow. For, again, we can do nothing to help him. All that we have done only adds to his sorrow, his pain, his suffering, his death. We are the cause even on our best days, even in our best works; for they are never perfect. We are his curse. And so we go up there with him, following him at a distance, as he carries his cross all alone. It is Jesus who must suffer and die. He, and he alone, must do it all, or we are doomed and damned. Just think of it! If he had required our help in order to accomplish our redemption, we would only have ruined it. For our work is, on its best day, stained by sin. Sinners—that's what we are. We cannot, therefore, do anything at all that does not carry the stench of sin, the smell of death, the sulfur of hell on it. We go up with him. But he must do it all, or we are lost. That is the glory hidden in the solitude of the cross, the solitude that Jesus must do it alone or we must perish.

Nothing will deliver him from the anguish that is his in the loneliness, the solitude, of his Lenten cross. Who will deliver us from ours? For as we follow Jesus up to Jerusalem in response to his call, we are like worms wriggling on the end of a hook. He has invited us to see what we did to him. He has called us to observe what we deserved. Who will deliver us from our sorrow in Lent? HE WILL! HE DOES! For as it is our greatest sorrow that we cannot help him in Lent, so too that is our greatest joy in Lent. Yes, it is our peace, our life, our salvation. Listen to him in his call to us to go up with him to Jerusalem. There is not one word of complaint that falls from his lips. There is not the least trace of bitterness or anger in his tone. He does not accuse us as we deserve. He does not shame us as we might expect. No, none of that. He alone will suffer, and he will suffer alone. And that is exactly the way he wants it to be. His march to Jerusalem is a march of doom for him but of triumph for us. It is defeat and death for him but a victory parade for us. His face is set with determination to do all that needs to be done to fulfill the Scriptures for us. His will is like iron and cannot be bent to turn him away from his purpose of paying the price of our wickedness and our total depravity. So full, so perfect, so complete is his love for us. So full, so perfect, so complete is his yearning for our salvation. He wants to do it! He not only does not need our help; he does not want it either! Every pore, every fiber of his being strains and stretches on the way to the cross and on the cross to accomplish our salvation. Without our aid, he made us. Without our aid, he redeems us too.

Oh, then let us go up to Jerusalem with him! Let us follow him in Lent, but not too closely as though we would help him. Let us go up with him and follow to the cross. Let us be filled with sorrow for our sin that caused it all. But then let us be filled with joy beyond all sorrow, that he did it all and he did it alone. Let us watch with him awhile and see how great his love is for us, how perfect his solitude for us, how complete his atoning sacrifice for us. For that is the glory hidden on the cross, the glory that he wanted and won, the glory of redeeming us by his work there. Let us watch and keep watching until we hear the victory cry: HE IS RISEN! HE IS RISEN INDEED! Amen.

Sermon 2
It Is Hidden in the Savior's Sighs

Text: Luke 22:39-46

    I. Love required his whole attention.
        A. Great love because of the coming cross.
        B. Great love because of those for whom he would bear it.
    II. Need requires our whole attention.
        A. When we do not take his cross seriously, we greatly increase the weight of our own crosses.
        B. His love on the cross not only atones for our failure but inspires us to follow after him.

As we continue to look for the glory of Christ hidden on the cross, let us go with Jesus and his disciples to the Garden of Gethsemane. There we will see how seriously Jesus takes his journey to the cross, as well as the sad consequences when we fail to take seriously that journey and the cross. We read from the gospel according to St. Luke, chapter 22, beginning at verse 39:

> Jesus went out as usual to the Mount of Olives, and his disciples followed him. On reaching the place, he said to them, "Pray that you will not fall into temptation." He withdrew about a stone's throw beyond them, knelt down and prayed, "Father, if you are willing, take this cup from me; yet not my will, but yours be done." An angel from heaven appeared to him and strengthened him. And being in anguish, he prayed more earnestly, and his sweat was like drops of blood falling to the ground. When he rose from prayer and went back to the disciples, he found them asleep, exhausted from sorrow. "Why are you sleeping?" he asked them. "Get up and pray so that you will not fall into temptation."

I.

In Lent, we are following Jesus to the cross. Lent is special. It is filled with glory. But the glory is hidden on the cross. Those who do not take it seriously will never see it, much less enjoy it or receive it. Tonight that glory is hidden under the sighs of the Savior. And there is nothing trivial about that. The sighs that end on the cross are the beginning and the middle, the heart and the core of what God has to say to us about ourselves and about himself. Let us follow Jesus this evening to the dark Garden of Gethsemane on the Mount of Olives. There we see how seriously Jesus took Lent.

He bids the disciples, and us with them, to watch and pray as he prepares for the great struggle that is about to begin. May we never think that the struggle was easy for him. Just look at him in the garden. He throws himself facedown on the ground. As the writer of the epistle to the Hebrews tells us, he prays with loud cries and groans. He sees all that is about to take place. Even as he prays, his dear friend Judas is in the process of selling him out for a few pieces of silver. The soldiers are on the way. Jesus sees it all. Soon will come the trial. Soon will come the spitting and beating. Soon there will be the flogging. Soon there will be the crushing weight of the cross. Then will come the nails in his hands and feet. Then a day of hanging on the cross naked, in shame, the object of ridicule and mockery. And then death. But that isn't even the half of it. Abandoned by all, comforted by none, all of the evil, all of the sin, all of the vice of the whole world will be dumped on him. And every bit of God's righteous rage against sin will be thrown into his face and onto his soul.

Oh, yes, Jesus took Lent seriously. What love he had for his Father! Who can begin to grasp or fathom it? For all of this he does out of love for the Father. Seeing all that he is about to endure, he cries out with groans and sighs to the Father he loves with every fiber of his being: If there is another way, Father, dear Father, . . . but your will be done. Three times Jesus cries out. An angel even comes to comfort, or strengthen, his human nature in the face of such agony. But does the angel lessen his pain? Not at all! Rather, the angel somehow gives strength to the human nature of Christ to bear and endure still more. He prays, he cries, he groans all the more at the dread prospect of his Father's anger and the torment ahead for his innocent body and soul covered with the sin of the world. It was certainly painful enough to endure the shame and the abuse of men. It was certainly painful enough to be abandoned by those he had helped and those he loved, to be abandoned by family and friends. But to be punished and then abandoned by his Father—who can even begin to comprehend what agony that entailed? And so he cries to his Father for relief. But only the angel comes. And then the angel leaves. The torment decreed for the sins of the world will not be taken away, nor will it be lessened in the least.

And what love for us! We are there in the garden with the disciples. And what are they doing? Surely they hear Jesus' cries. Surely they must see the blood and sweat that pours off his anguished brow. Surely they wrestle with God in prayer and smite their breasts during this great struggle taking place only an hour before the greatest struggle begins. Surely they take Lent and the cross seriously. After all, Jesus is going through all this out of love not only for his Father but out of love for them, for us.

But no! Look! The disciples are sleeping. They do not watch with Jesus. They do not join him in prayer. They do not struggle even to stay awake. Is that not astonishing? Saint Luke tells us that they sleep because of sorrow. The whole thing is just too much for them. A child cannot sleep on Christmas Eve because of the excitement of the coming Christmas Day. But the disciples, on the night before the suffering that wins salvation, sleep!

Wonder beyond wonder that Jesus does not at that point give up in disgust and say, "If that's all you care about Lent and about what I am going through for you, then forget it! I'll go back to the praises of the angels that I enjoyed before the world began. You disciples are not worth half, no, not the smallest fragment of the effort."

Oh, how such words would sting in our ears. For we know only too well the sleep of the disciples. With them we are experts when it comes to not taking Lent seriously. We know how to say to Jesus, "Well, Lord Jesus, I know that this and that is what you want me to do, but frankly it's just too much effort for me. Besides, I'm sure you understand. I'm sure you will forgive me. So, Lord Jesus, just excuse me while I go my own way, take a nap, a break from following after you. I certainly wouldn't want to suffer any lack or much inconvenience under the cross. No, not suffering but glory is what I want, glory that I can touch and taste and see. I'd much rather you give me time and treasure, friends and family, work and play, all that my heart desires so that I can do with them as I please, enjoy them for myself and those I love. You know, Lord Jesus, how it is."

Oh, yes, he knows. He saw it in the disciples in the garden. He sees it in us. And what does he say in answer? "Father, dear Father, with cries and groans and sweat like blood, I come before you and ask—ask that your will be done. While they sleep in indifference and carelessness, I beg of you, let me redeem them. And if this is the only way, then I obey! Just so long as their debt is paid and their ransom complete and secure." That is glory. That is the glory of the cross hidden in the Savior's sighs, the glory that redeems us for all eternity from death and the grave, from hell and eternal sighs of anguish and despair. Because of his great love for his Father and because of his great love for us, Lent and the cross absorb his entire being, every particle of his strength in his mind and body and soul.

II.

Oh, may we too take Lent and the cross seriously as we follow Jesus there in the garden. And how do we do that? How do we take it seriously? Jesus told the disciples, and he tells us: "Watch and pray so that you will not fall into temptation," into the devil's snare and trap. Again we have to pay close attention to Jesus' words here. He does not tell the disciples to watch and pray so that they can help him bear the cross for the sins of the world. No, never that! He must bear the cross for our redemption entirely alone. He tells the disciples to watch and pray because of the great danger and the great struggle that lies before them. They too must bear a cross. They too must endure a great battle. And the devil is waiting for them, eager to catch them in his snare and trap. If they do not listen to the words of Jesus, they will have no armor of defense. If they do not watch, that is, fill the eyes of their hearts and souls with him and what he is doing for them, then they will fall into the snare and trap of the devil. Without Jesus and his Word in the eyes of mind and soul, they will not cry out for help and none will come. Yes, without his Word and aid in answer to their prayers, they will suffer far more than they need to suffer in the coming hours and days.

For suffer the disciples must. The day will come when they will be despised because of Jesus. Yes, the day will come when

236

they too will bear a cross and their glory as children of God and heirs of eternal life will be hidden in sighs of pain and groans of sorrow. For all of them will be persecuted because of him. What groans and sighs await them even in the coming hours when they see Jesus arrested. Temptation comes. The devil attacks. And at Jesus' arrest, they all fall and fail. They run away and hide. How loving of them! How loyal! At the first whiff of trouble, they are gone. Peter, the strongest and boldest, denies Jesus with loud oaths and curses. The rest, except for John, just disappear into the woodwork. If they had only listened. If they had only watched with Jesus and prayed as he told them to do. They still would have suffered. But they would have suffered in hope, strengthened by his Word, supported every step of the way by his answer to their prayers for strength and help through that Word. Because they didn't listen to him, didn't fill the eyes of heart and soul with him, because they didn't cry out for help, they spent those next days with nothing to drink but tears and nothing to eat but despair.

So in whose footprints will you put your feet? Jesus bids you watch and pray as you listen to his Word and follow to the cross in Lent. The disciples take their feet out of the footpath to the cross and turn aside to sleep. If you join with the disciples, then you can be sure that when your time comes to carry a cross, you will carry it with much greater sorrow than is necessary. Worse yet, you may be so filled with sorrow at the cross of God's own sending that you cast it aside and never taste the glory hidden in sighs under the cross. You will fall and fail. You will run away and hide. You will deny him and pursue the sin of the moment rather than suffer with him while you wait for the glory of the resurrection.

Perhaps you already know that from bitter and painful experience. Think of the times in your life when you were tempted and you stumbled and fell. Why was that? It wasn't the will of God that you should fall. It was because you did not listen to him, did not watch with eyes fixed on him and his love for you. You did not pray, or if you did, you prayed for the secondary things as though those prayers were the most important ones. There is a time to pray for secondary things, and those prayers are indeed important. They are prayers for health and a measure of wealth; they are prayers for the warmth of family and friends. But more important is the prayer that Jesus bids us pray together with the disciples in the garden. It is the prayer that we will not fall into temptation. It is the prayer that we watch with him so that he and his grace fill our eyes and hearts and minds. It is the prayer that he would always be first and his Word most important to us. It is the prayer that in the hour of temptation to abandon him in times of persecution or to doubt his love in times of trouble—that in all such times we may cling to him and watch with him.

For we already know what it is like not to watch and pray. We already know what it is like to follow the example of the disciples and to fall asleep and push Jesus and his Word aside. The soul, after all, is like a vacuum. If it is not filled with the sight of Jesus and his grace, then very soon it will be filled with something else. Yes, very soon will come the tempter into the vacuum to engulf and fill the void with doubt, with fear, with lust, with pride, and with that whole host of sins that we know so well. Think of the times in your life when you were afraid that perhaps God had finally left you, had finally gotten sick of your excuses and now was going to let you stew in your own juices for awhile. You got sick. You lost a job. A loved one died. The past had shame in it. The future held fear. But Jesus said: Watch and pray! Listen to my Word and promise. Follow me to the cross; yes, clear your mind of everything else and consider it all as nothing so that you may join me under the cross.

If we do that, we will indeed still suffer. But we will suffer with Jesus. We will suffer in the confidence of the resurrection and the victory that he has won for us by his cross. We will suffer without despair. We will, in summary, experience the glory hidden with Christ in sighs under the cross.

Take Lent seriously. Take his cross seriously. May the incomparable love of Jesus in Lent inspire you to follow him up to the cross. For that is where he wants to find you and meet you and be with you: under the cross. We go to receive from him all the grace and benefit that he so yearned to win for us. We go to drown in the flood of his mercy. We go to live for him as he lived and died for us. Yes, we go to share in his heaven, since he has already endured hell in our place. He took it all so seriously. May we follow in his footsteps now and all the way through the portal of death and into the heaven he won for us in Lent! Amen.

Sermon 3
It Is Hidden in the Savior's Rejection by His Own

Text: Matthew 26:57-68

I. That rejection comes from those who should know better.
   A. They knew both the law and the promises by heart.
   B. They claimed love and loyalty to both.

II. Again we need to hear, "Watch and pray so that you will not fall into temptation."
   A. Hold to the truth by keeping your eyes fixed on Jesus and his Word.
   B. Watch and pray, lest you be among those who cause the cross instead of those who carry it!

We are drawing ever closer to the moment when all the promises are fulfilled. In our reading this evening, we come to one of the most appalling, one of the most shocking, one of the most painful points in the passion history. The Word of God had promised more than once, not only in the words of Jesus himself but in the prophecies of the Old Testament, that the Savior would suffer. But listen to the source of the suffering in the reading this evening. Who would have believed it? We read in Matthew 26:57-68:

> Those who had arrested Jesus took him to Caiaphas, the high priest, where the teachers of the law and the elders had assembled. But Peter followed him at a distance, right up to the courtyard of the high priest. He entered and sat down with the guards to see the outcome. The chief priests and the whole Sanhedrin were looking for false evidence against Jesus so that they could put him to death. But they did not find any, though many false witnesses came forward. Finally two came forward and declared, "This fellow said, 'I am able to destroy the temple of God and rebuild it in three days.'" Then the high priest stood up and said to Jesus, "Are you not going to answer? What is this testimony that these men are bringing against you?" But Jesus remained silent. The high priest said to him, "I charge you under oath by the living

God: Tell us if you are the Christ, the Son of God." "Yes, it is as you say," Jesus replied. "But I say to all of you: In the future you will see the Son of Man sitting at the right hand of the Mighty One and coming on the clouds of heaven." Then the high priest tore his clothes and said, "He has spoken blasphemy! Why do we need any more witnesses? Look, now you have heard the blasphemy. What do you think?" "He is worthy of death," they answered. Then they spit in his face and struck him with their fists. Others slapped him and said, "Prophesy to us, Christ. Who hit you?"

I.

Whenever and wherever Jesus and his cross appear, we should expect hostility, hatred, opposition, and persecution, not outward glory. The glory of Christ is hidden under the cross of rejection. That's what he promised. That is obviously a truism in Lent. For Jesus carries the cross and dies because of just such hatred and opposition. What is surprising, however, in our reading for tonight and, yes, in the whole history of the church, is the source of that hostility and rejection. Who is most hostile, most vicious, most filled with hatred toward Jesus and his cross? Exactly those who should be the first to welcome him, to believe in him, to love and trust and worship him!

That's who we see in our reading this evening. Jesus was arrested and taken before the high priest. The high priest was to be the man closest to God in the whole world. He brought the blood of sacrifice into the Most Holy Place, God's throne on earth, on the great Day of Atonement and sprinkled it twice on the mercy seat, once for the sins of the nation and once for his own sins. That sprinkling of blood was a picture of the work of the Savior, who would shed his blood to blot out sin and guilt once and for all. The high priest knew that. He was the overseer of all the ceremonies and sacrifices in the temple, most of which, in one way or another, pictured the coming of the Savior, whose one great sacrifice would redeem the world.

If anyone should have known that Jesus was the fulfillment of all those ceremonies and sacrifices, it was the high priest. As one who knew by heart all of the promises in the Old Testament that pointed to the Savior, the high priest's behavior should have been far different from the behavior we hear about in this reading. He should have stood up in front of all the people and shouted at the top of his voice the words of John the Baptist: BEHOLD THE LAMB OF GOD, WHO TAKES AWAY THE SIN OF THE WORLD! But just the opposite, exactly the opposite, is what we see and hear from the high priest. Totally contrary to the law, he presides over a kangaroo court in the middle of the night. He does not even act as an impartial judge. He has already made up his mind. Even before the trial begins, he declares that this Jesus must die because it would be better for him to die than for the high priest and his cohorts to lose their place and power. And now he goes so far as to arrange for and accept false witnesses who accuse Jesus of heresy and blasphemy. When they fail in their testimony, he charges Jesus to take an oath and identify himself. When Jesus declares that he is indeed the Son of God, the high priest cares nothing for all the proof of it. Instead, and completely contrary to the law, he rips his robes in rage and calls for the death sentence. It's shocking. Where is the glory that the Son of God should have from his own people, yes, from his own priests and official representatives on earth? It is nowhere to be seen. His glory is hidden in the rejection by his own.

But what of the rest of the officials, of the Jewish high court? That court consisted of the leading priests and Pharisees and scribes, all experts in the law and the promises of the Old Testament. So expert were they that they had all memorized word for word large parts of the Old Testament. What of them? If the high priest was corrupt, should we not expect an outcry from them, at least from the majority, at the very least from a few? But there is not a word of it. Not one rises to defend the law and legal process, nor is there a voice heard to defend Jesus. And again, that is not because they did not know what he had said and done. They had sent spies to watch his every move throughout the three years of his earthly ministry. They knew all about the raising of the young man of Nain and the daughter of the synagogue ruler. They knew all about the cleansing of the lepers, the giving of sight to the blind and hearing to the deaf. They knew all about the feeding of the thousands with a few loaves and some small fish. They had heard about the raising of Lazarus just outside of Jerusalem about a week earlier. All the evidence was there that this was indeed the Son of God, the promised Messiah. But they hardened their hearts against the prophecies about the Messiah that they knew by heart from the Bible. And they hardened their hearts as well to the evidence that Jesus was indeed that promised Messiah. They hardened their hearts and filled them instead with hatred that would only be stilled by Jesus' death. (Nicodemus was a member of this counsel. But it may well be that he was not called to this midnight meeting so that there would not be even his lone voice to protest.)

Jesus and his cross stir up hatred and hostility from the most surprising quarters. It was so in the first Lent. It has been so down through the ages. It is so to this day that his glory as God and Savior is hidden under the rejection by those who should know better, who should be the first to listen to his Word and follow it. The Jews continued their hatred of Jesus and his Word long after he was dead, as the book of Acts makes so tragically clear. And the rejection by most of his own people continues to this day. But it is by no means confined to them. Year after year after year, without interruption, one group after another rises up from inside the church to hate Jesus and to persecute his Word. If we had the time this evening, we could go through every century since Pentecost and would find that some of the most bitter persecutors of Jesus and his Word were those who claimed to be his followers. The Nicene Creed, which we all know by heart, was written to defend the truth that Jesus is true God and the only Savior against the Arian heretics who denied it and had taken control of the church in the fourth century. At the time of the Reformation, the persecution of the gospel and even wars against those who faithfully preached and taught it came at the insistence of Roman priests and bishops and popes.

Today in our country, to be sure, the gospel can be preached in all of its truth and purity. But that does not mean that everyone who calls himself a Christian loves the cross of Christ and its message that Jesus alone is the God-man born of the virgin and that he is the only Savior of the world. Quite the contrary, and you know it perfectly well, many churches that call themselves

Christian want nothing to do with that message. For some, Jesus is no more than a great teacher of the law who shows us how to live a good life. For some, Jesus is the one who made salvation possible and nothing more; if we follow him, we can finish the work he merely began by our own good works and merits. It may come as a shock to you to know that some so-called Lutheran publishing houses and their synods print and peddle books that even deny that Jesus was born of a virgin and rose from the dead. They publish and peddle books and magazines that openly reject most of the teachings of the Bible and, of course, the divine inspiration of the Bible itself.

We see it everywhere. Contrary to the Bible, a homosexual lifestyle is excused and defended, even made equal to marriage by churches calling themselves Christian. Abortion counseling is offered by many such churches. Many churches calling themselves Christian today go so far in their denial of Jesus that they even say that Jews and Muslims and ultimately anyone in any religion all worship the same God; they say such an outrageous thing even though those religions deny that Jesus is God and Savior. And many will argue that it doesn't matter at all what you believe, because whether there is such a thing as hell or even heaven is itself very doubtful.

Nor are any of these churches content with peddling their poison. Like the high priest and the Jewish high court, they heap scorn and ridicule on the Jesus of the Bible and on those who still proclaim the message of Christ and him crucified for the sins of the world. Such believers, they say, are narrow-minded bigots from the dark ages and the world would be better off without them. And all this in the name of religion. All this even while wearing a cross around the neck and claiming to be Christian. Isn't it shocking? Isn't it tragic?

II.

It truly is shocking and tragic. But it is more than that. It is a warning to us. As Jesus told us in Gethsemane, "Watch and pray so that you will not fall into temptation" (Mt 26:41). There is no guarantee that we will always belong to the right church. Nor is there any guarantee that our church will forever teach God's Word in all of its truth and purity. The high priest was in the right church. The heretics who attacked Jesus at the time of the Nicene Creed started out in the right church. At the time of the Reformation there was only one recognized church. But those churches all fell away. They all turned aside from the Word and ended up being numbered with those who despise the hidden glory of the cross. And yes, the Lutheran churches of Germany and the rest of Europe and many in this country as well have also, for the most part, fallen away. Watch and pray therefore. Keep your eyes fixed on Jesus and his Word, and see to it that your church does too! For the simple fact of the matter is that all too often we too are lazy and careless about holding fast to all that God has revealed in his Word. All too often we too are inclined to take a smorgasbord approach to what God says in his Word. When the law stings, we are tempted and easily fall into the temptation to say to ourselves, "Well, it isn't really all that bad that I don't care for what God has to say about marriage or church fellowship or purity of eyes and mind or stewardship, or . . ." —well, you can fill in the blank. When we take a casual approach to his Word like that we join with those down through the ages who thought they knew better than God and who refused to take him and all of his Word seriously. Yes, and we run the horrible risk of losing all of that Word and its saving benefit.

Jesus went through rejection by his own to save us all from that dread fate. Even for us when we have joined with those in our text who should have known better he endured the shame and abuse of his passion. Oh may our hearts break with sorrow at the times that we have been casual and lazy about his Word. Oh may we fill our eyes with the vision of his rejection by his own as we repent of the times that we too have failed to follow him faithfully by clinging faithfully to his Word. And then, purged of that dread crime by his blood, may we resolve to follow yet again such a compassionate Savior who still comes to us in that Word with his grace and pardon.

We do not hate false teachers or followers of false teachers in other churches. We have no desire to persecute them. But we also have no desire to invite them into our churches and homes, nor to let them stay, should they arise from our own midst. Jesus said, "I am the way and the truth and the life. No one comes to the Father except through me" (Jn 14:6). Jesus said, "If you continue in my word, you are truly my disciples" (Jn 8:31 RSV). Jesus said, "Watch out for false prophets" (Mt 7:15). St. Paul said repeatedly—and he was echoing the words of all the prophets and, of course, of Jesus himself—that we should have nothing to do with false teachers and false teachings.

Therefore watch and pray. Keep your eyes fixed on Jesus and his Word. Out of love for those deceived by false doctrine, we reject the heresy that all teachings are basically the same and that it's only important that you at least believe something. No! That's poison! That's deadly error. We warn against it. We warn against it out of love for those poisoned by it. Some people may think that rattlesnakes will not harm them. That doesn't make a snake any less deadly. Nor is it an act of love to tell such people that as long as they don't believe the snake will hurt them, everything is well and they are safe. The loving thing is to warn against the snake and flee from it, not embrace it or hope it won't bite.

Yes, we need to watch and pray so that we are not sucked into the notion so common among those who call themselves Christians today that doctrine doesn't matter. We need to watch out that we are not seduced by such an attitude and become angry when our own church rebukes error and insists on teaching all of the truths of the Scriptures, no matter how unpopular they may be, no matter how many people may not like it. For the sad truth is that sometimes the biggest problem that a congregation or church body has is with its own members who want to soft-pedal and compromise the truth of God's Word. In their weakness, such members have turned aside from the hidden glory in favor of the glory they want to see; they want the glory of being popular or the glory of the easy path that runs away from the cross to whatever is convenient. They imagine that what we believe, teach, and confess is up to us, that it is some kind of smorgasbord or buffet menu from which we can pick and choose whatever suits our fancy at the moment.

Watch Jesus before the high priest and the Jewish council, and pray that in his Word you find and keep the whole of God's truth. Watch Jesus before the high priest and the Jewish council, and pray that you may be filled with such love for him that

245

you willingly take up the cross and follow him. For you can be sure that just as Jesus and his faithful church have been ridiculed and persecuted when they followed the truth and carried the cross, so too will you taste that hostility that comes from faithfulness. Don't be scared off by it. Don't be surprised by it. For that is what Jesus has promised.

But he has also promised that he will not forsake you or abandon you when you cling to him and to his Word. There is glory in that rejection, since it is a rejection that we share with him and that he shares with us. He has promised, and he will never lie to you, that even in persecution you will learn more and more of his love and grace. He has assured you, and the witness of the church says that it is so. As you bear the cross after him, your knowledge of his love and grace will only deepen and increase—grace heaped upon grace, as St. Paul says. These may indeed be hard lessons to learn. People don't want to hear these lessons. But Jesus goes the way of the cross out of love for us to teach them. He goes out of love for us on the way of the cross to bring us salvation by his sacrifice for us and by the word of his sacrifice for us. Oh, to see Jesus and to see him only. Oh, to follow him up to the cross, gladly bearing it after him in love and faithfulness to him who loved us and gave himself for us. May God grant this to each of us for Jesus' sake! Amen.

Sermon 4
It Is Hidden in the Savior's Rejection by the World

Text: John 18:33–19:1

   I. The world does not understand the message of the cross, nor does it want to.
      A. The message of the law it despises.
      B. The message of the gospel only provokes even greater hostility.
   II. We go up to his cross under the cross of that hostility.
      A. The cross has two beams; one is the hostility of our own nature, and the other is the hostility of the world and culture around us.
      B. Christ endured the humiliation of hostility and rejection, and so do we.
      C. His humiliation and ours is God's way of glorifying his Word.

In our meditation this evening, on the way up to Jesus' cross and under our own, we consider an aspect of our cross bearing that we share with Christ and that he shares with us. It is this aspect of cross bearing: The cross always brings rejection, and to our astonishment, that rejection has glory hidden in it. We began to see that in our meditation last week; Jesus and his cross were rejected by the very ones who should have understood and embraced Jesus first. Tonight we see that the cross brings rejection from another still larger quarter: the cross brings rejection from the world. For the world neither understands the cross nor wants to understand it. Listen to a portion of St. John's record of Jesus' trial before the world in the court of the Roman governor Pontius Pilate:

> Pilate then went back inside the palace, summoned Jesus and asked him, "Are you the king of the Jews?" "Is that your own idea," Jesus asked, "or did others talk to you about me?" "Am I a Jew?" Pilate replied. "It was your people and your chief priests who handed you over to me. What is it you have done?" Jesus said, "My kingdom is not of this world. If it were, my servants would fight to

prevent my arrest by the Jews. But now my kingdom is from another place." "You are a king, then!" said Pilate. Jesus answered, "You are right in saying I am a king. In fact, for this reason I was born, and for this I came into the world, to testify to the truth. Everyone on the side of truth listens to me." "What is truth?" Pilate asked. With this he went out again to the Jews and said, "I find no basis for a charge against him. But it is your custom for me to release to you one prisoner at the time of the Passover. Do you want me to release 'the king of the Jews'?" They shouted back, "No, not him! Give us Barabbas!" Now Barabbas had taken part in a rebellion. Then Pilate took Jesus and had him flogged.

I.

Could there be a sharper contrast in all the world than the one we see here? On the one side is Jesus. He testifies that he is a king but that his kingdom is not of this world. He testifies that all who are on the side of truth listen to him, yes, listen to him in the sense of hearing and holding to his Word, in the sense of believing him, trusting him, and following after him.

But was there ever a more pathetic sight? Was there ever a more pathetic claim? Has anything in the world ever looked more ridiculous? Jesus is a king, handed over by his own people who scream for his death. Jesus is born to be the King whose kingdom consists of those who love the truth—and there is not one person who defends him or the truth; there is not one who speaks out in his favor, who is willing to come forward and declare himself a follower of this King. Jesus is the King; but those who should have been first in his kingdom cry out for Barabbas, a rebel and companion of murderers and thieves. Such a one they prefer to the King of truth! Jesus is a king now in the hands of a petty Roman official. Jesus the King had already been beaten by his own people and spat upon. And soon he will endure still worse at the hands of Pilate's soldiers. Some king! Some kingdom! Some truth to which this King bears witness! That's the King on one side.

Pilate stands on the other side as the spokesman and representative of all the kingdoms of the world, yes, of all of us as we are by nature. He views and judges this Jesus with his eyes and his reason. It may surprise us at first that unlike the Jewish high priest and court, Pontius Pilate actually was interested in and wanted to do justice. But more than justice, he was interested in and loved his own position and his own convenience. Doing justice lost out. Out of exasperation with all the bother that this king is causing him, Pilate orders him flogged. He comes to the conclusion that the whole message is nothing but foolishness. It is a foolishness that is a nuisance and a bother. This Jesus and his truth are inconvenient, and a mob is forming that could prove troublesome. Pilate sees no criminal in Jesus and no behavior in Jesus that deserves punishment. Nevertheless, he orders that Jesus be flogged, a punishment that all by itself was so gruesome and painful that it often killed its victims. And soon after the flogging, Pilate orders the execution of this king.

Why such hostility? Why such anger? Why such violence against something and someone that on the outside seems so weak and frail, even foolish? It all hinges on that one little word that Jesus spoke to Pilate, the word *truth*. Jesus said that he was the King of truth, the one who had come into the world to bear witness to the truth! Pilate, however, wanted no truth from this Jesus. He had already made up his mind, in fact, that there really is no such thing as truth; there is only me; there is only the moment. There is no truth; there is just my needs, my wants, my will, my goals, my ambition, my pleasure, my power. Those things are all the truth that Pilate wants and all the truth that everyone else wants too. Any other truth is bound to get in the way of those things that we consider the only truths and the only realities. Pilate doesn't even want to think about the possibility that there might be something else, something more. For if there is a truth beside me, more than me, he thinks, it will require that I give up my single-minded devotion to me in favor of something or someone else.

If Pilate would have listened, instead of just rejecting Jesus and the truth out of hand, would things have turned out different? No. They would have been no different. For the message of Jesus and his cross, the heart and core of the truth to which Jesus bears witness, always provokes hatred and hostility from the world. The

truth that Jesus came to give to the world is the truth evident
already in the Garden of Eden. It is the truth that human beings
are totally depraved and corrupt and fallen in their total devotion
to self. It is the truth that even in their best works, they offend
the holiness and justice of God. It is the truth that on our best
days, the best of us deserve nothing but hell for ever and ever.
That truth is irritating and rubs us all the wrong way. Even
though the evidence of this truth is strewn generously over the
pages of history, I still don't want to hear it. Though the evidence
is right in front of me when I look honestly into the mirror of
God's law, I want to hear nothing from that mirror either. Away
with this truth! Away with the King who proclaims it!

But wait, wait! There is more to the message of the King of
truth than the guilty verdict over all of us and all our works. He
comes chiefly and primarily with this greatest truth of all: that he
himself is the solution to the problem of our sin and guilt. The
truth about us is the problem; the truth about him is the only
solution. And how will he solve the problem of sin and guilt? Will
he give us a new law to keep? Will he tell us that our sin and guilt
don't matter after all? Will he bid us to just do the best we can and
God will be satisfied and overlook the rest? Is that the great truth
that he brings? If that were the truth that Jesus brought, the
people would not have flogged him. For that's what people want to
think; they want to think that no matter how bad they may be,
they still have enough good or enough potential to save themselves. Had Jesus taught that, the people would not have crucified
him. But the King of truth declares that he himself is the whole
and complete, the only solution to the problem of sin and guilt, to
the penalty of death and hell that all deserve. The solution is that
he alone will embrace all the sin and guilt of the world. The solution is that he and he alone will suffer the penalty of death and
hell for us as our substitute. The solution is that salvation, therefore, will be an altogether free gift, won by the crucified, deserved
for us by the crucified, given in the message of the crucified. But
tragically, the truth of the gospel that saves is even more despised
than the truth of the law that condemns.

So here is the great mystery and the profound truth: So
depraved is mankind that by nature we hate to be told the truth
that we are depraved; and so great is our corruption that by

nature we hate still more the truth that the only solution to the punishment we deserve is Jesus, the King of truth. You would think that people would stampede to this Jesus who delivers from death and hell. If we offered them free gas or free health care or free money, we would be trampled in the stampede. But free salvation? Free heaven? Free rescue from hell? No, not that! Away with him! Give us Barabbas, a crook and a murderer, rather than this Jesus! Him we want to crucify!

II.

We noted at the beginning of our sermon this evening that Jesus is not the only one who must bear the cross, though it is his cross alone that saves. Those who follow to the cross must also follow under the cross. That is the mark of the Christian, the sign of the cross. For wherever the King of truth appears with the message of truth, the one and only truth, there will be hostility, opposition, and often enough, even violence. As a cross has two beams, so the hostility to the cross has two beams as well. The first beam is the one that we carry from our own nature. Pilate dismissed Jesus with the words "What is truth?" Pilate didn't want an answer. He already assumed that there was no answer outside of himself. That's what our own flesh says too. Don't bother me with ideas about right and wrong that come from God, that come from the Bible. There is no right and wrong. There are only values. Today I like this, tomorrow that. People shouldn't commit adultery; but if my children, my friends, or finally I myself decide to live outside of marriage in a relationship reserved for marriage, well, who's to judge? People shouldn't hold grudges or gossip. But you don't know what was done to me! People shouldn't steal or cheat. But the government wastes my money and businesses charge too much anyway. Besides, people cheat and steal from me; I just want what's coming to me. People shouldn't be arrogant and self-righteous, but let's face it, we really are better than most, aren't we?

Then comes the confession in the liturgy: "I, a poor miserable sinner." "No, no," objects our flesh, "I don't want to hear about that. It's so depressing, such a downer." Then comes the message of forgiveness: "All you need bring to the cross of Christ is your despair of any good or merit in you; this will be his answer:

'I forgive you; I wash it all away in my blood; I pay for it fully; redeemed by me, you are restored as a dear child of God!'" But the flesh likes that news even less! "I work hard. I deserve what I get. God is at least a little bit lucky that I'm on his side, and he should feel at least a little flattered that I believe in him at all, given the world we live in today. And if he doesn't treat me right, I'll fix him. I won't believe in him anymore, and I'll quit the church!"

So the first beam of the cross that we Christians carry is the beam of our own sinful nature that hates the truth of the law and despises the truth of the gospel. The second beam is the hostility of the world, of all in our culture who simply can't stand the message of truth that Jesus is and came to bring us. Our world wallows in vice and wears corruption as if it were a badge of honor. The corrupt and perverted of the world declare their right to be corrupt and even demand that the rest of us respect both them and their perversion. And woe betide anyone who says, "But the Bible declares that all who do such things will go to hell." And woe betide the one who says, "Jesus is the only solution and the only Savior and the only way to heaven and blessedness." "No, no! Away with such a one," the world declares. "If that's what you want to believe yourself, well, go ahead and be a fool. But don't go running around saying that that is the only truth, the truth that saves, the truth that, if rejected, dooms and damns the one who rejects it! Away with such a one from the earth!"

So we see Jesus today in our reading. He is the King. He is the one who brings truth, the only truth. But his glory and the glory of the truth that saves is hidden under the cross. He is despised and rejected by his own. And he and his message provoke the hostility of the world that he came to save. We see how hidden his glory is and how glorious the truth he brings is as we watch his reaction when he and the truth are spurned and spit upon. He endures it! He takes it! There is no lightning bolt from heaven to strike the crowd with the penalty that it deserves. There is no earthquake under Pilate's feet to shake him up enough to make him listen to the truth that Jesus has come to proclaim.

And why not? Wouldn't it better if there were a lightning bolt? Wouldn't the truth at least get a hearing if there were an earthquake under Pilate's feet? Yes. And wouldn't our own witness to the gospel work better if we could send a few lightning bolts of our own to destroy the wicked and the mockers, at a least a few of them, and then knock some sense into the rest of them? And wouldn't people be more willing to listen and to believe if just once in a while we could have a magnificent miracle or two to grab their attention?

The resounding answer to all those questions is NO! Christ bore the cross of shame and humiliation. The time will come for his exaltation and for judgment. But that is all in his hands and not ours. We journey under the cross as we go up to the cross. We share the weakness and the humiliation until the time of exaltation comes on the Last Day. And why is that? Because our glory too is hidden under the cross of rejection. Jesus wants his Word working quietly in hearts to get all the credit for creating faith when and where the Spirit works and wills it. Yes, he wants us also to recognize that it is a miracle of the first order when we believe his Word, a miracle wrought by the gospel message, not by our razzle-dazzle, our cleverness, or our might and merit. It is the hidden power of the cross that works its way in those who follow under it. The whole world wants to be rid of the cross and its truth and has tried to be rid of it for almost two thousand years. But nevertheless, the message is proclaimed by those following under the cross, and in some it still bears its precious fruit; it still works to create faith even in someone like the thief who died next to Jesus.

Yes, it is the glory hidden in the message of redemption in Christ alone that creates saints who lay their whole lives of sin and shame at the foot of Jesus' cross. There is still heard in the world the triumph song of the thousands who rise up again, still under the cross, to sing the praises of the Lamb that was slain and has redeemed us by his blood. And their joy is the product of the glory hidden in the only Savior and the one and only truth. They are not left to guess whether or not they may be right. They do not depend on a poll or public opinion or the view of the smartest or the most pious. No, their certainty rests on the Word of God and the work of God, even under the cross of hostility and persecution. Heaven and earth may pass away. But that will never pass away! Oh, may we ever remain in the blessed number of those who know that glory hidden under the cross. Amen.

Sermon 5
It Is Hidden in the Savior's Stumbling

Text: Mark 15:17-21

    I. See—he stumbled under the crushing weight of the cross.
        A. He could have used his almighty power to carry the cross with no more trouble than it would be to carry a twig.
        B. How, then, would he show the depth of our need and the greatness of his love? Therein lies his glory!

    II. We will too.
        A. While he could have prevented his stumbling, we cannot altogether prevent ours.
        B. We stumble because of our inborn weakness, and we stumble because of our own pandering to that weakness.

    III. We need his help beneath the weight of the cross.
        A. He stumbled—he knows the weight of your cross.
        B. He stumbled—he is at your side in his Word and sacraments to wash off the dirt of the street and to lift you up again as you continue the journey under the cross to the empty tomb. Therein lies our glory!

This evening we are nearing the end of our journey up to the cross and under the cross. The journey to this point has been deadly serious, and it is this evening too. For following him at a distance, it is now becoming quite clear that God is not going to do anything to prevent the completion of this dread drama. Jesus' glory has been hidden in rejection by his own. His glory has been hidden by the rejection of the world. There will be no legion of angels coming to the rescue. There will be no uprising in his behalf by the hundreds and the thousands that Jesus has helped or fed or healed. No, the holiness of the church will not intervene to save him. No, the Roman sense of justice will not kick in either to prevent this horrible miscarriage of justice. For look what happens on the journey this evening. Gasp in horror as you behold it. See how deeply hidden is the glory of the Son of

God and the Savior of the world under the cross. Let St. Mark paint the picture for you. He tells us in the 15th chapter, beginning at the 17th verse:

> They [that is, Pilate's soldiers] put a purple robe on him, then twisted together a crown of thorns and set it on him. And they began to call out to him, "Hail, king of the Jews!" Again and again they struck him on the head with a staff and spit on him. Falling on their knees, they paid homage to him. And when they had mocked him, they took off the purple robe and put his own clothes on him. Then they led him out to crucify him. A certain man from Cyrene, Simon, the father of Alexander and Rufus, was passing by on his way in from the country, and they forced him to carry the cross.

I.

Is it not an astonishing thing? It is just as Jesus said it would be. The soldiers mock him. Again he is spit upon. Again he is beaten up, after having been scourged. To make sure that his humiliation is complete, these hired hands of the Roman governor, himself a hired hand, bow down in mock homage to the Creator of the world and the preserver of the universe. The angels, who love him perfectly and have worshiped him since their creation, do not intervene. The Father himself, who has declared this to be the Son whom he loves and in whom he is well pleased, does not send thunderbolts to destroy these tormentors of his Son. His glory is completely hidden under bruises and blood, under spitting and shame and abuse of every kind.

And now that his humiliation is just about as low as it can get, they take him out to crucify him. But not even that part of the journey can be uneventful. Jesus has had no sleep and probably nothing at all to eat or drink since the Passover meal the night before. The scourging has left him seriously dehydrated. Under the blood of his wounds there is nothing but black and blue from the beatings. And now they tie onto his arms and shoulder the wooden cross beam for him to carry to the place of execution. But he cannot do it. The Creator of the universe stumbles in exhaustion. The one who carved out the mountains and fashioned the depths of the seas by his word falls under the weight of the cross.

Again we gasp in horror. There is no one to help. The angels do not help. The Father has already begun to abandon Jesus. But what about all those he has helped? Is no one there to jump forward and say, "Here, please, let me carry it for him!" Where are the lepers he cleansed? Where are the blind and the deaf to whom he gave sight and hearing? Where is the young man of Nain whom he raised from the dead? Where is Jairus, whose daughter he had raised? Is there not even one from among the thousands he fed with a few loaves and fishes who will at least show some compassion at this point and come forward to help? Where are the disciples? Where are his relatives? Is there no one at this moment who will help? No. There is not one. And most astonishing of all is this: Jesus does not help himself! He was in these moments still the almighty Son of God. He could have used the power that he still possessed and never gave up to make the load lighter. If he had wanted to, he could have carried that cross with no more effort than it would take to carry a twig.

But look at him there on the way of sorrows. No one helps him. And he does nothing to help himself to make his burden lighter and his pain easier to bear. Since someone is drafted to carry the cross for him, he must have stumbled under the weight of the cross and fallen down. The soldiers may kick and prod and beat him as much as they like, but he will continue to stumble and fall down. So the soldiers, not wanting this filthy business to occupy them any longer than necessary, grab someone from the crowd. Simon from the coast of Cyrene is passing through. He apparently knows nothing of what is going on or the reason for it. And he seems to care nothing at all about the one suffering and stumbling and falling. The soldiers seize him. Out of no regard for Simon and still less regard for Jesus, they put the cross beam on Simon's shoulder to speed up the parade on the way to the execution.

This is worth emphasizing: There is nothing to suggest that the soldiers grab hold of Simon out of any pity for Jesus; they had already shown their contempt for him just before this sorry procession began. They just want to get the job done, and the sooner the better. Nor does anything suggest that Simon saw himself as a helper of Jesus in this sad spectacle. He was drafted. And even then, the help he gave is help that hastened the journey to the place of execution—hardly what we would call help. We can barely grasp how people could be so cruel, so heartless. We cannot get our minds around it that not one of those Jesus helped or healed, not one of those who said they loved him, did anything at all on this way of sorrows to help him. But what may leave us most puzzled of all is why he did not do something to help himself. Would it have been such a crime to quietly use the divine power that he still had to stand up straight and tall and then to march with triumphant mien to the altar of the cross? Would it have been so terrible to spite the devil and all those who hated Jesus with at least some show of dignity on his way to death? After all, he had shown a glimmer of glory in Gethsemane when they came to arrest him; he had made them all fall backward to the ground when he told them who he was. Additionally, he had performed the miracle of healing Malchus, whose ear Peter had chopped off. Yes, he had even ordered the soldiers to let his disciples go, and they had obeyed his command. Would it now be so terrible just to let another glimpse of that glory shine through, instead of this disgusting scene of humiliation?

But no. No one helps him in his torment, and he does not want anyone to help him. He does not even help himself, not in the slightest. That's how much he loves us. That's his glory. It is not a glory to be seen and wondered at. It is a glory that uses every moment to show his love for us. He wants us to see and know that the price he pays for our salvation is full price, not bargain-basement, knock-off cheap. The suffering decreed for the sinner already in the Garden of Eden was real. The suffering, therefore, of the one who stands now in the place of sinners must be real too. And so he stumbles under the crushing weight of the cross. He falls down on the pavement and stains it with his blood. Note it well: he did not stumble morally by cursing his tormentors in the court of the high priest and then in the courts of Pilate and Herod. He did not stumble spiritually by hurling lightning bolts of terror and torment at those who beat and scourged and spit on him. No, it is just as Isaiah had prophesied: He goes as a quiet lamb to the slaughter. But he does not go as an unfeeling superman. He does not go as a senseless brute. He stumbles. He falls. He lets us see his glory in the suffering that pays for our redemption.

II.

For he knows that we too will stumble. We too will fall. He wants the sight of his stumbling and falling to be a consolation to us. He wants the sight of it to encourage us with the thought that he understands and knows our pain at such times. The epistle to the Hebrews puts it so well: "We do not have a high priest who is unable to sympathize with our weaknesses, but we have one who has been tempted in every way, just as we are—yet was without sin. He is able to deal gently with those who are ignorant and are going astray, since he himself is subject to weakness" (Heb 4:15; 5:2).

For like Jesus, we had the power to avoid stumbling and falling. We noted it already in Gethsemane. If we had just watched with him, filled our eyes with him and our minds and hearts with his Word, if we had just prayed for his help and gracious presence in the hour of trial, we would not have stumbled. We would not have fallen. Unlike Jesus' stumbling, our stumbling and falling is moral, is spiritual. And also unlike Jesus, we should have used the help that he gives to prevent such stumbling and falling. But we haven't done that. Instead we pander to our own weakness. We think that we can play with the devil. Just a little greed. Just a little getting even. Just a little gossip, a little lie, a little here, a little there. I'll think about something unclean, just for a little while. I'll toy with a grudge, nurse and feed it, just for a little while. It feels so good to look down on this one and to despise that one just for a little while. How nice it is just for a moment not to serve, not to follow in the footsteps of Jesus, not to love and obey him but to love and obey—ME.

III.

And so, through our own fault, we stumble. We fall. The soldier of conscience may be near at hand to kick us while we are down. Others may cry out: "Look at the hypocrite! He's no better than we are. His Christianity is all playacting; when it's convenient, he puts on the show, and when it's not, he turns it off." Oh, how blessed we are when conscience kicks us while we are down. How blessed we are when others shame us because we have stumbled and fallen into hypocrisy. For down on the street, kicked and prodded by conscience, ridiculed and shamed by those who should have expected better from us, we may at last see Jesus. To bear the punishment of the stumbling that is our own fault, he stumbled. To endure the eternal shame that we deserve because we loved to fall, he fell. Thinking of you and yearning for your salvation, he let himself be kicked. And he did it so that he could meet you there in the street of your shame and in the gutter of your guilt. And from his stumbling and falling, you would know that he understands yours and loves you in spite of it. Yes, he loves you and raises you up again to begin your journey under the cross all over again. With the water of your baptism, he washes you from the filth and the grime of your fall, though no one washed him from the filth and the grime of his. With the wine of his blood, he refreshes your parched soul, though no one offered him so much as a drink of water when he was thirsty. He feeds you with the bread of his body to renew your strength, though no one gave him even a crust of bread to quiet his hunger.

Simon of Cyrene was forced to carry the cross for Jesus when he stumbled and fell. But Jesus willingly, eagerly comes to your side to pick you up and carry you when you stumble and fall, even though your stumbling is your own fault. Is that not an amazing thing? Yes. And is it not reason to love him all the more as you follow after him in Lent? Fill your mind with the vision of this glory hidden for you in his stumbling. Let your heart and soul be filled with the grace and mercy that has always been there for you when you fell. And then, maybe, just maybe, you will not stumble so often and fall so far.

And then, maybe, just maybe, you will even join those who, like you, have stumbled and fallen. You will join them not in their sin but with Jesus in helping to raise them up. You will seek your glory in loving service to those who, like you, have stumbled and fallen. You will join them, the members of your family, your friends, those with whom you have contact. You will join them to do what Jesus wants to do—not scold and lord it over them, not ridicule and abuse and kick them when they are down, not constantly remind them of everything they have ever done that was foolish and wrong. No, like Jesus you will join them in love to raise them up. You will join them in forgiveness. You will join them to help them bear the cross as Jesus has so often and so generously raised you up. For we are on the way to Golgatha. We are on the way to the triumphant cry of "It is finished!" We are on the way to the victory of the empty tomb and the shout that sounds down from the street through the ages, the cry of "He is risen!" Oh, may the victory procession be filled with those who stumbled and fell; may it be filled with those who were raised up and washed and renewed by Jesus, who stumbled and fell; may it be filled with those whose sorrows we have shared, whose guilt we have forgiven, and whose crosses we have helped to carry out of love for Jesus, who carried his for us and for our salvation. Amen.

Sermon 6
It Is Hidden in Powerful Words

Text: Luke 23:32-43

I. On the cross there is glory hidden in words.
  A. Everyone else's words are pathetic, shameful.
  B. Jesus' words alone are filled with grace and beauty, and that in the midst of deepest degradation.
II. That glory hidden in words is powerful beyond imagination.
  A. But those words are not mere sentiments; they give what they say!
  B. That miracle is repeated time and again in every one of our church services: Beautiful words from lowly men that accomplish powerful things.

We have almost come to the end. The humiliation of the Savior is just about complete. He has stumbled his way up to the altar of the cross. Without anyone to plead his cause, to defend him or help him, he has been nailed to the tree. And now in his last hours of deepest degradation, the glory of the cross shines brighter than the noonday sun. Listen to St. Luke's description of that degradation, and listen for the glory hidden in it. We read from Luke 23, beginning at verse 32:

> Two other men, both criminals, were also led out with him to be executed. When they came to the place called the Skull, there they crucified him, along with the criminals— one on his right, the other on his left. Jesus said, "Father, forgive them, for they do not know what they are doing." And they divided up his clothes by casting lots. The people stood watching, and the rulers even sneered at him. They said, "He saved others; let him save himself if he is the Christ of God, the Chosen One." The soldiers also came up and mocked him. They offered him wine vinegar and said, "If you are the king of the Jews, save yourself." There was a written notice above him, which read: THIS IS THE KING OF THE JEWS. One of the criminals who hung there hurled insults at him: "Aren't you the Christ? Save yourself and

us!" But the other criminal rebuked him. "Don't you fear God," he said, "since you are under the same sentence? We are punished justly, for we are getting what our deeds deserve. But this man has done nothing wrong." Then he said, "Jesus, remember me when you come into your kingdom." Jesus answered him, "I tell you the truth, today you will be with me in paradise."

I.

We have reached our goal in Lent. We have followed Jesus up to the hill called the place of the skull. At the beginning of Lent, he called us to follow him there, not so that we could help him but so that all alone he could find glory. That glory is the glory of being our Savior. It is the glory of redeeming us without our help or aid. It is the glory of offering up to God a perfect, complete, all-sufficient sacrifice for the sins of the world, for your sins and mine. And now he is fast reaching his goal of attaining that glory, the glory of becoming the world's one and only Redeemer.

But, oh, how deep the humiliation that covers the glory and hides it from our eyes! He looks like the worst criminal, because that's who were crucified—the worst of criminals. Even the Law of Moses had said it: "Cursed is everyone who is hung on a tree" (as quoted in Gal 3:13). He looks like the most despised of men, and he is, just as Isaiah had prophesied. There is no one to help. He looks like the weakest of all men. He does not seem able even to help himself.

Where then is the glory? How will we find it in this disgusting vision that St. Luke has painted for us in the text for this evening? The glory is in the words spoken by Jesus. They are words with a glory that outshines the splendor of the sun at noonday. The glory of Jesus' words in our text shine all the more brightly when we contrast them with the words of everybody else who had something to say in those opening hours of the crucifixion. Did you hear them? There are the rulers, the holy men of Israel. Why couldn't they just leave him alone in his agony? They had gotten their way. They fully expect to be rid of him soon. But, oh, no. They have to show up at the execution, and as we say, rub salt into the wounds. They preach to the crowd gathered there, some of whom had wondered if Jesus might be the promised Messiah. They preach to the soldiers who had been ordered to carry out the execution. They preach to anyone who just happened by to gawk at this gruesome scene. With scorn and loathing and contempt, they stand there and proclaim: "Look at him there, all you who pass by! Look at him! No Savior, this one! No, he is a fraud and cheat. Prove us wrong, Jesus! If you are the Son of God, come down, come down from the cross!" The cruelty of their words and the injustice of their words is underscored when they even admit that he was, at the very least, a good man. They say, "He helped others." Well, the obvious question is, if he helped others, why are you killing him? If he helped others, why do you have no pity when he is unjustly put to such a cruel death? The words of the rulers are wicked and show the wickedness of those who speak them.

The soldiers heard the sermon of the rulers. They shout their amen by joining in the mockery. Here these hirelings of the Roman government continue what they had begun earlier in the hall of Pontius Pilate. There they had given Jesus the crown of thorns and put a reed in his hand. There they had fallen down before him and called amidst laughter and blows, "Hail, King of the Jews!" And now to pass the time, they keep it up. No pity. Not a shred of human decency is to be found in their words either.

Then there are the words of one of the two men crucified with him. They are both criminals whose punishment is well deserved. If they say anything at all, at least from them we might expect a shred of sympathy and understanding. For evil though they be, they are suffering outwardly the same torment that he is. But no, even one of them joins in the chorus of ridicule.

So the picture of human depravity is now complete. Friends have failed him. Family is of no use to him. The official church, his church, has handed him over to heathens for judgment. The state has failed to do justice and instead has committed the greatest injustice ever seen. And now every shred of what should be common human decency has been stripped away in the words of those who surround the cross on that dread day.

What will Jesus say? Will he at last call down curses from heaven on his tormenters? Will he fill his mouth with words of abuse to match those of the ones who mock him? After all, what more can they do to him than they have already done? It is not as though things could get any worse. So what will he say? Can you believe it? Can you even imagine it? This is what he says, not to them but to God: "Father, forgive them, for they do not know what they are doing." But, we call out, didn't they know what they were doing? The chief priests and elders hired false witnesses against him; they knew what they were doing. The Roman governor even declared earlier that Jesus had done nothing worthy of death; nevertheless, he sentenced Jesus to death. Pilate knew he was doing an injustice. How could Jesus say that they don't know what they are doing? And then to even ask God to take pity on the tormentors of his Son and forgive them! Have you ever heard the like? Can you imagine it? Can you picture yourself behaving that way with even a fraction of the abuse and the injustice that Jesus endured? How different this man of sorrows from anyone who ever lived, that he could say such a thing!

Then there are his words to the thief on his right. That crook, that criminal, is the only one there who spoke words that recognized the truth. He considered all that he himself had done to deserve what he was getting on his cross. He saw Jesus' behavior and heard Jesus' words in contrast to all around him. It would seem that this criminal must have known of Jesus' works and Jesus' message more than he saw that day. But be that as it may, he is moved to cry in his own torment words of faith: "Jesus, remember me when you come into your kingdom." And then listen to Jesus' remarkable reply to this remarkable prayer from the crook on his right: "I tell you the truth, today you will be with me in paradise." Had Jesus said nothing, given his own pain and sorrow, we would not have been surprised. Had Jesus anything to say at all, if we were writing the script, it may have been something like this: "Here you are suffering what you deserve to suffer, and you have the gall to ask such a thing of me? You will rot in hell forever together with all of these people around me, just as you deserve and just as they deserve." But no! Nothing like that comes from the mouth of Jesus. Instead, he promises the criminal a gift, a free gift, a gift totally unmerited and so obviously undeserved, a gift for which the thief can never repay him even in the least. Jesus promises him heaven! That heaven will be his not after he has suffered a while in some imagined purgatory. It will be his that very day.

II.

What glory there is in those words of Jesus in the hour of his deepest humiliation! They are words more beautiful than any ever spoken by anyone, made the more beautiful by the contrast with the words of those around him. But the glory in those words is much, much more than beauty. Those words that Jesus spoke that day were filled with power unequalled and unimaginable. Think about that for a moment. The words of the rulers, of the soldiers, and of the one thief who mocked could inflict pain and, no doubt, did increase the pain of the suffering Savior. But those words had no lasting power. Jesus' suffering would come to an end when he breathed his last. Ah, but the words of Jesus on that day are filled with power. He prays, "Father, forgive them." No more powerful word has ever been spoken. For the Father, who himself is about to abandon his Son, heard that prayer and answered it. He heard and answered not just for those surrounding the cross that day. He heard and answered it for the whole world, for each and every one of us! Just think of it. An answer to Jesus' prayers and cries in the Garden of Gethsemane must wait until Easter Sunday. But here in the depths of his suffering, he prays, "Father, forgive them." And then he finishes paying the price of that forgiveness in the suffering yet to be completed on the cross. Father, forgive them, he prays, and the Father accepts the payment for the sins of the whole world. It is just as St. Paul was to say later in 2 Corinthians: God was reconciled to the whole world by the payment Jesus made for the sins of the world. That is what Jesus himself had promised Nicodemus when he told Nicodemus that God loved the world enough to give his one and only Son for its redemption. That's the message of the whole Bible. That's the heart and core of Christianity. Christ was praying for our forgiveness there on the cross.

And God answered his prayer. The whole world was redeemed in these sacred hours of his sacrifice. Only those who reject what he did, who throw it away in unbelief, miss its saving benefit. They perish, not because God wants them to perish, not because their sins were not paid for here. They perish not because God refused Christ's prayer for them. They perish solely because of their own rejection of the gift, the redemption won for them.

The thief on the cross hears words equally beautiful and equally powerful. Jesus did not lie to him or merely express a

265

pious wish for him in that dread hour. Jesus gave the thief what he won for the world. He gave him the paradise of the saints and angels. He gave him heaven at the moment of the thief's death as a testimony to the rest of us that heaven was won for all of us too. And that gift is ours full and free, no matter how far we have fallen or how often.

Oh, yes, there is glory hidden in these words. And that glory has not yet ceased. So powerful are these words of Jesus that they give to this very day what Jesus prayed for on that day. You hear it in the liturgy week in and week out, as thousands upon thousands have heard it for two thousand years. The pastor is just a lowly man. He has no glory of his own. But what glory hides underneath that lowliness, the glory of Christ's call, the glory that gives the pastor the command to declare as Jesus' spokesman: "I, by virtue of my office as a called servant of the Word, announce the grace of God to you; in the stead and by the command of my Lord Jesus Christ, I forgive you all your sins in the name of the Father and of the Son and of the Holy Spirit." That majestic moment in the liturgy was bought and paid for on the cross. That powerful moment in the liturgy is still, to this very day and as long as the world will last, the Father's answer to Jesus' prayer that day. Jesus still prays it. He still holds before his Father the payment made. And the Father still accepts that payment for all of your sins and all of mine.

Oh, what glory shines there in those words most beautiful and most powerful but still hidden beneath the shame of the cross. As our journey up to the cross in Lent draws to its close, fix your eyes on Jesus alone. As our pilgrimage reaches its holy goal, may his words open your ears and your heart and your mind and your soul. May they fill you with sad and solemn repentance for your role in his suffering. For we have not come to the cross to help him. The role of Redeemer is his and his alone. Then may these words also fill you with joy unspeakable. He has prayed for you instead of for himself. He has paid for your admission to heaven by his own suffering of hell. And the Father has answered Jesus' prayer for you. As far as God is concerned, your entrance into heaven is as assured as was that of the thief. That is the glory hidden on the cross. That is the glory hidden in these words of Jesus our Savior and Redeemer, Jesus our light and life, Jesus our joy, and Jesus our resurrection! Amen.

Sermon 7: Maundy Thursday
It Is Hidden in the Savior's Feast

Text: Matthew 26:26-30

I. It is a feast which is so simple that we may miss its glory.
   A. The new feast is hidden inside of an old feast and is its perfect fulfillment.
   B. But it is all so simple and so common that many altogether miss its glory.

II. It is a feast that is itself the price of our salvation.
   A. Its glory lies hidden in the reality of who is given in the feast.
   B. Its glory lies hidden in the reality of why he is given in the feast.

In Lent this year we have been considering this general theme: Behold the hidden glory of the cross. As we have followed Jesus through this holy season, one thing that stands out as striking is this simple truth: The more common and the more lowly the words and works of Jesus, the more glorious and the more powerful they are. That is nowhere more evident than it is on this most holy day, the day on which Jesus instituted the Sacrament of the Altar. You doubtless know the words of institution by heart; for you have heard them hundreds of times since childhood and even memorized them in confirmation class. Listen to those words yet again. Note both the utter simplicity of the words and acts. And note as well their splendor, their glory. St. Matthew tells us in chapter 26, beginning at the 26th verse:

> While they were eating, Jesus took bread, gave thanks and broke it, and gave it to his disciples, saying, "Take and eat; this is my body." Then he took the cup, gave thanks and offered it to them, saying, "Drink from it, all of you. This is my blood of the covenant, which is poured out for many for the forgiveness of sins. I tell you, I will not drink of this fruit of the vine from now on until that day when I drink it anew with you in my Father's kingdom." When they had sung a hymn, they went out to the Mount of Olives.

I.

Could anything have been more simple? Jesus is with his disciples in a borrowed room. They have come there to celebrate the Jewish festival of Passover. They have come to the yearly remembrance of Israel's delivery from Egyptian slavery. They have come to recall how glorious it was when the angel of death passed over the houses of the people of Israel who had their doorposts painted with the blood of the lamb being eaten inside. They remembered how that angel of death brought death to the first-born of every household in Egypt that did not have its doorposts painted with the blood of the lamb.

Passover was the central festival of the Jewish calendar. Everybody looked forward to it. So too did Jesus' disciples. But this Passover was different. In the middle of the Passover celebration, quietly, with no fanfare or fuss at all, Jesus did something new, something different. He instituted a whole new feast. But he did it so simply that we have to wonder if the disciples, at the time, got even a fraction of the significance of what was happening. We strongly suspect that they did not. For as usual, their minds were on other things. They had been so busy arguing with one another about which one of them was most important that no one took on the task of feet washing before the meal. Servants or hosts would do that when people came in from the dusty outdoors. But no one did it that night; no one wanted to be the servant of the others. No one, that is, except Jesus, who took on the task himself and washed the feet of the disciples.

Then Jesus spoke of his coming death. But again, it was Passover, a celebration. Who wants to talk about such things at a celebration? And Jesus spoke about betrayal, about the one who was that very night going to sell him out. The disciples were mystified and did not understand. So much was crowded into the evening, so much celebration of Israel's past, so much confusion about the present, so much wrangling over the future.

And in the middle of it all, again with no fuss or fanfare, Jesus creates a new feast. It is so simple, so easy to pass by and treat it as though it were nothing. He took bread, the plainest bread possible. He broke the bread and gave it to them to eat. He declared as he did so: "This is my body!" He didn't explain it. He didn't say that it was a symbol for his body. No, the words are plain and clear: "This is my body." He didn't tell them either to save it up or put it on parade or worship it. He just said, "Take and eat." And then with equal simplicity, he took a cup of wine, the cup used in the Passover celebration. And he just said, "Drink from it, all of you. This is my blood of the covenant, which is poured out for many for the forgiveness of sins." Again he makes no further explanation of what he means. He does not have to. The words are plain and clear. "This is my blood," he declared. He didn't say that it was a symbol for his blood. Neither did he say that it was something to be worshiped and adored. No, just "Drink from it, all of you."

Yes, it is all so simple that we may miss the glory in it. For glory it has, glory beyond all telling. Here is the Lamb for sinners slain, the Lamb whose blood redeems the world. Yes, here in this new feast is the solution to the sins the disciples were committing that very night. For Jesus comes in this feast to give forgiveness. That's what he said: "This is my blood . . . for the forgiveness of sins." Here is the Lamb who gives himself as food for life eternal, not merely as paint for the doorpost. But so many miss the glory. Indeed, the very fact that we see the feast celebrated not just on this most holy day but many times during the course of the year may cause us to think that it is nothing special. The common conversation in many Lutheran homes before a Communion service goes something like this: "Are we going to Communion today? Well, let's see. Did we go last time? No? Well, then I suppose we should go this time." Perhaps even this evening before you came to church, someone said, "Well, it's Maundy Thursday; that means we have to go to Communion; everybody goes to Communion on Maundy Thursday." Yes, it's all so simple that we easily treat it like an empty ceremony whose purpose we have long ago forgotten.

But Jesus makes the purpose clear. And Jesus shows us the glory that is here. Listen, listen to what he said. Let the words be inscribed on your heart in the blood that is here in the Sacrament. Let it be the Bread of Life he intended for you. Write its holy truth in your memory and never let it go. Jesus said, on the night of his betrayal. Jesus said, on the way to the cross. Jesus said as his last will and testament. Jesus said, "THIS IS MY BODY. THIS IS MY BLOOD, GIVEN FOR YOU, GIVEN FOR THE FORGIVENESS OF SINS.

II.

Way back when the disciples were squabbling with one another, way back when Jesus got not a shred of sympathy or understanding from them, way back when Jesus saw with perfect clarity what was coming to him in the next 20 or so hours, way back on that night in which he was betrayed, Jesus spoke his last will and testament. He gave no stocks or bonds. There is no family silver to bequeath, no family china, no homestead. There is nothing in Jesus' estate at all that is worth talking about—except, that is, Jesus himself! And so in his last will and testament, having nothing else to give, he gives himself! "This is my body; this is my blood given for you," he declares. Yes, and who is the "for you"? Why, it is you; it is me. On this most holy night of nights when there was so much on Jesus' mind; on this most holy night of nights when the scourge and the crown of thorns, when the nails and the spear were already clearly before his eyes; he thought about—you. He spoke his last will and testament, and he made you his beneficiary. Having nothing else to give you, he gave himself to you and for you.

For look at the feast. Listen and wonder at its glory. "This is my body; this is my blood." We do not eat and drink a symbol in this feast. No, it is the real, the true, the living Son of God and Mary's son. It is the same Jesus who spoke that night and who on the next day offered himself up as a sacrifice for the sins of the world. Yes, it is the same Jesus who was still thinking about you on the next day when he cried out from the cross, "My God, my God, why have you forsaken me?" And the answer, of course, to this most painful question is this: God would forsake him because God wanted your salvation. God would forsake him because Jesus wanted to suffer the torments of hell itself on the cross for you, for me. All around him the people cried out, "If you are the Son of God, come down." Why didn't he? Because the night before, he had willed and bequeathed himself to you. Why didn't he? Because the night before, he had declared in his unalterable will that he should never be separated from you. And the only way that that goal could be reached, the goal that we be forever united for time and for eternity in this sacred supper, was for him to be abandoned by the Father. The only way was for him to pay for the sin that separated us from God. The only way was for him to endure the torment of hell on the cross as our substitute.

And so, in anticipation of what he is going to do on Good Friday, Jesus declares to us on the night before, "This is my blood of the new covenant, which is poured out for many for the forgiveness of sins." Ordinary food and drink have, by God's design, the ability to preserve our bodies and to give them strength. But look what is in this food and drink! It preserves not just the body but the body and the soul for life eternal. That's why the church fathers called it the "medicine of immortality." For here is Jesus the living bread from heaven. Here is Jesus the cup of salvation. Here is Jesus, who now gives us the very price that he paid for our salvation—his true body and true blood. He declares that it works; it works now and forever for the forgiveness of sins. That's why he came down from heaven in the first place, to win our forgiveness. That's why he suffered and died, to win our forgiveness. That's why he has ruled all things in heaven and on earth, so that in Baptism he could wash us clean, and in this Supper he could feed us with himself, to preserve our union with him for time and for eternity.

The world passes the Lord's Supper by with disdain. Many a Christian dismisses it as unimportant, not really worth bothering with. But we are looking for the glory hidden in the cross. And here it is! Glory worth more than all the wealth of the world. For Jesus, our God and Savior, is here. Glory that lasts for all eternity. For Jesus, the risen ruler of the universe and of time and of eternity itself, is here. Glory that is more precious than all the medicines ever invented. For Jesus is here with himself as the medicine that bestows eternal life; for where there is forgiveness of sins, there is life and salvation.

Therefore, come with hearts that are broken because of sin and guilt and shame. Therefore, come with souls that are starving for food that will strengthen for the ongoing battle with the devil, the world, and the sinful nature. Therefore, come with a heart parched with a thirst for salvation. Come and eat and drink the price of your salvation in this feast of feasts. Then go. Go to hold him fast who had nothing else to give this most holy night than himself. Go and hold him fast who, on the night in which he was betrayed, had no one he would rather think about than you. Go and forget him never, who in his last will and testament made you for all eternity his heir of the heaven he would purchase with his body and his blood, the very same that he gives you this night. Go with the gift of his body and blood that strengthens and preserves you for life and for life eternal. Amen.

Sermon 8: Good Friday
It Is Hidden in the Savior's Promises

Text: John 19:31-37

    I. The promises fulfilled there break the heart of God.
       A. Just think: These promises were all made by God himself.
       B. These were promises that Jesus himself had given and approved.
    II. With those promises fulfilled, all promises will surely be fulfilled.
       A. He has made promises to you for this life.
       B. He has made promises to you for all eternity.

We have come to the end of our Lenten pilgrimage. Forty days ago we heard and heeded the call of Jesus: we are going up to Jerusalem. We have followed after him looking for the glory hidden on the cross. And today that journey has reached its goal. Listen to its end. Listen to the summation. Listen and look for the glory hidden on the cross. We read from John's gospel, the 19th chapter, beginning at verse 31:

> Now it was the day of Preparation, and the next day was to be a special Sabbath. Because the Jews did not want the bodies left on the crosses during the Sabbath, they asked Pilate to have the legs broken and the bodies taken down. The soldiers therefore came and broke the legs of the first man who had been crucified with Jesus, and then those of the other. But when they came to Jesus and found that he was already dead, they did not break his legs. Instead, one of the soldiers pierced Jesus' side with a spear, bringing a sudden flow of blood and water. The man who saw it has given testimony, and his testimony is true. He knows that he tells the truth, and he testifies so that you also may believe. These things happened so that the scripture would be fulfilled: "Not one of his bones will be broken," and, as another scripture says, "They will look on the one they have pierced."

I.

Our journey ends as it began. When Jesus began his Lenten pilgrimage, he declared that he was going up to Jerusalem to be mocked and spit upon. He was going up to be handed over to the Gentiles. He was going up to be beaten and crucified. He was going up to die and then, after three days, to rise from the dead. And he said on more than one occasion that all of this was done to fulfill the Scriptures.

And that is the glory on this most solemn day of the year. Jesus did it! He fulfilled the Scriptures. Ponder that for a few moments. Every step of his journey, yes, going all the way back to his birth in Bethlehem, had been foretold in the Old Testament. One promise after another depicted the journey of the Son of God from heaven to hell, from the glory that he had in eternity to the horror of hell's essence when he is abandoned by his Father on the cross. Just think of how heartrending these events that take place on this holy day are to God! But God had promised every single one of them. David, in Psalm 22, was inspired to write of this day when Jesus would be crucified, when his bones would stick out so that they could be counted, when his clothes would be won by gambling soldiers at the foot of the cross. Isaiah had pictured this day so graphically in chapter 53, the day when God's Suffering Servant would be despised and rejected, would have no form or beauty that we would want to see. Later Isaiah spoke of the blood-spattered garments. The passages referred to here in the gospel of John are promises from God that go all the way back to the time of Moses and that end with Zechariah, one of the last Old Testament prophets.

Try to wrap your mind around it! God promised all this misery for his Son. The Son of God agreed that all this should take place and happen to him. And every step of the way, the Father ruled over history and the Son directed his own footsteps, so that not one, not a single one, of the promises God made concerning his Son would fail. Who ever heard of such a thing? To make promises and to keep them, yes, we have heard of that. But to make promises that are filled with torture and ridicule and suffering and pain and to keep them, that is something else. To make such promises and keep them when there was no one who could force you to keep promises like that, that is something else. To make a promise to your own hurt when you don't have to and then to make absolutely sure that not a bit of the hurt is left unfelt, unsuffered—who ever heard of or can imagine such a thing? But that is exactly what happened in the journey of Christ that ended on Good Friday. He promised that he would come of his own free will. He promised that he would suffer the torments of death and hell, not because he deserved any of it but for us and in our place. And he kept his word. He kept it down to the last detail. He kept it perfectly.

All that remains is to keep the promise of the resurrection. And we do not doubt for a second that he will fulfill that promise too. For if Jesus kept all these promises that cost him so much, then surely he will not let fall idly to the ground the promise of his triumph over the grave on Easter Sunday.

But there is still more glory for us to see on the cross on Good Friday. For all of heaven and hell, all of time and eternity, is wrapped up in the promises that we see fulfilled on the cross. And those promises have to do with us, with you and me. Jesus had promised it himself to Nicodemus in John chapter 3; he had promised that he would be lifted up on a tree and that all who believe in him will have everlasting life. That promise extends to each one of us. We see him on Good Friday fulfill the promise that he would be lifted up on the cross. He kept his word. And now his word promises us everlasting life.

How can you doubt it? If he did the one thing: suffered on the tree, as he promised, he will surely do the other: give eternal life to all who trust in him alone for their salvation. For that's the whole reason why he kept the promise. It would be silly for any of us, let us say, to pay for a coat at the store and then leave it there. Jesus has paid the price for your salvation by the hard labor he endured. It would be ridiculous in the extreme for him to pay so high a price and then not get what he paid for—your redemption and salvation. No, you can be sure of it. He kept the promise to pay the price of it. He will keep the promise as well to give you fully and freely what he paid for: your redemption, your forgiveness, your peace with God and even with your own conscience.

Is that not glory on the cross? God has kept the promises there that break his heart as he sees the torment of his Son. The Son of God has kept the promises there that leave him bleeding, that leave him dead. The Holy Spirit has kept the promises there that he made through the mouths of the holy prophets in the Old Testament, going all the way back to the Garden of Eden. Not one of those promises has failed. Not one of them has been left incomplete in any way. And all of them were expensive to no one but God. Having kept these hard promises, we can be sure that what he wanted to accomplish by this hard labor has been accomplished: our salvation!

II.

Nor is that all. All through the Bible, God makes promises to you, beautiful promises, one right after the other, that cover the whole of your life, that cover you even after you are dead. Behold the glory on the cross. If God kept his promises there, promises so hard and painful, then you can be sure of this: He will keep all of his other promises to you as well. For example, he promised through the apostles Peter and Paul that Baptism would wash away all your sins for all eternity. Here on the cross, the promise is paid for. In your baptism, God keeps his promise and adopts you there for his own; he washes you clean of the sin and guilt in which you were conceived and born; he washes you clean of every stain of a lifetime and promises to be your dear Father for the sake of the Son who suffered and died. Then he promises you, in the closing words of Jesus himself just before his ascension and in so many other places in the Bible, that he will never leave you or forsake you.

Oh, to be sure, we deserve to be forsaken. For in spite of the love and the promises he kept in Baptism, we have been all too eager to wander away, we have been happy to stumble and fall, and we have rejoiced to rebel and leave the Father's house. But, nevertheless, just as the father in the parable of the prodigal son, God has stood waiting, waiting, waiting. And then, when the bitter consequences of our sins have come home to roost and we are in despair, there is the Father, waiting, calling, embracing, pardoning, receiving us again and with tears for the sake of his Son who suffered.

Nor is that all. When it is your turn to suffer pain, he does not forsake you. When all around you leave, he remains. When sorrow shadows your every move, either because of your own sins or those of others, he does not abandon you. For he has promised it. A mother, he said, may forget her suckling child, but he will never forget you; your names are written on the palm of his hand. He promised that the mountains could fall down and melt into the ocean, but his love would remain for you forever. He promised that all things would work together for your ultimate good, that he himself would be with you to the end of your days. He promised it, and on the cross he paid for it. He promised, and on the cross he kept his promises so difficult and so expensive. All these promises he has kept and will always keep. For he is not a man that he should lie. He is faithful to his word and keeps it ever. Did you not see it, even last night? He promised to feed you with his body and his blood through the lowly elements of bread and wine. He promised there to give you again the forgiveness of all your sins. And he kept his word.

Nor is that all. His promises go all the way to the grave and through it. For Jesus promised it when he said, "Because I live, you will live also." Even the grave will not rob us of our life in Christ and our life with Christ. For as he would keep his promise to triumph over his own grave on Easter Sunday, so he will keep his promise to give us the victory over our graves as well. As we have risen with him from death in Baptism, so we will rise with him in the glory of the resurrection that he has promised us on the Last Day.

It is Good Friday. The hill of Golgatha is veiled in black, as the sun refuses to shine on the body of its suffering Creator. It is Good Friday, and those who saw what happened that day went home smiting their breasts in anguish at the sight. It is Good Friday, and our churches too are dark and draped in black, if draped at all. It is Good Friday, and we too go home in our own way smiting our breasts at what we have done to him; he pays for our sin with his passion. But at the same time, we go home with hearts throbbing with hope that cannot disappoint and with joy that will never fade and with life that does not end. For we have seen the glory hidden on the cross. We have seen the glory that is his promises kept. We have seen the glory that his promises to us have all been fulfilled there on the cross. We have seen the glory so that we, therefore, can be certain that he will always keep all of his promises to us. Go home now in the sorrow of repentance. Go home now in the joy of forgiveness, and wait with quiet confidence for the cry that will rise three days hence. For then will be fulfilled that great promise of his resurrection, when we rejoice to hear again: HE IS RISEN! HE IS RISEN INDEED! For all of this has happened that the Scriptures should be fulfilled. Amen.

Sermon 9: Easter Sunday
It Is Hidden Even in the Savior's Triumph

Text: Matthew 28:1-10

  I. Where is his glory to be found on Easter Sunday?
     A. Not in sight!
     B. Only in the fact proclaimed in the Word!

  II. Look for glory where he has promised you will find it.
     A. Go where he has told you to go.
     B. There and there alone you will find true glory that
        knows no limit and no end.

CHRIST IS RISEN! HE IS RISEN INDEED! Listen to the report and pay attention to the story so that your hearts may be filled with undiluted joy and your souls with unmixed gladness. St. Matthew reports it in chapter 28, beginning at verse 1:

> After the Sabbath, at dawn on the first day of the week, Mary Magdalene and the other Mary went to look at the tomb. There was a violent earthquake, for an angel of the Lord came down from heaven and, going to the tomb, rolled back the stone and sat on it. His appearance was like lightning, and his clothes were white as snow. The guards were so afraid of him that they shook and became like dead men. The angel said to the women, "Do not be afraid, for I know that you are looking for Jesus, who was crucified. He is not here; he has risen, just as he said. Come and see the place where he lay. Then go quickly and tell his disciples: 'He has risen from the dead and is going ahead of you into Galilee. There you will see him.' Now I have told you." So the women hurried away from the tomb, afraid yet filled with joy, and ran to tell his disciples. Suddenly Jesus met them. "Greetings," he said. They came to him, clasped his feet and worshiped him. Then Jesus said to them, "Do not be afraid. Go and tell my brothers to go to Galilee; there they will see me."

I.

Could there be a more glorious day than this? Was perhaps the first day of creation more glorious, when God simply spoke and created time and space and all matter out of nothing more than his words? Was maybe the fourth day of creation more glorious, that day on which God, just by speaking, created the sun, the moon, and the stars and flung them into the positions and courses that they hold to this very day? Were those days more glorious than this one? Oh, no! A thousand times no! For as glorious as was the day of creation and the day on which the sun and moon and stars were made, creation and everything in it will one day collapse and be changed by God with no more effort than taking off a coat. Ah, but this day! This day will shine for ever and ever in its glory and supreme importance. What about the Last Day, the day when Christ will come again with all the saints and angels, the day on which all will rise from the dead and face the judgment seat of God? Is that day more glorious than this one? Oh, no! Again, a thousand times no! For apart from this day, that day would not be glorious at all to us. Apart from this day, the Last Day would be filled with horror and terror unimaginable, and we would hear the voice of thunder say, "Depart from me, you cursed, to that place of dread prepared for the devil and all his angels." No, this day, the day of Christ's resurrection, is by far the most glorious day in all of time and in all of eternity. CHRIST IS RISEN! HE IS RISEN INDEED! May you love and treasure this day beyond your highest good as a day more glorious than your birthday, your wedding day, the day of the birth of your child, even the day of your death and your own entrance into glory. All through Lent we have been looking for the glory hidden on the cross. And now on this day, that glory of the cross, that glory on and in the cross, reaches its incomparable climax.

But notice yet again what we have noticed all through Lent. Every step of the way in Lent there was glory, but it was glory that was hidden. And even today, this most glorious day of all time and eternity, the glory of Christ is hidden. Did you catch that in St. Matthew's report? Who appears as glorious in that report? It isn't Jesus! It's an angel. The angel descends from heaven, knocks open the grave, and sits on the stone that covered its opening. Where is Jesus? He has already done his great works, and he has done them hidden from sight. On Easter Sunday his body and soul were reunited in the grave. No one saw it. On Easter Sunday, as St. Peter reports in his epistle, the risen Christ descended into hell and proclaimed there his great victory over sin, death, and hell. No one on earth heard the shrieks of rage and the impotent howlings of the devils that day. It was hidden. Then, before the angel came down from heaven, Jesus came out of the grave while the stone was still firmly fixed at its entry. But again, the glory was hidden. The only one that appears glorious in St. Matthew's report is the angel who rolled away the stone. His appearance was like lightning, and his face, white as snow. The visible effect of that visible angel was glorious too. Those tough soldiers who knew how to stare death in the face were no match for the glory of the angel. Stunned and terrified, they fell to the ground like dead men.

When the women arrive at the tomb, the soldiers have apparently recovered and have already run into the city to report to the chief priests. But the angel, so glorious in appearance, is still there. He speaks to the women who had come expecting to anoint the dead body of Jesus and thereby finish the funeral that had been left unfinished on Good Friday. To their amazement, the stone has been rolled away, and there is only this angel who frightens them also by his glorious appearance. His message, however, is far more glorious than his appearance. "Go in and look," he tells them. "See, he is not here in the house of the dead. He has risen, just as he said he would. Go and tell the disciples. He will see them in Galilee, just as he said he would!"

But isn't that all still a bit of a disappointment? Don't we want to see Jesus, the risen Jesus, on this most glorious day in all the world, looking even more glorious than the angel? Don't we want to see him robed in splendor, with his face shining like the sun and his garments white as the light? Don't we want to see him looking the way he will look on the Last Day and the way St. John saw him toward the end of his life and recorded what he saw in the opening chapter of the book of Revelation? Shouldn't our sight of him on this most glorious day match the glory of the event?

The answer is no! We see his glory on Easter Sunday in the way he shows that glory to the women at the tomb. After they ran from the tomb at the command of the angel, Jesus appears to them. And how does he appear? With his glory hidden! Oh, thank God for that! For if the appearance of an angel in glory caused the soldiers to fall down as dead men and filled even the hearts of the women with fear, what, then, would become of us if we would see Jesus in all his resurrection glory? Would we not freeze in terror and die of fright right on the spot? What joy would there be for us sinners then? But no. This day is a day of joy for the heart and gladness to the soul. And it is that not least because Jesus, on this day, still hides his glory. Unlike mere mortals, he has no need to put his best on display and make sure that everyone is impressed by his might and his majesty. He does not want to intimidate us by that kind of appearing. There will be a day for his appearance in majesty and glory, the Last Day. But not today. Not on Easter Sunday.

So even on Easter Sunday, he hides his glory. He appears to the women in the same humble form that they knew and recognized during the preceding three years. How different their reaction to his appearance than the reaction to the angel's appearance. There is no dread, no fear, no terror, no running. They run to him, not away from him. They fall down before him in worship and adoration. Filled with joy that cannot be concealed, they hold him by his feet. How they must have drenched the ground with their tears of gladness! For he is risen! He is risen indeed! And he has not come to terrify but to comfort and console. The work he finished on Good Friday is well and truly finished. Sin has all been paid for, covered in his blood. And now is the great day to proclaim the glory of that victory.

And the glory is hidden, hidden in his words. In two short sentences, he sums up the whole glory of Lent, the whole glory of Easter, the whole glory of the gospel. He tells the women, "Do not be afraid. Go and tell my brothers to go to Galilee; there they will see me."

Don't be afraid! What a beautiful summary of our Easter joy and of the whole of the gospel. Without Good Friday and Easter Sunday—the two cannot be separated without missing the point of both of them—we would have in this life nothing but fear. Fallen with Adam and Eve in the garden, we were separated from God by our sin. Death was our lot in this life, and hell, our future in the next. But Jesus died and has risen. He did exactly what he said he would do and what was prophesied concerning him already in the Garden of Eden. He went into battle for us on the cross. And he won. Easter Sunday is the proof of it. He paid for our sin. Don't be afraid; he conquered hell. Don't be afraid; he has triumphed over the grave. Don't be afraid.

But how can I know that he did it for me, even for me? For conscience still condemns, and temptations still gnaw and nag. Listen to Jesus' second sentence to the women: "Go and tell my brothers!" What an astonishing thing! He calls the disciples his brothers! But all they did was sleep in the Garden of Gethsemane after he warned them that they should watch and pray. All they did was run away at the first opportunity, when the soldiers came to arrest Jesus. All they did was behave no better than Peter, who denied him with oaths and curses in the courtyard of the high priest's palace when a servant girl accused him of being a follower of Jesus. They certainly do not deserve now to be called his brothers, do they? No. And that's exactly the point. That's exactly the glory of Lent and of Easter. The disciples don't deserve it, and neither do we. For we are no better than they. But we are no worse either. Their sins are gone, and our sins are too. They are buried in Jesus' grave. St. Paul says the same about our sins: they are buried in Jesus' grave when we are baptized. And now with the sins covered and hidden away, there is no reason why he should not call the disciples brothers. And yes, there is no reason why he should not call us his brothers and sisters. That's just another way for Jesus to say, "Don't be afraid!" You are by faith and through your baptisms now dear, precious, beloved children of God. For behold the glory of Easter! Jesus died. Now he has risen and will never die again! We are redeemed! We are reconciled! Our sin is gone! Hell is conquered! The grave is destroyed!

II.

And see how gentle Jesus is with us, how kind and considerate. Does he make it known with the glory of the angel that would scare us to death and send us running away from him in terror? No, he still hides his glory. He hides it in his Word. That's where we will find it all. Did you notice how that point was emphasized in the Easter story? Jesus promised that he would rise. And he tells the women to report it to the disciples. He does not appear to them right away. He wants them to depend on the Word. He emphasizes that again when he tells the women to add this detail: he will see the disciples in Galilee. That is what he promised them earlier. Again, he wants them to learn the lesson well, to depend on his Word. For soon his visible presence will be withdrawn when he ascends into heaven on the 40th day. But his real and abiding presence he will not take away. He will be with them until the end of time, again just as he promised, in his Word and sacraments.

So, then, do you want to find the glory of Easter? You've come to the right place! For here where his Word is proclaimed and his sacraments celebrated is where you will find his glory. It is in the Word that drives away our fears. For to you no less than to the disciples, he says this day, "Don't be afraid. I am not coming to you this moment in majesty and might that terrifies. I am coming to you with hidden power and glory in my Word. That Word announces and declares that sin is forgiven. Don't be afraid. Tomorrow you will still have problems and temptations aplenty. Don't be afraid. I have died, and see, I am alive. I will not leave you or forsake you. Ah, but still the grave lies ahead of you and you must die. Don't be afraid. I conquered it all in my death and resurrection. Because I live, you will live also. Death, the last enemy, has been defeated, and the grave is the portal to life eternal."

Go ahead then. Just as the disciples saw Jesus in Galilee and even before that—he always gives even more than he promises— so you too will see him in splendor in heaven. Yes, and you will even share in his glory. For you are his brothers, his sisters. Nothing that he has will he hold back from you. And every step of the way, whenever you can, come to his Word and return to his sacraments, so that through the whole journey you may taste and see the glory that is hidden on the cross, the glory that is his resurrection and the promise of your own. FOR CHRIST IS RISEN! HE IS RISEN INDEED! HALLELUJAH! Amen.

Other books in the
Impact Series

- *Baptized Into God's Family: The Doctrine of Infant Baptism for Today* (15N0543)
- *Biblical Interpretation: The Only Right Way* (15N0571)
- *Feminism: Its Impact on Marriage, Family, and Church* (15N0713)
- *Gospel Motivation: More Than "Jesus Died For My Sins"* (15N0732)
- *Law and Gospel: Foundation of Lutheran Ministry* (15N0548)
- *The Pentecostals and Charismatics: A Confessional Lutheran Evaluation* (15N2049)
- *Sanctification: Christ in Action* (15N0458)
- *A Tale of Two Synods: Events That Led to the Split Between Wisconsin and Missouri,* (15N0711)
- *What's Going On Among the Lutherans? A Comparison of Beliefs* (15N0544)

Order online at **www.nph.net**, or call **1-800-662-6022**
(Milwaukee area 414-475-6600 ext. 5800),
8:00 A.M. to 4:30 P.M. CT weekdays.